Ascend

The Catholic Faith for a New Generation

Jan 9 2010

To John and Peggy

Ascend
The Catholic Faith for a New Generation

Eric Stoltz
Vince Tomkovicz

PAULIST PRESS
New York/Mahwah, NJ

The scripture quotations contained herein are from the New Revised Standard Version: Catholic Edition Copyright © 1989 and 1993, by the Division of Christian Education of the National Council of the Churches of Christ in the United States of America. Used by permission. All rights reserved.

Book and cover design by Eric Stoltz

This book is published with ecclesiastical permission granted by Dr. Michael Downey, Cardinal's Theologian, Archdiocese of Los Angeles.

Library of Congress Cataloging-in-Publication Data

Stoltz, Eric.
    Ascend : the Catholic faith for a new generation / Eric Stoltz and Vince Tomkovicz.
       p. cm.
    ISBN 978-0-8091-4621-5 (alk. paper)
    1. Catholic Church--Doctrines. 2. Theology, Doctrinal--Popular works. 3. Christian life--Catholic authors. I. Tomkovicz, Vince. II. Title.
    BX1754.S77 2009
    230'.2--dc22   2009018998

Published by Paulist Press
997 Macarthur Boulevard
Mahwah, New Jersey 07430

www.paulistpress.com

Printed and bound in the United States of America

"I came to bring fire to the earth,
and how I wish it were already kindled!"

JESUS

(Luke 12:49)

Contents

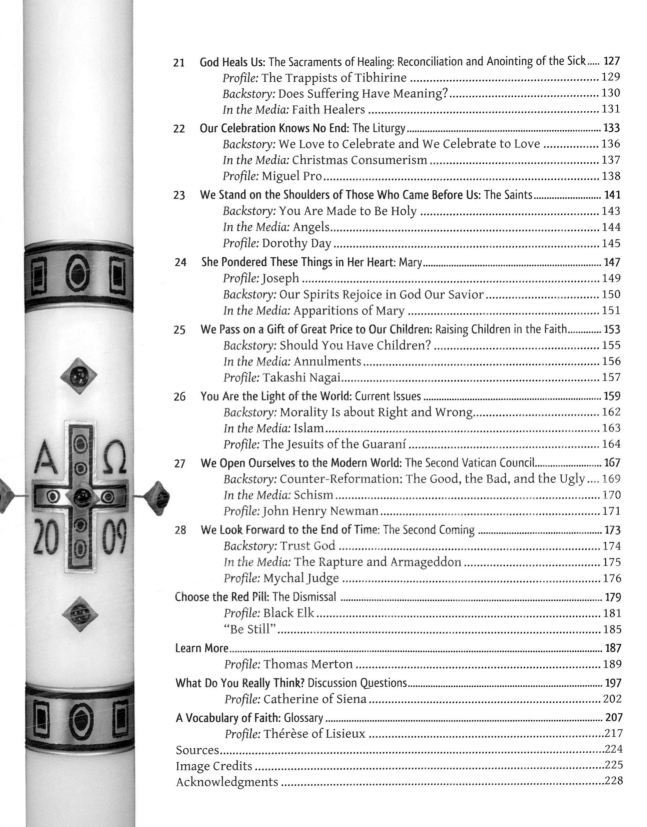

He has told you, O mortal, what is good;
and what does the LORD require of you
but to do justice, and to love kindness,
and to walk humbly with your God?

MICAH 6:8

Introduction

LOVE, GRACE, AND PEACE TO YOU

Christianity gets something of a bad rap today. Those who scramble to be interviewed in the media as representing Christianity are sometimes the least Christian of all. They often list rules or spew hatred. As more and more news formats are designed not around "talking heads," but around "shouting heads," this is perhaps inevitable if lamentable.

So when one hears of "Christians" doing something, one might assume it involves some sort of intolerance. Fundamentalists have arrogantly insisted that the term *Christian* applies only to them. Unfortunately, the media have accommodated them. A comparable scenario would be for Rhode Island to rename itself "The United States of America" and tell you, "We're Americans. You're Californians."

Of course, the rise of modern fundamentalism has not only affected Christianity. Muslim fundamentalists have hijacked the perception of that faith so that a tiny percentage of Muslims have given Islam a violent face. Jewish fundamentalists are working to make Judaism synonymous with some of the extreme policies of the State of Israel.

Catholics especially have been affected by this hijacking of Christianity in the United States by fundamentalists. "We're Christians. You're Catholics," we're told over and over again. Such statements show not only intolerance, but also ignorance of history and theology!

Unfortunately, we ourselves must sometimes admit to some deficiency in our knowledge of history and theology. This book is one way you can be a part of the solution: by advancing your own understanding of Christianity. Maybe you had religious education classes as a child, but you realize you need a better understanding of what Christianity teaches for your life today.

This book is for you because you have faith and you want to grow in your faith. But the world intrudes. Your job is demanding or your children require a lot of time. Maybe your church doesn't have an adult faith formation program, or it's scheduled at the same time as your daughter's ballet class. Or you missed the first session because you had a business trip to Cincinnati.

Maybe you're not Christian, but curious. This book's for you, too.

Perhaps you thought you might pick up a book at the bookstore. It was full of polysyllabic words like *hypostatic union* and *mediatrix* that made Christianity seem kind of academic and boring.[1] And you set aside that book to watch *The Daily Show with Jon Stewart*, never to pick it up again. Been there, done that.

So here's your chance. This book can be put in a backpack or a carry-on bag to read on a plane. You can slip it into your briefcase to read at lunch. It will even fit in your purse so you can read a

---

1 *We throw in some words like this occasionally in footnotes. The footnote can be your friend. We'll also use footnotes to offer more background, tell a joke, define terms, gripe, cover our...well, you get the drift.*

chapter while you're waiting for your kid's soccer practice to end. Doesn't fit? Get a bigger purse!

Later on you can pick up your Bible to read some of the scriptural passages referred to. You can check out the Learn More section and maybe order a couple of the books that sound kind of interesting.

And that's the key: explore those aspects of the Faith that appeal to you. Each Christian has different interests; these may come to us from the Holy Spirit, and they vary in each of us. It's up to you to discern what aspects of Christianity rock *your* world. Then go out and rock the *whole* world!

May the Lord be in your heart and mind as you read this book, enabling you to be a confident and compassionate Christian in the modern world.

How to Use This Book

Use the chapters as starting points

We didn't want to make this book complicated, so it's written in an easy style with short chapters. So this book isn't a comprehensive explanation of the Christian faith. But we did want to make sure you have some suggestions for how to learn more than we can put in such a compact book. Here's how we've done that:

In the text of the main topic, there are times when we refer you to a fuller treatment of a subject in scripture. In these cases, the citation is provided like this: John 1:1-18.

Also in the text of the main topic, you will see some words in **boldface**. This means they're defined in the glossary. We only do this the first time the word is used.

Books that will help you to learn more about a subject area are listed by chapter in the section at the end of the book entitled, oddly enough, Learn More.

If you're reading this book as a group (like a book club, adult education class, or even RCIA), we provide a section at the end with discussion questions. If you're reading it alone, you may find these questions helpful for reflection.

If you're interested in learning about other books or resources available, go to www.catholicstory.org. There's also a blog there you may find helpful as an extension of this book.

If you like this book (and we hope you do!), consider giving a copy to a friend. Remember what Jesus told us:

Go therefore and make disciples of all nations, baptizing them in the name of the Father and of the Son and of the Holy Spirit, and teaching them to obey everything that I have commanded you. And remember, I am with you always, to the end of the age. (Matthew 28:19–20)

Is this book only for Roman Catholics?

No. The authors are Roman Catholic deacons; let's be honest about that up front! However, the vast majority of what's in this book is equally applicable to Eastern Catholics, Orthodox, Anglicans (Episcopalians), Lutherans, and members of other traditions who consider themselves Apostolic Churches. We've attempted a presentation of Christianity rather than concentrating on disagreements. Probably less than 5 percent of this book is specific only to Roman Catholics. Where practical, we denote that by prefacing any such statement with something like "As Roman Catholics we believe...." So even if you're not of the Roman tradition, this book is for you.

What's your agenda?

In our polarized society, one often assumes anyone who speaks about religion has a hidden agenda. We've tried to steer clear of that. Our purpose is to provide young adults living in cities with a contemporary look at Christianity from a Catholic viewpoint so they can be more knowledgeable about their faith and live it more wholeheartedly.

What's the idea behind this book?

Some of us grew up with catechisms that presented the faith in one way for everybody. Often these were lists of questions and answers. This isn't that kind of book, so be not afraid! Our concept for this book grew out of our work in jails, where we needed brief explanations of Christianity that were easily understood. It has since grown into this book, an exploration of Christianity in manageable chunks, tailored to the needs of specific individuals, one they can read on a plane or in the park or a café or wherever they are.

Should I know anything before I read this book?

No. Just get started! Enjoy it with an open mind.

And thus the paths of those on earth were set right, and people were taught what pleases you, and were saved by wisdom.

Wisdom 9:18

O God, you are my God, I seek you,
my soul thirsts for you!

Psalm 63:1

God Speaks to a Longing in the Human Heart

KNOWLEDGE OF GOD AND REVELATION

We're hardwired for God. By nature we humans are religious beings. From the most ancient times, humans sensed that some divine power guided their lives. They knew there was a difference between right and wrong. Many early cultures tried to deal with this belief in the divine by looking to various gods. They hoped these gods would protect them and bring them things like fair weather, good health, bountiful harvests, successful hunts, fertility, and prosperity.

Our early ancestors imagined these gods had power over natural events—such as rain, for example—in their area. These tribal gods supposedly watched over a specific clan or place. People thought they had to appease the greed and pride of these gods with costly gifts and elaborate rituals. Often the power of one local god over another was tested through war. We call the belief in many gods **polytheism**.

In some areas of the world, great religious thinkers questioned polytheism. Through the light of **reason**, they developed teachings that sought to answer the great questions of the ages: Why are we alive? What is the meaning of suffering? How should I treat others? These are the great **natural religions** that sought the transcendent in ways other than sacrifices to **idols**.

When the evolution of the human race had reached a certain point, **God**, in his[1] infinite

wisdom, acted. He decided to reveal himself to humans as the one all-powerful God who created the universe and rules over everything. Psalm 115

God Reveals Himself to Abraham and the Israelites

The first messengers God chose to reveal himself to were Abraham and his wife, Sarah. God called Abraham from his home to travel to a place God would show him. In this place, God promised to make Abraham a father of many nations. His name was changed from Abram to Abraham, "Father of Many," to reflect this **covenant**.

God said Abraham's descendants—those who worship the one true God—would be as numerous as the stars in the sky. Genesis 15:1–6 God's promise has come true. The belief in the One God expressed in Judaism, Christianity, and Islam can now be found in every nation and culture of the world. We call the belief in one God **monotheism**, and Abraham was the first monotheist. God's relationship with Abraham was a critical moment in the ongoing **revelation** that began with our first parents.

---

1 OK, hold on now. We all know God has no gender, right? So why does this book use masculine pronouns for God? Merely for convenience and readability. To just keep saying "God" over and over without using pronouns can get a bit unwieldy, we think. If you disagree, please bear with us. Blame it on the English language. We do.

God taught Abraham many things. For example, God did not want human sacrifice as practiced by many religions at that time. Genesis 22:1–18 Abraham's sons, Ishmael (the father of the Arabs) and Isaac (the father of the Israelites, the **Jews**), passed on Abraham's monotheism to their descendants. It wasn't easy for them to keep their faith in one God. Polytheism still had a strong attraction for the Israelites because the neighboring tribes were all polytheistic. In any game of you-show-me-your-god-and-I'll-show-you-mine, the Israelites always lost! Their God wasn't an idol you could touch and see.

The Israelites Write It All Down

The Israelites became the first to worship the one God in a world filled with thousands of tribal gods, a relationship memorialized in the central Jewish prayer called the *Shema*: "Hear O Israel: The LORD is our God, the LORD alone!" (Deuteronomy 6:4). To Isaac, his son Jacob (later named Israel), and their descendants, God made a special promise: he would be their God, and they would be his people. They became God's **Chosen People**. Exodus 6:2–8

As the Chosen People experienced the wonder and awe of God, they told stories about God to their children and grandchildren. Deuteronomy 11:18–21 Eventually they developed an alphabet, and they began writing down these stories of God's power and love. In this way, our **scriptures** came into being as a joint effort between God and the human authors he inspired.

God Throws a Curveball

The Chosen People continued to learn more about God over hundreds of years. They continually expressed amazement at God's loving power. Psalm 105 But even they were not prepared to understand the wonderful plan God had for humanity.

The **Lord** is a God of surprises! Just as God chose the time when humans were ready to accept the idea of one God, he chose a time to show his love for humanity in the most intimate way possible. God became one of us.

ABRAHAM

Abraham is the father of three religions: Judaism, Christianity, and Islam. Half the world recognizes him as its spiritual father.

Thousands of years ago, God began a special relationship with Abraham (then called Abram). God called him to leave everything he knew at his home in present-day Iraq and to go to another land where he would discover what God had in mind for him. One of the most famous lines in the Bible says simply, "So Abram went, as the LORD had told him;..." (Genesis 12:4).

Abraham didn't really even know who God was, but he had faith. That's why he left everything he knew behind and followed God's will.

Because of Abraham's faith, God worked wonders. Through him God changed the world. We are also called today to live by faith, to take chances on God, to leave the comfortable behind.

You can read the story of Abraham in Genesis, chapters 12—25.

profile

As the ultimate form of revelation to all humanity, God chose to reveal himself in the life of **Jesus**. As the Gospel of John says, "For God so loved the world that he gave his only Son, so that everyone who believes in him may not perish but may have eternal life" (John 3:16).

In this way, God completed thousands of years of revelation with a real shocker. Everything we need to know about God we can learn through the life, teaching, and suffering of Jesus. We call this amazing revelation of God the **incarnation**, which comes from a Latin word meaning "becoming flesh." That's why we call Jesus *the Word made flesh*. John 1:1–18

The early **Church** recorded the teachings and life of Jesus and the marvelous effects of these truths on the early community of believers. These new writings became part of revealed scripture, the **Bible**.

So Now What?

We have the riches of the Jewish scripture to guide us, our ancient **Christian** writings and the very person of Jesus as the Way, the Truth, and the Life. We Christians are able to change our own lives and even the whole world. Such is the power of God sharing himself with us through revelation. So we begin a journey through **salvation history**, the story of God's involvement with us from the time he set forth the Law for the Jews; became incarnate in the saving life, death, and resurrection of Jesus Christ, established the Church and will come again at the end of time.

A look at the major world religions

Judaism (dating from around 1300 BCE[2]) is the first monotheistic religion. There are about 14 million Jews in the world today, divided among the Orthodox, Conservative, Reform, and Reconstructionist branches. The Jewish scripture is called the *Tanakh*, which is the Christian Old Testament.

Christianity (dating from around the year 33) developed from Judaism and accepts Jewish scripture. The main difference between Judaism and Christianity is that Christians believe Jesus is divine, while Jews say he was only a great teacher. Today there are about 2.1 billion Christians, divided among the following traditions: Catholics (1.1 billion), Orthodox (324 million), Anglicans (80 million), mainstream Protestants and the newer Evangelical, Pentecostal, Dispensationalist, and Fundamentalist movements (710 million). The Christian scripture is called the Bible and includes the Jewish Old Testament and additional Christian writings called the New Testament.

Islam (dating from the year 622) recognizes most basic Jewish and Christian beliefs and worships the same God as Jews and Christians, except that Muslims honor Jesus as a great Prophet who was not divine. Muslims (followers of Islam) also love and respect Mary, the mother of Jesus. Today there are about 1.5 billion Muslims in the world, divided between the majority Sunni and minority Shia sects. The Islamic scripture is called the *Qur'an*, a collection of revelations to the Prophet Muhammad.

---

2 BCE stands for "Before the Common Era," the period covered by the older term BC, "Before Christ." In the same way, CE means "Common Era," the period also called AD, or Anno Domini, "The Year of the Lord" in Latin. BCE and CE are used in a pluralistic society. Besides, we now know that Jesus wasn't born in the year 1 AD! The exact date of Jesus' birth is unknown.

backstory

Buddhism (dating from around 520 BCE) seeks to deal with the question of suffering by recommending detachment as taught by the Buddha ("Enlightened One"), whom Buddhists revere not as a god, but as a teacher. To be a Buddhist does not require believing in God. Today there are about 376 million Buddhists in the world.

Hinduism (dating from about 1500 BCE) encompasses many faith traditions, some of which revere many gods. Hindus often comfortably accept many religious ideas. There are about 900 million Hindus in the world.

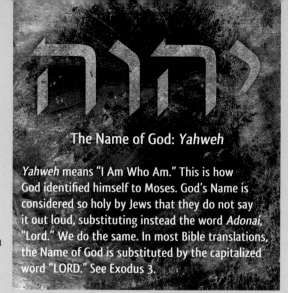

The Name of God: *Yahweh*

Yahweh means "I Am Who Am." This is how God identified himself to Moses. God's Name is considered so holy by Jews that they do not say it out loud, substituting instead the word *Adonai*, "Lord." We do the same. In most Bible translations, the Name of God is substituted by the capitalized word "LORD." See Exodus 3.

Fundamentalism refers to conservative movements found primarily in Judaism, Christianity, and Islam. It reacts negatively to social change by looking back to an imaginary era when everything was supposedly better. It anticipates a violent end-time. Fundamentalists see things in black or white and insist on a literal reading of their religious texts. They're opposed to other faith traditions. Fundamentalism causes division rather than dialogue and consequently hinders development of true peace within the human family.

EXTRATERRESTRIAL LIFE

Is there life outside Earth? If so, doesn't this disprove the existence of God?

Catholic tradition takes no position on whether there may be other intelligent physical beings in the universe. That's a question for science, not religion.

The Church doesn't decide scientific reality, but we do analyze it. So the discovery of intelligent life elsewhere in the universe wouldn't disprove the existence of God. God is the maker and ruler of all Creation and may have created many other worlds and races we are not yet aware of. Among these possible beings, some may be in need of redemption and some may not. We humans are a particularly violent and selfish lot; beings in other parts of the universe may not be as prone to evil as we are.

So if folks like Yoda really exist, one thing we can be sure of: God loves them as he loves us. Whatever their understanding of the divine, whether more advanced than ours or more primitive, God is the Father and Creator of them as well.

in the media

a LATIN cross

2

O LORD, our Sovereign,

how majestic is your name in all the earth!

PSALM 8:1

From Age to Age God Gathers a People to Himself

THE HEBREW TESTAMENT (OLD TESTAMENT)

"In the beginning when God created the heavens and the earth." These are the first words of the Book of Genesis. Thus begins the Hebrew Testament, one of the wonders of world literature and the account of God's involvement with humanity. In its grand sweep, the Hebrew Testament contains a variety of books that record laws and messages from God, minutiae of liturgical rites, stories that address fundamental questions, the words of the prophets, poetry, proverbs, and even an erotic love poem thrown in to boot.

In the history of the world, there's probably never been a collection of works that has inspired more commentary, more art, more music, more academic study than the **Hebrew Testament**. OK, yes, and not a few cheesy movies as well.

Jesus was intimately familiar with the Hebrew Testament.[1] As a faithful Jew, he had committed large parts of it to memory, and he quotes from it continually in the **Gospels.**

The books of the Hebrew Testament record the stories of salvation history. They chronicle the covenant God made with the Jewish people, a covenant he has never revoked.[2] Jesus said of his mission: "Do not think that I have come to abolish the law or the prophets; I have come not to abolish

but to fulfill" (Matthew 5:17). "The law or the prophets" are books in the Hebrew Testament (see Backstory).

The Law (Hebrew: Torah)

The first five books of the Hebrew Testament contain a rich collection of stories that ground our Faith and chronicle the very roots of God's involvement with humanity. These five books—Genesis, Exodus, Leviticus, Numbers, and Deuteronomy—are also called the **Pentateuch**, Greek for (you guessed it) "Five Books." Among the stories in the **Torah** are the accounts of the Creation, the Flood, the calling of Abraham, the lives of the **patriarchs** and **matriarchs**. There's also guidance for how the Israelites were to live their lives.

When reading these books, it's especially important to realize that many of the events described are not to be taken literally. For example, if after reading the first of two different Creation stories in the Book of Genesis, we are left believing the world was made in six 24-hour days, we've missed the entire point of the story! The

1 Many people today (your authors included) prefer the term Hebrew Testament over Old Testament because to say something is old can seem to imply it is no longer relevant, or it has been replaced. That's not true; the Hebrew Testament is the living and vital Word of God, still guiding our lives today.

2 Some people think that Christianity has "replaced" Judaism. This idea, called "supersessionism," is rejected by the Roman Catholic Church.

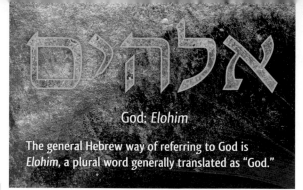

God: *Elohim*

The general Hebrew way of referring to God is
Elohim, a plural word generally translated as "God."

purpose of the story is to say that God created the world and to give us a sense of wonder and awe at his work, not to explain exactly how that occurred. It's also helpful to remember that ancient peoples had a much looser idea of history than we do today and were less concerned with recording facts than with explaining relationships.

The Prophets (Hebrew: *Nevi'im*)

To secular society, a prophet is someone who sees the future. But that wasn't the role of the Hebrew prophets. They did not see the world as it would be, but as it should be. It was their role to be a voice for the **outcasts** of society, especially the poor, the widow, the orphan, and the immigrant. The prophets participated intimately in God's justice and compassion. The prophets couldn't endure "business as usual" when the status quo was unjust. What seemed to others as "just the way things are" for the prophets was a cosmic affront to God. And they let people know that, regardless of whom they angered. As you can imagine, this did not make the prophets popular, especially with religious and government leaders. The prophet's career path did not exactly entail a generous retirement plan.

The Writings (Hebrew: *Ketuvim*)

Also included in the Hebrew Testament is a wide range of books of different genres. There are histories, wisdom books, and collections of poetry. If you're looking for the stories of King David, Solomon, Samuel, and other great figures, you'll find them among these books. There are stories of war, adultery, deceit, betrayal, and just about every human experience you can imagine. Turn

off the reality shows and get a dose of reality from scripture.

The wisdom books such as Proverbs and Wisdom contain many sayings that you may recognize. Also among these books is the magnificent Book of Psalms, the world's greatest collection of poetry. The Psalms cover every imaginable human emotion, from exultation to abject despair. For thousands of years, they have been among the most treasured prayers of Jews and Christians, and they somehow retain their majesty in every language. Those in love may be surprised when they read the Song of Songs, a book of erotic poetry in which the Church sees a spiritual significance. The relationship we are all called to have with God may be likened to the union of a lover and beloved.

Getting in Touch with Your Roots

The Hebrew Testament is an amazing witness to the workings of God in all aspects of life. Every Christian should be familiar with these stories. Some people try to "read the Bible through" starting at Genesis and continuing on.[3] That works for some, but not for everyone. Don't feel like you have to read everything. There will be no test! Remember, it's like a library. Sample a prophet or a book from the Torah and then maybe browse through some of the proverbs. If you hear an interesting reading at Mass, try reading the book it was taken from. There is no rule for how to read the Hebrew Testament; find a way that works for you.

....

3 *Someone once bragged, "I've read the Bible all the way though eleven times!" To which we wanted to reply, "Interesting. And yet you're still selfish and intolerant!" We actually said something like "Good for you!" Better to read the Bible in small doses and reflect on what you read than to treat it as a marathon.*

backstory

In the beginning,

What Is the Bible?

The Bible isn't one book, although it certainly looks like one. It's really a collection of many books that together tell us the story of how God works in our lives and in the lives of people who came before us.

The Bible is divided into two main sections.

The Hebrew Testament contains writings from before the birth of Jesus. These books tell the story of how God chose a people, revealed himself, and was involved in salvation history. In Judaism, these books are known by the Hebrew acronym *Tanakh*, a word made up of the first letters of the Hebrew words for Law, Prophets, and Writings (*Torah*, *Nevi'im*, and *Ketuvim*).

The *Law* is the Torah, the first five books of the Hebrew Testament, which hold a special place of honor. The *Prophets*, as the smarter ones among you may already have guessed, are the writings of the prophets. The *Writings* are made up of history, wisdom, and poetical works. Now that's pretty straightforward so far, but here's where it gets complicated.

Catholic and Orthodox versions of the Hebrew Testament also include the **deuterocanonical** books.[4] These are writings commonly accepted at the time of Jesus, but which Jews and some Christians no longer include in the Hebrew Testament. They're the books of Tobit, Judith, Wisdom, Sirach, Baruch, 1 Maccabees, 2 Maccabees and portions of Esther, Jeremiah, and Daniel. Some Christians refer to the deuterocanonical books as Apocrypha, but we Catholics use that word for a type of nonscriptural literature.

The New Testament covers those events that occurred with the birth of Jesus. The New Testament covers a period of about a hundred years, ending with the Book of Revelation.

---

4 *Just when you thought this was already confusing, various Orthodox Christian traditions also include other deuterocanonical books in the Hebrew Testament.*

The most important part of the New Testament is the four Gospels: Matthew, Mark, Luke, and John. They're the most important because they recount the life and words of Jesus. Each of the four Gospels is written from a different point of view and for different purposes. Think of them as different directors' takes on the same story; each movie will have a different approach and feel.

Following the Gospels is the Acts of the Apostles, stories about the early Christian community attributed to the author of the Gospel of Luke.

Next are different letters[5] written by early Church leaders to Christians in different places, and other letters written to the whole Church, called the "catholic letters."

The last book of the New Testament is Revelation, a mystical account of the struggle between the Church and its enemies, especially the Roman government.

The Bible has much deeper meaning than might appear on the literal level. Many of the stories told in the Bible were intended to teach lessons rather than record actual events. An example of this would be when Jesus taught by telling stories called parables. Luke 10:25-37

The words of the Bible are sacred because they're the words of God. Even though humans wrote scripture, it was God who guided the authors. When you read the Bible remember that it is God speaking to you through the sacred text. Psalm 19

Thomas Merton wrote:

By the reading of Scripture I am so renewed that all nature seems renewed round me and with me. The sky seems more pure, a cooler blue, the trees a deeper green, light is sharper on the outline of the forest, and the hills and whole world is charged with the glory of God, and I feel fire and music in the earth under my feet.

Now that sounds like a good way to approach the reading of scripture.

5 *The letters of the New Testament are sometimes called "epistles," from the Greek word for* letters.

EVOLUTION

Is it wrong to believe in evolution?

Most Christians believe the Bible is not a scientific book. The Book of Genesis, which contains two entirely different stories of the Creation, isn't meant to be a literal report of actual events.

The purpose of the Creation stories in Genesis is to give us a sense of awe at the fact that God created the universe, not explain exactly how God did it. As Christians, we believe without a doubt that God created the universe, but we do not pretend to know how.

Why do we need to know exactly how God created the universe? Such questions do nothing for our faith. They only make people argue, as you've no doubt noticed if you've ever listened to talk radio.

Maybe evolution is an ongoing process of creation. God continues to create the world. Even today, volcanoes create mountains, rivers carve canyons, and earthquakes change the landscape. Maybe God is doing the same with living beings.

If someone gets all bent out of shape by insisting that God created the world in six days, ask yourself, How does this affect my relationship with God? Will I love God more if he created the world in six days or millions of years?

God created the universe. Period. What more do we need to know about it to live a life of faith?

in the media

HOSEA

The Prophet Hosea was chosen by God to understand God's relationship with humans in a very down-to-earth way. God wanted Hosea to understand how painful it is to God when humans reject him.

God told Hosea his relationship with Israel was like a marriage where the wife is unfaithful. So Hosea could understand how God felt, God said to him, "Go marry a whore." No, really.

So Hosea married a woman named Gomer who slept around the whole time they were married. But Hosea loved Gomer deeply, so of course that made her betrayal even harder for Hosea. He experienced some of the pain that God feels when he loves us and we do not return that love.

If you've ever had someone cheat on you, you know a little bit how God feels when we turn our backs on him, just as Hosea learned.

You can read the story of Hosea and his unfaithful wife in the Book of Hosea.

profile

One generation shall laud your works to another,
and shall declare your mighty acts.

PSALM 145:4

Revelation Is Alive and Working in Our Own Lives

SCRIPTURE AND TRADITION

Ever been blown away by beauty? Sometimes when we're really aware of all the wonderful things in the universe, we can feel the closeness of the One who created us and everything around us. These times can be so powerful that we never forget those memories. Maybe you've had such an experience in your life! Some call it touching the face of God.

If we think of how the universe and life are all put together, it is hard to imagine that it all happened by chance.[1] It's more believable to think that a higher power was at work in making the entire universe and keeping all things in existence. Psalm 148

It's true we can know God exists by life experience and reason alone. But that's more intellectual knowledge, insufficient to truly know God. The only way to know anything for sure about God— as much as we humans can know anything about someone so far beyond our words —is through divine revelation, the way God has made himself known to us. Like Judaism and Islam, Christianity is a **revealed religion**. Revelation means to unveil (or uncover). Revelation is God's way of sharing with us who he is. It's God's way of letting us know that he wants us to share in the divine life forever.

Revelation Happened over Thousands of Years

From the beginning of time, God showed his loving kindness to humans. This started with Creation and continued through people mentioned in the Hebrew Testament. People like Abraham, Moses, the Israelites who are God's Chosen People, and the prophets.

When God became one of us in the person of Jesus, God's revelation reached its fullness. The followers of Jesus saw all that Jesus did and were witnesses to God's revelation in the person of Jesus. The passing on of this saving story has continued from the time of Jesus to the present day by the teachers of the Church, the **bishops**.

Scripture and Tradition: Like Two Headlights

Our Christian scripture began as stories told by people long before they were written down. We call this **oral tradition**. For example, after the **Ascension**, various stories of Jesus were told over and over for a long time before they were written down; the Church existed for some time before the **New Testament**.

Not all these stories ended up in the Bible. In fact, stories about Jesus and his teachings—and the ways in which the early community of believers

----

1 *By saying this, we don't mean to endorse the idea of "intelligent design." That's just a backdoor way to teach "creationism," which holds that the Bible is to be read literally in regard to scientific matters. Rather, we mean to say that God is involved in all life but may not be dictating every detail of how nature works.*

understood them—were still being told in the Church after the writing of the Gospels and the other books of the New Testament. This means stories of Jesus were told in two ways. First orally, or what we call "tradition," and second in writing or what we call "scripture." When we use the word *tradition* this way, we don't intend the usual secular meaning of the term, as in customs or conventions. We mean those things we have learned from Christians who lived before us, *some* of which are written in scripture. As the epilogue to the Gospel of John says, "But there are also many other things that Jesus did; if every one of them were written down, I suppose that the world itself could not contain the books that would be written" (John 21:25).

Tradition and the scripture that flowed from it work together to provide a more complete picture of who God is and what God wants us to know.

Sacred scripture is the inspired Word of God, written by human authors guided by the Spirit of God. And tradition tells us more about God. For Catholics,[2] it's the job of the successors of the original **Apostles**—the bishops—to keep, explain, and spread the Word of God by preaching and teaching.

So we, the Church, understand God's revelation both by what was written in sacred scripture and by the beliefs handed down and lived called tradition. Scripture and tradition together guide us in the Christian life.[3]

....

2 *Please note that we've made careful distinctions among the three terms* catholic, Catholic, *and* Roman Catholic. *They don't all mean the same thing! With a small c,* catholic *means "universal" or "all embracing" and encompasses more than institutional Catholicism. With a capital C, it refers to the communion of twenty-three Churches in union with the Bishop of Rome, one of which is the Roman Catholic Church. For a list of all the Catholic Churches, see the glossary. Anglicans and Lutherans may also use the word with a small c to refer to the apostolic tradition they share with Catholics and Orthodox, so they would not capitalize this particular instance as we have here.*

3 *The other Abrahamic religions have similar setups. Jews, our elder brothers and sisters in faith, are guided by both* Torah *and* Talmud *(rabbinical commentary similar to our idea of tradition). Muslims are guided both by* Qur'an, *the holy book of Islam, and* Hadith, *which is also roughly equivalent to our Tradition.*

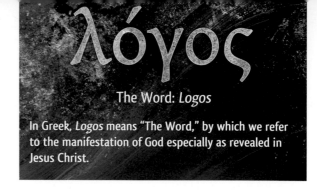

The Word: *Logos*

In Greek, *Logos* means "The Word," by which we refer to the manifestation of God especially as revealed in Jesus Christ.

When we think about tradition, we need to remember something Jesus said to his followers: "When the Spirit of truth comes, he will guide you into all the truth" (John 16:13). With these words Jesus promised that the Holy Spirit, God's Spirit, would help the Apostles understand and pass on the truth to those who would come after them.

Scripture: Inspired and Inspiring

The human authors of scripture were guided or inspired by God. That means they wrote only what God wanted them to. There's an important distinction among how Catholics, Orthodox, Anglicans, and most mainstream Protestants understand inspiration compared to the view held by some other Christians: we do not believe scripture was dictated word for word by God. Rather, God utilized the skills and talents of the authors, who wrote their own words, shaped by their own experiences, as well as the culture and knowledge of their own times. To understand parts of scripture, we need to know something about the time and culture of the author.

God inspired the words of the Bible. They're free from any error in all the important things—you know, the reason you read scripture to begin with. Everything the Bible tells us about why we were created, how we should live our lives and how we will live with God forever after we leave this world is true.

While the words of the Bible are free from any error about how we are saved by God, the Spirit of God did not protect the original writers from scientific or historical errors. Scripture is not intended to be a scientific treatise or a history book in the way we understand history today.

After all, we're not reading the Bible to learn about science, are we? If you want to learn about science, don't read scripture, watch *Nova*.

How the canon of scripture came about

The Church existed before there was a New Testament. In fact, the Church produced the New Testament. At the time the Church began, there wasn't even complete agreement on what books should be included in the Hebrew Testament. So how does it happen that today Christians have agreement (well, sort of) on what constitutes the Bible? The list of books included in the Bible, called the *canon*, was a long time coming.

First, let's look at the Hebrew Testament. For hundreds of years, there were some books everybody agreed were accepted as scripture, like the first five books of the Bible, the Torah. But once you got beyond these books, there was disagreement.

One of the most important sources of scripture at the time of Jesus was a Greek translation of the Hebrew scripture called the *Septuagint* (meaning "seventy" in Greek because the story was that seventy scholars worked on it between the third and first centuries BCE). As good Jews—for that's what they considered themselves—the first followers of Jesus considered the Septuagint the authoritative *Tanakh*. This was the version they spread to the Gentile[4] world.

Meanwhile, back at the ranch, Jewish scholars of the time were not entirely convinced all the books in the Septuagint really belonged in the canon of Jewish scripture. Around the year 100, Jewish scholars began to come to a consensus that some of the books in the Septuagint shouldn't be included in the Jewish canon. But Christians didn't get that memo. By then we were mostly Gentiles and no longer a part of mainstream Judaism, so we continued to use the Septuagint as our version

....

4 *Gentile: anyone who's not a Jew. If you've ever hear someone call you a goy, that's Yiddish for Gentile. So now you can say to your Jewish friends, "What do I know, I'm just a goy!" You'll get a good laugh and maybe an invitation to a bris. The plural of goy is goyim.*

backstory

of Hebrew scripture. This canon included the deuterocanonical books mentioned in the previous chapter and was used by Christians until the time of the Protestant Reformation, when some Protestant scholars urged a move to the by-then long-established Jewish canon, discarding these deuterocanonical books.

The story of how the canon of the New Testament was established is similar. The early followers of Jesus, after his resurrection and ascension, had no Christian scripture. They relied on oral transmission of stories for what they knew of the life and teachings of Jesus. Around the year 60 or so, people began writing these stories down. Church leaders also wrote letters to far-away Christian communities; those letters were saved and cherished as important sources of Christian teaching.

There was a proliferation of these stories, generally called "gospels," and these letters, as well as various instructional documents, and mystical writings called "apocalypses." This situation created a problem. Some of these gospels presented very different views of Jesus from what was generally accepted by believers. Some of the letters circulating were of suspect origins. So what was a good Christian to accept and read?

The idea of a standard canon of Christian scripture was kicked around for some time. By the time a list of these contents of the New Testament was set in the year 380, it reflected a consensus established by common usage over quite a while.

Dozens of early Christian writings, called "apocryphal books," weren't included in the canon. One occasionally hears breathless media reports of a "Lost Gospel" or "Forbidden Book," but these are books we've known about for centuries. They weren't included in the New Testament for good reasons. You can buy them today online or in a bookstore. Read a couple and you should be able to see right away why the early Church didn't include them. They just don't jibe with what we know about Jesus.

BIBLE TRANSLATIONS

I'd like to buy a Bible, but I'm confused about all the different translations available. Why are there so many? Help!

When you're looking to buy a Bible, there are a few things to think about. The first is that it be a Catholic version; in other words, it includes the deuterocanonical books (see chapter 2), which some versions refer to as "including the apocrypha." Then come two considerations based on your personal needs: readability and study.

You're buying a Bible to read it. So you should make sure the version you choose is easy to understand. All the "thees and thous" of the King James Version, for example, may sound familiar and comforting, but will you easily understand what you're reading? One popular option for Roman Catholics is the Revised New American Bible. This is the version used for the readings at Mass for Roman Catholics in the United States, so when you read this version you might connect more easily with what you hear in the liturgy.

Another popular translation is the New Revised Standard Version, used in the liturgy of the Episcopal Church, Eastern Churches, and in the Roman Catholic Church in Canada, the United Kingdom, and other countries.

There are many contemporary translations that emphasize readability over accuracy, like the Good News Bible, which are fine for everyday use as long as you realize their limitations.

The second consideration is study. If you want a deeper understanding of the Bible, you'd probably want a version with plenty of footnotes and introductions to each book. Most versions offer many editions that provide different levels of background information. Some versions, like the New Jerusalem Bible, place accuracy over readability and provide lots of explanations reflecting the best biblical scholarship.

Most modern translations were developed by teams of scholars from various Christian traditions and Jewish scholars, who made significant contributions to translating the Hebrew Testament. Most are very good. Compare versions by looking at one of your favorite passages and see which version speaks to you best. You can always supplement any translation with a good commentary, like the *Collegeville Bible Commentary* (or if you are of a scholarly bent, the *New Jerome Biblical Commentary*), to provide plenty of background and explanation.

profile

MOSES

Moses was born when the Israelites were slaves in Egypt. To save his life, his Hebrew mother found a way to give her baby to an Egyptian princess, who raised him as her own son. He lived a life of privilege and didn't identify much with his own people.

As Moses became a man, he became aware of how much the Israelites suffered as slaves under the Egyptians. This injustice enraged him. He killed a man he saw beating one of his people. He fled into the desert and there, on the lam, God spoke to Moses.

God told Moses to tell Pharaoh (the king of Egypt—a title, not the king's name) that God wanted the Israelites to be free. Moses famously commanded Pharaoh, "Let my people go!" Of course this was the last thing Pharaoh intended to do, just as Americans were loath to give up the free labor of their slaves. So to show Pharaoh the power of God, God worked some amazing miracles. It wasn't pretty for the Egyptians. Pharaoh finally gave in and Moses led his people from slavery to freedom. This is the event commemorated by the Jewish celebration of *Pesach* (Passover) and has been invoked by people everywhere who long for liberation, such as those active in civil rights movements. Moses was a great leader and an example of the faith and courage we need to follow God, even when the powerful are against us.

You can read the story of Moses in the Book of Exodus.

You open your hand
satisfying the desire of every living thing.

PSALM 145:16

God Believes in Us Before We Believe in Him

FAITH

Have you ever had faith in someone? Maybe in a friend you know who will be there for you no matter what? We look at our past experience with a person to know if we can expect him or her to be there in the future. That's faith. We have faith in nature, that the sun will rise and set, or that water and trees will be there to clean the air we breathe and maintain life. We come to believe in truths bigger than ourselves by faith. Faith challenges us to believe more than what we know for sure.

Faith[1] is given to each person who responds to the gift of grace, freely offered by God, through which we come to know him and respond to him intimately. Faith is a bridge between those things we can see and touch and those things we cannot see but we know are there. Scientists tell us there are tiny particles called atoms that make up all things. Have you ever seen one? Faith is knowing they're there.

We have the advantage of knowledge from those who've come before us. We can't test everything for ourselves. So faith allows us to believe, even though we don't have firsthand knowledge of how all things work. Example: Do you really understand how your body and mind work? Yet we know they do and we rely on and have faith in them every day of our lives.

Faith Gives Us the Big Picture

Faith also means believing it's possible to have a relationship with God, to believe that something much bigger than us is responsible for Creation. Jews, Christians, and Muslims all say there's rational evidence of God's existence and the way God works in the lives of human beings.[2] Still, if you're looking for hard scientific proof that God exists beyond any doubt, there is none. You couldn't prove the existence of God to the satisfaction of a court of law. We know God exists and has a plan for us by the gift of faith. Scripture has many stories of how God has worked in the lives of people who've had faith.

We Can't Earn Faith

For those of us who follow the teachings of Jesus Christ and call ourselves Christians, the truth about God is seen in the life of Jesus, in his death,

....

1 OK, here's more about capital letters. When we refer to "faith" with a small f, that's the gift we receive to believe. When we talk about "the Faith" with a capital F, it means the whole body of our Christian teachings and way of life.

....

2 For example, many sections of the Qur'an describe the wonders of the natural world, noting they are "signs for rational people." See Sura 2:164 for one such instance.

rising from the dead, and his return to his Father. 1 John 1:1–4

In the early Church, faith allowed the followers of Jesus to carry on after his death and resurrection. Faith is a free gift of God, available to anyone who wants to receive it. We don't "earn" faith. While faith is a gift from God, we respond to that gift by how we live our lives. Ephesians 2:1–21

Faith is one of the most powerful ideas and teachings of Jesus. In the Hebrew Testament the word *faith* is used only twice, but the word *faith* appears 245 times in the New Testament.

The classic Christian explanation of faith is in the Letter to the Hebrews (11:1): "Now faith is the assurance of things hoped for, the conviction of all things not seen." Hebrews 11:1–39

Faith Is a New Way of Living

There's a lot of talk about faith in God and what God's really asking of us. People wonder, Does God want us just to have faith alone? This would mean believing that God exists is enough. Or, Does God want our faith to be shown in our actions? This means because we have faith in God and understand what God wants us to do, we live our lives in a different way and look out for the needs of others.[3] James 1:19–27

Scripture challenges us to have faith and to let our actions follow our beliefs. Galatians 3:1–29 Just believing God exists makes no difference unless we act on that belief. In the same way, just saying we believe in the teachings of Jesus isn't enough unless we act on those beliefs. James 2:14–26 Having faith isn't something we can attribute to our own virtue or intelligence; it's a gift from God we can take no credit for. Nor can we pat ourselves on the back when we turn our faith to action; we're merely doing our Christian duty. Luke 17:7–10

....

3 *You may have heard that Protestants and Catholics were in opposing camps about the nature of faith and how we respond to it, expressed as "good works versus faith." That was never totally true, but a lot of people of both traditions thought it was. In 1999, the Vatican and the World Lutheran Federation signed a joint declaration stating that Catholics and Lutherans are of one mind on this issue. In 2006, the World Methodist Council also agreed to the statement.*

God Never Promised You a Rose Garden (Well, actually, he did...)

It's not always easy to live by faith. When we go through bad times, we may wonder where God is or why God allows bad things to happen. These times can make us question our faith. Matthew 13:1–53 Hey, look at the life of Jesus. He didn't have it all that easy either. The leaders of his own people rejected him, conspired against him, and eventually got him put to death. John 1:1–14 And you want the easy way out?

Jesus never promised faith would make all our problems go away. Some people say it like this: "Jesus doesn't offer us a way out, but a way through." Jesus did say that if we remain faithful to God, when our earthly life is over we will live forever in **heaven** where there'll be no more suffering, but true **peace** and justice. Romans 8:14–39

SAINT PAUL THE APOSTLE

THE JUST SHALL LIVE BY FAITH †

PAUL

A Christian manifesto

A "creed" is a statement of belief. It comes from the Latin *credere*, "to believe."

We believe God became human in the person of Jesus. Early creeds expressed their beliefs about Jesus and God. 1 Corinthians 15:1–9 One early statement of Christian faith is the proclamation that "Jesus is Lord" (Romans 10:9).

After Christ returned to heaven, the Church was trying to make sense of all that Jesus said and did. There was a problem in teaching the gospel to the Roman world. The early Christians were being persecuted, and there were different versions of Jesus' life and teachings. This created a lot of confusion over just what it was that Christians believed.

In the year 313 the emperor Constantine legalized Christianity in the Roman Empire. (Soon after, it became the official state religion, not exactly a good thing.) But Constantine discovered there were disagreements in the Church over many issues.

Constantine asked the bishops to hold a council in Nicaea in the year 325. He wanted all these arguments settled. At this council the bishops reached agreement on the Nicene Creed. This was a clear statement of what the Church believes. Most Christians recite this creed every Sunday:

> We believe[4] in one God, the Father, the Almighty,
> maker of heaven and earth, of all that is, seen
>   and unseen.
> We believe in one Lord, Jesus Christ,
> the only Son of God, eternally begotten of the
>   Father,
> God from God, Light from Light, true God from
>   true God,
> begotten, not made, one in Being with the Father.[5]
> Through him all things were made.
> For us men[6] and for our salvation he came down
>   from heaven:
> by the power of the Holy Spirit he was born of the
>   Virgin Mary, and became man.
> For our sake he was crucified under Pontius
>   Pilate; he suffered, died, and was buried.
> On the third day he rose again in fulfillment of
>   the scriptures;
> he ascended into heaven and is seated at the
>   right hand of the Father.
> He will come again in glory to judge the living
>   and the dead,
> and his kingdom will have no end
> We believe in the Holy Spirit, the Lord, the Giver
>   of Life,
> who proceeds from the Father [and the Son].[7]

....

4 By the time you read this book, this may be changed to "I believe" in the Roman Catholic liturgy. Although the original Greek is "We believe," some people today want the liturgy to conform as closely as possible to the later Latin version.

5 Again, by the time you read this, the Creed in the Roman liturgy may say "consubstantial with the Father." It means the same thing as "one in being."

6 Men here is used in the archaic English sense, meaning "humans."

7 "and the Son": These words were added to the Roman liturgy around the year 1000. They're not used in the Churches of the East.

profile

Saul, a Syrian Jew, was a big-time persecutor of the followers of Jesus. He was even the official witness at the stoning of Stephen, a deacon who was the first Christian martyr.

One day while traveling on a road to Damascus, Saul suddenly saw a blinding light. He heard Jesus ask him, "Why are you persecuting me?" Saul was blinded and led into the city, where he was found by one of the disciples of Jesus. When he got his sight back, he was baptized and began to preach about Jesus all over the Roman Empire. He became known as Paul.

Paul was a radical. He said that everybody, not just Jews, should hear about Jesus. He made three missionary journeys, preaching and teaching about Jesus. He was put in jail for preaching the Good News and eventually received the death penalty.

Much of the New Testament is made up of letters from Paul. He was responsible for formulating a lot of what we Christians believe.

Like us, Paul never met Jesus face to face. But his encounter with Jesus on the road changed his life forever. Paul set an example for us. Where have you met Jesus in your life, and how have you changed or not changed through knowing the Lord?

You can read about Paul in the Acts of the Apostles.

backstory

With the Father and the Son he is worshipped
  and glorified.
He has spoken through the Prophets.
We believe in one holy catholic[8] and apostolic
  Church.
We acknowledge one baptism for the forgiveness
  of sins.
We look for the resurrection of the dead,
  and the life of the world to come. Amen.

....

8 Note that in the Creed, catholic is spelled with a small c. Here
it does not refer primarily to the institutional Catholic Church,
but rather the original Greek meaning, "universal," including all
Christians baptized into the one Body of Christ.

We agree: *Amen*

Amen (ah-MEN) is a Hebrew word used as a way of agreeing to what you've just heard. The English meaning of the word *Amen* is "Yes," "Truly," "So be it," or "Let it be." The same word is used in Arabic by Muslims, pronounced *Amin* (ah-MIN).

ATHEISM

My friend says she's an atheist. How should I act toward her?

An atheist doesn't believe there's a God. That's different from an agnostic, who's not sure if there's a God.

It's the gift of faith that allows us to believe in God. In that belief humans find the purpose for which they're created and are bound together by all the things God has done through the ages.

If someone doesn't believe in God, then the question of why we were created becomes more challenging. Is the human only a highly intelligent animal whose existence stops at death? Or are we created in the image of a divine being who longs to be in an eternal relationship with us?

Most atheists have a personal moral code. These beliefs are often taken from acceptable behavior in any society. Many atheists are kind and honest people. Some are kinder than many Christians!

Many people become atheists because of the bad example of some Christians. In this way, we are sometimes to blame when people stop believing in God. Because some Christians act like jerks, some people assume the whole idea of God is a farce!

The example we give by our lives is very important. Thomas Merton warns us, "Do not be too quick to condemn the man who no longer believes in God: for it is perhaps your own coldness and avarice and mediocrity and materialism and selfishness that have chilled his faith."

in the media

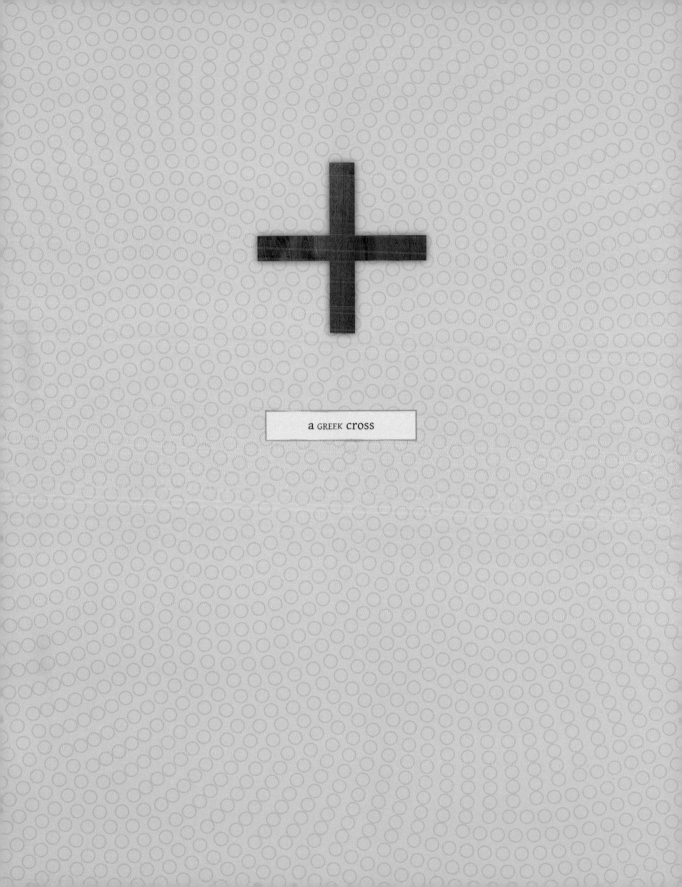

a GREEK cross

You hem me in, behind and before,
and lay your hand upon me.

PSALM 139:5

God Is Love

GOD THE FATHER

Maybe your dad was just plain mean. Perhaps he wasn't very loving or wasn't there when you needed him. Or maybe you didn't have a dad growing up. If your own dad is great, fantastic, you are indeed blessed! Still, we all long for the ideal father, who will teach us, protect us, care for us, spend happy times with us, and hold us when we are hurt or depressed. Even though our own human parents may fail us, God is always the perfect Father.

We don't call God **Father** to imply that God is male. The point is that God is our parent. Some people prefer to think of God as Mother, and that has real advantages—and deep roots in scripture. But because it's our tradition, we especially think of God as Father.

God is Father for two reasons. First, he's the parent of everything that exists because he created it. Second, he's our own Father because he loves us and cares for us.

God Made Everything

Before there was anything, before there was even time, there was God. God can do anything.[1] God is the source of all life, all goodness, all truth, all beauty, all love.

In ways we don't fully know, God created the universe from nothing through Word and Wisdom[2] and keeps it going through his loving kindness. He made everything that exists, no matter what it is. Everything God made is good. Each of us is alive because God wants us to be alive. As Benedict XVI said, "Each of us is willed, each of us is loved, each of us is necessary." Psalm 104

The Book of Genesis (1:27) tells us God made humans "in his own image." This means each of us has a share in the life of God. Our **soul** is that integral aspect of us that's spirit, that gives life to our body and is eternal. In the Creed, we profess that body and soul will be reunited for eternity. Psalm 139

God Is Love

God is total love. Every time we experience love, we taste a little bit of God. The first love we feel is from our parents, and this is why we call God

---

1   So there's always the kid in religious education class who asks, "If God can do everything, can he make a rock so big even he can't lift it?" If you were the kid who asked this question, by now you surely understand that God has a reason for everything he does and doesn't sit around trying things just for fun.

---

2   Word = Christ; Wisdom = Holy Spirit.

Father. His love is a parent's love that wants only good for all people. 1 John 4:7–21

God Is Just

God requires us to treat each other with justice, because it's God himself who established justice. God is always on the side of the oppressed. When the rich let the poor starve, when the powerful beat down the powerless, when one race discriminates against another, God is on the side of those who suffer. Those who oppress others must answer to God, no matter who they are. Matthew 25:31–46

God Is All about Second Chances—and Third, and Fourth...

Many times we probably did things that hurt our own parents. Amazingly, they forgave us. God our Father does the same. No matter what we do, God is always ready to forgive us unconditionally, without any "ifs." God does not "test us" to see what we will do. Even if we deserve to be punished for what we've done (or, more often, not done), God is ready to forgive without punishment. Psalm 103 God never holds a grudge. God never tries to get even. Because he is Love, God waits quietly in sorrow for us to return to him. And because we're made in his image, God requires that we act with mercy and forgiveness toward others. Matthew 18:21–35

God Answers Prayer

Prayer is a conversation with God. In prayer, we open our hearts to God in happiness and in sadness. In prayer, we stand naked before God, leaving aside our pride, and we submit ourselves to God's loving plan.

At times we may ask God for certain things to happen, things we think will be best for us or others. As you've probably figured out by now in your own life, we don't always know what's best. God, however, does. Prayer isn't a magical way to get what we want. God isn't a candy machine in the sky that shoots out cars and health and money whenever we put in a quarter. When we ask something of God, we must realize God knows better than we do what we need and what will make us happy. He'll always answer our prayer, but maybe not in the way we expect. Luke 12:22–34

God Wants a Relationship with You

Being the Creator and able to do anything isn't enough for God. He doesn't sit around and just enjoy his power. The one thing God wants more than anything is to have a loving relationship with you, Father to child. He wants to hear your desires, to hold you when you cry, to rejoice with you when you are happy, to show you the sun in your darkest night.

It's amazing. The most powerful being in the universe wants you above all else.

Experiencing the Trinity in our lives

For hundreds of years, people have tried to explain the Trinity. Many of the world's greatest theologians have written massive books about the Trinity. Along the way, they used some pretty long words, and when they couldn't find a word that meant what they wanted, they made up a new one!

But understanding the Trinity doesn't have to be so difficult. Partly that's because we're not expected to totally understand the Trinity. We call some truths of our faith **mysteries,** and the Trinity is one of these mysteries. When we use this word, we don't mean it like a murder mystery that you try to solve. In the Church, a mystery is something we can think about over and over again, and each time we understand a little something just by thinking about it. We're not supposed to "solve" it.

Even the simplest way to explain the Trinity has some tough ideas: the Trinity is One God in three persons. That's how we usually explain it, but that word *person* can be a problem. We don't mean

backstory

Born in the Darfur region of Sudan, Bakhita was abducted at the age of nine and sold into slavery. She endured a childhood of extended, horrifying torture and misery that would seem to be devoid of all hope.

Eventually, she was purchased by a kindly Italian diplomat who enrolled her in a Catholic school in Italy. Bakhita was excited by what she learned in school. She immediately recognized the God who comforted her in her difficult life: "the saintly sisters, with a patience that was truly heroic, instructed me in the faith. They helped me know God, whom I had experienced in my heart since childhood, without knowing who he was." She wrote, "I remembered how, as a child, when I contemplated the sun, the moon, the stars, and all the beautiful things of nature, I was wondering, 'Who is the master of it all?' And I felt a keen desire to see him, know him, and pay him homage."

Baptized Josephine, she won her freedom and entered a convent. There she lived a simple life of prayer and service that inspired all who met her. As she lay dying in 1947, she became delirious, reexperiencing her life of slavery. She screamed, "The chains are too tight; loosen them a little, please!"

Slavery still exists in our world today, not only in places like Sudan where Josephine was first abducted, but also in American sweatshops and in the red-light districts of our cities. God, as the loving Father Josephine knew, will comfort the enslaved in their misery, but we are called to free them from their oppressors as well.

JOSEPHINE BAKHITA

profile

a human person or a humanlike person. Those paintings of God as an old man with a long beard can lead us down the wrong path.

So what is the Trinity?[3]

To gain some insight into the mystery of the Trinity, we can look at different ways humans have experienced God. It's a mistake to think of the three persons only as aspects or roles of God; that idea's been discarded by Christians before us as incomplete. But for the moment, let's run with this idea of *experiencing* the Trinity.

From ancient times, we had an experience of a loving God. When Jesus came, calling God "Father," we had an experience of God as one of us. And especially after the resurrection of Jesus, we had an experience of God as a Spirit among us that spreads the message of God throughout the world.

---

3   *The great theologian Augustine was once walking on the beach, contemplating how to explain the Trinity. He saw a young boy scooping water into a hole and asked him what he was doing. "Putting the ocean into this hole," the boy replied. Augustine pointed out that was ridiculous; the hole could not contain the ocean. "Neither can you explain the Trinity," said the boy. Smart kid!*

So, we have the Father, the Son, and the Holy Spirit. All are different ways we name God, but there is still only one God.

The Father created the universe. He put a Law in our hearts. He watches over us with loving care and gives us what we need.

The Son is Jesus Christ, God's love expressed in a human. He saves us from our sins. He is our brother and our Lord at the same time.

The Holy Spirit guides us individually and as the Church. The Holy Spirit is the source of all knowledge and wisdom and creativity. The Spirit gives us faith and inspires us to express our faith in many ways.

These three persons exist in a dynamic community of love. The Father is the Lover, the Son is the Beloved, and the Spirit is the Bond of love among them, so the whole is greater than the parts. This "community of love" is a pattern for many aspects of the Christian life. We call this approach to community **Trinitarian**.

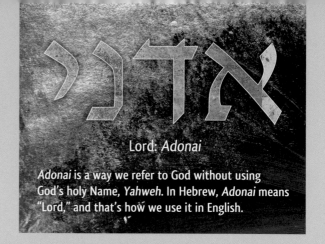

Lord: *Adonai*

Adonai is a way we refer to God without using God's holy Name, *Yahweh*. In Hebrew, *Adonai* means "Lord," and that's how we use it in English.

Of course, there's more to the Trinity than what we can say in this space, but this is a good start. Because the Trinity is a mystery, you can fill in some of the blanks yourself by thinking about ways God has acted in human history and in your own life.

SPIRITUAL BUT NOT RELIGIOUS

I went on a date with a guy who said he was spiritual but not religious. What's that all about?

Considering some of the idiotic things that have been said and done in the name of religion—and Christians are no exception—it's not surprising that some people of good will choose to distance themselves from religion while keeping their options open with God. Or your friend may have experience only with a church where he experienced toxic self-hatred, intolerance, or hypocrisy. Or maybe it was just plain boring. We Christians can be pretty good at making exciting things boring.

We'll assume your friend is trying sincerely to connect with God in various ways. But religion has more to offer than truthiness, bad art, or soul-draining homilies. A good parish will offer engaging preaching, liturgy that provides a transcendent experience, programs to learn more about our Faith, and opportunities to help those less fortunate than we. Our Christian tradition offers insights from thousands of years, so we don't have to reinvent the wheel ourselves. Christianity offers ways to approach regular prayer, so we can grow in our relationship with God. And as Christians, we're not saved by ourselves, but in community.

These are some good aspects of religion those who claim to be merely "spiritual" are missing out on. Maybe if he found a more with-it parish, your friend could take advantage of these opportunities and get beyond the negative religion he has experienced in the past.

Some people who say they're "spiritual but not religious" only say that so they don't seem insensitive. These are the ones who would rather just watch a football game on Sunday when there's a good parish nearby. Let's hope your friend isn't one of those!

a BYZANTINE cross

I wait for the LORD, my soul waits,
and in his word I hope...

Psalm 130:5

Jesus Changes the World

THE SON OF GOD

Jesus was a troublemaker. During his life, he made loads of enemies. The priests especially despised him because he didn't follow the rules. So they tried to frame him. They asked him trick questions to see if they could trap him. Finally, the religious leaders paid one of his friends to turn in Jesus. They got Jesus sentenced to the death penalty, and the Roman governor executed him. They thought they'd won. But as so often happens, God had other plans.

What they didn't realize was that God had sent Jesus to the people. Jesus was a Jew, and many of his people were crazy about him. But the leaders were out of touch with the people. They wanted Jesus to just shut up and follow the rules. They didn't understand Jesus had come not only to change their rules, but the whole world. Luke 4:14–21

When they got Jesus sentenced to death, the leaders thought that would put an end to Jesus and his message. Instead, it began a revolution that would spread to every part of the world. This revolution wasn't violent or angry. It's a revolution of love and justice and **forgiveness** in the face of hate and injustice and revenge. This revolution is Christianity.

Jesus: Totally Divine, Totally Human

Jesus was born a human like the rest of us. In this way, he's our brother. His parents cared for him, loved him, and taught him to follow the Jewish religion. But Jesus was also sent to us by God in a special way. In fact, God loves humans so much that he became one of us in the person of Jesus. So Jesus is totally divine and totally human. One of the Hebrew titles of Jesus explains this well: *Emmanuel*, which means "God with us." Colossians 1:15–20

There was one thing about how Jesus was born that's different from the rest of us. His mother, Mary, gave birth to Jesus without having sex with a man. This miracle is called the **Virgin Birth**. God did this to show that Jesus was divine—his own Son. Luke 1:26–38

Jesus Is the Way

In his life, Jesus set an example for us. He didn't just talk the talk, he walked it. He knew the religious leaders wanted to kill him, but he did the right thing anyway. The example Jesus gave us is as powerful as his words. Jesus didn't come just to teach us "fun facts" about God we could use on *Jeopardy* or in crossword puzzles. He came to teach us a way to live our lives. In fact, the first followers of Jesus, before they were called Christians, called our religion "the Way." By learning about Jesus and how he lived, we learn how to live our own lives. That's why some people, when faced with a

THE SAMARITAN WOMAN

The Samaritans were people in Jesus' time that no "good" Jew would talk to. They were the outsiders, the heretics. And, of course, in Jesus' time, women had no status in society. Most men paid little or no attention to women, as they were considered to be owned by men.

So you can imagine what a ruckus there was when Jesus one day sat down to chat with a Samaritan woman. This was a total double don't! She was shocked he would even speak to her. Even his disciples freaked a little.

Jesus didn't care who was in or who was out. To him, everybody was equal. He talked with the Samaritan woman, and she believed he was sent by God. She even went back to her village and told everyone about him.

Jesus told her his teaching was like water that would make you never be thirsty again. It's water for everybody who's thirsty, even those disrespected by "important" people.

You can read the story of Jesus and the Samaritan Woman in the Gospel of John 4:1–42.

profile

decision, ask themselves, "What would Jesus do?"
Matthew 11:28–30

Jesus Is the Truth

Jesus brought us a message. His message is the love of God and neighbor and how to live that way. But Jesus is more than a messenger of truth. He himself is the Truth. The teachings of Jesus aren't true just because Jesus was smart. They're true because God is Truth and Jesus is God. When people go against the teachings of Jesus—for example, by starting wars—they're not just disagreeing with some nice guy called Jesus. They're acting against everything God stands for. To pick and choose from the teachings of Jesus isn't right. Everything we learn from Jesus is one single Truth. John 8:31–32

Jesus Is the Life

Jesus said he came to give us a full life. He wants us to enjoy life and be happy. But some people think following Jesus means they have to give up fun and be unhappy. These folks need an attitude adjustment. All those things they think make life fun but are against what Jesus taught will in the end always make them unhappy. The **world** tells us we'll be happy if we have cooler clothes or a hotter car or more sex or if we get even with others. But these things don't really make us happy for long. Billionaires are often unhappy, and very poor people are often very happy.

Jesus teaches us what's important in life for the long haul. He promises us that if we follow him, we'll be happy not only in this life, but forever. Matthew 19:16–30

Jesus Can Change You and the World If You Let Him

Change is hard. Especially when all around us people say we're idiots to believe in Jesus and follow him. Some people take the easy way out. They say they believe in Jesus, but then they don't follow him. Or they only come to Jesus when they want something. It's not always easy to follow Jesus all the time, but the more we try, the happier we become.

Jesus is the Way, the Truth, and the Life. He gives us everything we need to be truly happy. John 14, 15, and 16

All you need is love

Looking for love? All of us are. Even most of our songs are about love. That's because love is the greatest desire of every human being. Everyone craves love. Scientists have shown that for newborn babies, love is more important than food.

The problem is, many people try to find love the wrong way. The whole reason Jesus came to us was to teach us about love.

We all love those who love us. But Jesus said that's not enough: "If you love those who love you, what good is that? Even bad people do that." It's true, isn't it? Even the Nazis would spend the day killing thousands of people and then go home to be loving husbands and fathers. If all people say about you when you die is that you loved your family, is that enough?

Jesus was radical about love. He even said we should love our enemies!

One time someone asked Jesus which of the 613 Jewish commandments was the most important. Jesus, who usually did things his own way, didn't choose one of the 613 laws as his answer.

Instead, he boiled down all the laws to loving God and loving our neighbor as much as we love ourselves. We call this teaching "the Great Commandment." Mark 12:28–34

The world usually thinks of love as either sexual love or the love of family. Jesus, however, said the greatest love is to give up your life for others. Giving up your life doesn't always mean dying; it can also mean spending your life in service to others.

As Christians we're called to look beyond the love the world gives us, to seek the love Jesus

backstory

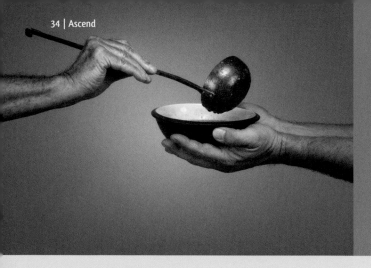

Jesus' Hebrew Name: *Yeshua*

Jesus is the Latin version of the Hebrew name *Yeshua*, which means "God saves." Another English form of this name is Joshua.

offers. If we believe what the world tells us about love, we'll never be really happy. Only the love that Jesus offers will make us happy.

One of the best guides to what love is was written by Paul. 1 Corinthians 13

Paul said that even if one is a great theologian, a mystic, a miracle worker, or a martyr, but does not have love, one is nothing. He said love is patient and kind. Love isn't pompous; it's not proud. It's not rude, selfish, or angry. Love doesn't bear a grudge.

Paul said the greatest things ever are faith, hope, and love,[1] but love is the most important.

....

1   Faith, hope, and love are called the "theological virtues." All virtue and morality is derived from them.

Some people—Christians and non-Christians alike—make it seem like Christianity's nothing but a lot of stupid rules.[2] They don't understand what Christianity's all about. But sometimes we Christians are to blame for this misunderstanding. When Christians are truly living according to God's will, others will say about us, "See how these Christians love everybody!"

Start with love. That's how we serve God—who is love—and our neighbor.

....

2   This isn't to say we don't have our share of stupid rules. But these rules are changeable, while the essence of our Faith is not. Who will change these rules? You will!

THE DA VINCI CODE

I read *The Da Vinci Code*. Don't the facts in this book show Christianity is a lie?

We've read *The Da Vinci Code* and seen the movie. It's a good story. It's interesting, exciting—a real page turner. But it's a novel. We also like *The Lord of the Rings*, but we don't go looking for hobbits.

This isn't the place to go into detail about this story. Even though it's fiction, some of the more absurd claims in it have been floating around for a long time, like the idea that Jesus was married to Mary Magdalene. Like the anti-Semitic hoax *The Protocols of the Elders of Zion*, these stories rear their ugly heads every so often. Sadly, there are always people anxious to believe them.

A lot of people have tried to answer these claims. Of course, that does nothing. People who believe in conspiracy theories won't accept an explanation from the people they think are involved in the conspiracy! "Ah, but that's what you're supposed to say, isn't it?" they say with a knowing wink.

So instead of answering all these claims, let's look at it this way: Suppose for a minute everything in *The Da Vinci Code* was true. How would that change the teachings of Jesus? How would that change the way you should live your own life? The answer, of course, is not at all. Such controversies are only a distraction from the message of Jesus. Imagine what could be accomplished if all the time and effort spent on arguing about that book were directed toward helping the poor!

in the media

a CELTIC cross

When you send forth your spirit, they are created;
and you renew the face of the ground.

Psalm 104:30

The Breath of God Gives Life

THE HOLY SPIRIT

You can give life. You've heard about mouth-to-mouth resuscitation. To do this, you exhale your breath into an unconscious person's mouth. Your breath can bring the person back to life and allow him or her to start breathing again. You really breathe life back into a person who would otherwise have died! This idea of breath as life is as old as scripture, and it's one way we explain the Holy Spirit.

In the very beginning of the Bible, God creates the human person. We read in Genesis 2:7, "The Lord God formed man out of the clay of the ground and blew into his nostrils the breath of life."[1] God blew Spirit into the human person at the moment of our creation.

The Holy Spirit Animates the Christian People

But the Spirit does more than just make us physically alive. By the power of the Holy Spirit we receive the gift of faith and are able to know God. You know God exists in three "persons": Father or Creator, Son (Jesus) or Redeemer, and Holy Spirit.

While it was Jesus who was seen by his apostles and disciples, it was the power of the Holy Spirit that allowed Jesus' followers to see him as the Son of God. So while Jesus is the Word of God in human form, the Holy Spirit allows us to have faith to know Jesus as Lord.

The word *Spirit* used in relation to the Holy Spirit comes from the Hebrew word *ruach*, which means "wind" or "breath." The idea of the Holy Spirit was also present in the Hebrew concept of

Shekinah, the presence of God among the people, which had a feminine identity. Early Christians sometimes referred to the Spirit as *Sophia*, the Greek word for "wisdom" (also feminine, so there is precedent in the Christian tradition for referring to the Holy Spirit as "she"). We as the Church know that Jesus spoke of the Holy Spirit; you can read this in Matthew 28:19. Jesus also called the Holy Spirit the "Paraclete." This Greek word means "one who is called to your side" as if to be there to always help you.

And that's exactly what the Holy Spirit does. The Holy Spirit guides not only individuals but the Church as a community. Romans 8:1–27 In fact, our English word *inspiration* literally means to have the Spirit enter into us.

We Learn about the Spirit in Symbols

Water is used in baptism as a sign of the Spirit's action. Through a special blessing the priest or deacon asks God to send the Holy Spirit into the water. Being dunked (immersed) into this water is a strong sign of dying and being reborn. In baptism we are reborn as Christians with God's Spirit, giving a new kind of life to our spirit or soul. Romans 6:3–11

---

1 Again, we caution you against reading this story literally. Think about the deeper meaning.

Oil (made from olives) is used when we celebrate the sacrament of confirmation. In this sacrament, a Christian is anointed with the oil called "Chrism." To be anointed means to be set aside and made sacred. In fact, the word *Christ* comes from the Greek word for "anointed," meaning Jesus was set aside for a special purpose. So in anointing, we are set apart to follow the example of Jesus, the Christ. Romans 8:28–39

In the waters of baptism and through confirmation a person receives the fullness of God's Holy Spirit. The Spirit walks by your side, allows you to be in a strong relationship with God, and gives you wisdom and courage to live as a follower of Jesus Christ. In short, the Spirit is life!

Fire is another symbol of the Spirit. Fire changes things. The heat of fire produces energy, and God has unlimited energy. The fire of the Spirit in you can change your life. On Pentecost the apostles received the Holy Spirit as tongues of fire that came to rest on them. Acts of the Apostles 2 At first they were afraid and unsure what to do after Jesus left. But after they received the Holy Spirit, they had the courage, wisdom, and faith to go out and change the world. Matthew 28:16–20

The Spirit will give us the same courage, wisdom, and faith to change our world and our lives. With the power of God's Spirit alive in you, nothing is impossible. Wisdom 7:22–30

I've Got to Be Me

Our spiritual life grows through the power of the Spirit. Yet the Holy Spirit does different things with different people. 1 Corinthians 12:1–31

To one is given through the Spirit the utterance of wisdom, and to another the utterance of knowledge according to the same Spirit, to another faith by the same Spirit, to another the gift of healing by the one Spirit, to another the working of miracles, to another prophecy, to another the discernment of spirits, to another various kinds of tongues, to another the interpretation of tongues. (1 Corinthians 12:8–10)

When we allow ourselves to be open to the gifts of God's Holy Spirit we become more and more like Jesus. We become people of love and peace. We treat each other with respect and dignity. We find it easy to love others as much as we love ourselves. We live our lives as true children of a loving God. 1 John 4:7–13

What can you see yourself doing with the gift of God's Spirit? The possibilities are exciting and endless!

SPEAKING IN TONGUES

A coworker told me "speaking in tongues" is the sign of a real Christian. Is this true?

Before Jesus returned to heaven, he promised to send us God's Spirit (the Paraclete) who would be with us forever. On the day of Pentecost Jesus made good on that promise.

That day, the disciples all began to speak in different languages they didn't know before. When they went outside to preach to the crowds, everyone understood what the disciples were saying, even though the people were all from different nations gathered to celebrate the Jewish festival. It's important to understand God allowed this powerful sign to show the power of the Spirit. It's called the gift of tongues.

Today some people say they can "speak in tongues." God may allow this to happen so we can see proof of the Spirit alive and among us. We should be open to this possibility.

However, some preachers, who may be more into putting on a show, seem to cause others to "speak in tongues" at will. Remember, it's God who is in control of this event if it in fact happens. It's also important to remember that on the Day of Pentecost, the apostles spoke in tongues so they could be understood. It's not clear how speaking a language no one can understand is the same as using a known language to teach others the Good News of Jesus Christ.

Use your judgment when you encounter speaking in tongues (also called *glossolalia*). What is its effect? Does it set up one group of Christians as superior to others? Or does it inspire people to reorient their lives to service? If it makes only for a spectacle, it may fall into the category of "things that make you go, *hmmm.*"

in the media

How you can be a wise person

Wisdom is a gift of the Holy Spirit. In fact, an ancient title of the Holy Spirit is Holy Wisdom, or *Hagia Sophia* in Greek. The church in Istanbul that was the greatest church in the world for nearly a thousand years was named for the Holy Spirit under this feminine title. To have wisdom is to have good judgment, to be able to make good decisions. It's knowing when we're doing the right thing. 1 Corinthians 2

Wisdom is different from intelligence or education. While it may be founded on experience and knowledge, wisdom is a higher form of knowing. Maybe you know someone, like your grandfather or aunt, who always gives good advice. Even though they might not have "book smarts," they understand what's important in life. They interpret and evaluate knowledge and experience to arrive at a state of wisdom. Wisdom in people like this shines out. Everybody knows they're wise, and people respect what they say. Or at least they should.

Being wise, as God wants us to be, makes our lives rich. The more confident we become of our wisdom, the more confident we become with ourselves. Others who see we are wise will look up to us—but maybe not at first. Jesus always acted with wisdom.

There are books in the Bible called "wisdom literature." You can look through the Books of Job, Psalms, Proverbs, Ecclesiastes, Song of Songs, Wisdom, and Sirach. These writings give you an idea of the tradition of biblical wisdom.

Wisdom isn't something we just get one day. We gain wisdom by looking at our lives, knowing people we admire and confiding in them, and learning from our mistakes. All these things give us ways to check ourselves, to see what worked for us, what didn't work. The wise person has

the ability to step back and evaluate how she and others are living and draw conclusions from that insight. We need to understand how we make decisions for ourselves and for others. We need to ask ourselves if these decisions will allow us to live in freedom and know they will.

True wisdom is a gift from God. As with any gift, we can choose to use it or we can put it away and disregard the giver. A lot depends on how we value the gift. We can't live a life filled with good things if we don't use the gift of wisdom. One of the saddest things to see is people facing the same problems over and over their whole lives. They're like hamsters on a wheel. God doesn't want us to be hamsters. Even Jesus had to grow in wisdom before he could begin his mission. Luke 2:22–40 If it was necessary for Jesus, why are we any different?

Pray that when you receive the gift of wisdom you'll use it well and be able to pass it on to those who are not yet wise. True wisdom will make you a fearless, confident leader and a trusted confidant. People will look up to you because you'll be filled with the Holy Spirit. 1 Kings 3:5-14

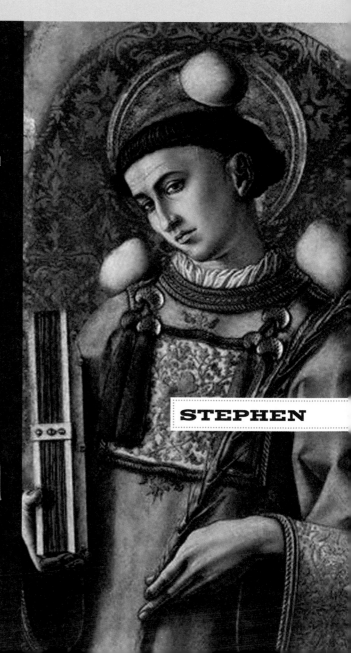

STEPHEN

Stephen was chosen by the Apostles to serve the early Christian community. He and six other men were the first deacons. He was filled with the Holy Spirit. He worked miracles to help people and he loved the poor.

Those who were not believers recruited false witnesses who testified against Stephen.

At his trial, Stephen gave a speech in his defense. He said he was only doing these things because he loved God and the people and wanted to serve them. He said the judges weren't following God's law. This made the judges furious. They sentenced Stephen to the death penalty.

A crowd stoned Stephen. All the while he was being tortured, Stephen shouted praises to God. A martyr is a person who gives up his or her life for the Faith, and Stephen was the first Christian martyr.

You can read the story of Stephen in the Acts of the Apostles, chapters 6 and 7.

profile

ΠΕΝΤΕΚΟΟΤή

50 Days: Pentecost

The Greek word *Pentekoste* means "fiftieth day." This was the Jewish Feast of Weeks, or *Shavuot* (fifty days after Passover) when the Holy Spirit came to the followers of Jesus.

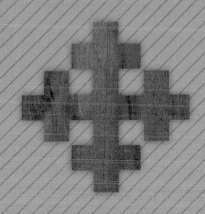

a COPTIC cross

Your kingdom is an everlasting kingdom,
and your dominion endures throughout all generations.

PSALM 145:13

The Kingdom of God Is Here and Now

TEACHINGS AND MINISTRY OF JESUS

Magic and miracles. What's the difference? Magic is a skillful illusion. By tricking our eyes, the magician gets us to think something happened that didn't really happen at all. A miracle is much different. While we can see the miracle, there's no natural explanation as to how it really happened. To believe in a miracle requires faith.

Jesus began his ministry by working many **miracles.** He made the blind see, the deaf hear, sick people were cured, even the dead were brought back to life. Did Jesus do all these things because he felt sorry for these people? That's part of it, but there is much more to the miracles of Jesus. The miracles of Jesus were powerful signs that the Messiah (the one sent by God) had come and the **Kingdom of God**[1] had arrived. Mark 1:40–42

Jesus' cousin John the Baptist had been telling people that someone would soon be sent by God. So one day John's followers came to Jesus and asked him if he was the one sent from God. Jesus said, "Go and tell John what you have seen and heard: the blind receive their sight, the lame walk, lepers are cleansed, the deaf hear, the dead are raised, the poor have good news brought to them." Luke 7:18–23

These people may not have understood what Jesus was telling them. But long before Jesus lived, the prophet Isaiah said this: "Then the eyes of the blind shall be opened; and the ears of the deaf unstopped; then will the lame leap like a deer, and the tongue of the speechless sing for joy."[2] Isaiah 35: 1–10 The prophet was talking to the people of his time but also looking ahead to a time when God would send the one he promised would save his people.

So Jesus' answer to John's friends is really a way of saying, "Yes, I'm the one you've been waiting for, I'm here to save you."

The Kingdom of God Is upon Us

The miracles of Jesus tell us that God's Kingdom has arrived. Yet these miracles didn't last forever. Those whom Jesus raised from the dead would have to die again. Those who were cured would eventually die of other causes. People who witnessed these signs were challenged to think about what they meant.

The miracles of Jesus challenge us as well. We are asked to open our eyes to things that blind us. Things like selfishness, prejudice, hatred, and violence. We need to hear more clearly, too, so we can understand others who are not like us. And we also need new life in us so our hearts will be open to everyone. These are all ways that we can

---

1 Some people prefer to use the term Reign of God because it's gender neutral. That's cool. It means the same thing. We use Kingdom in this book because so many Christian writings use this term.

2 Are you sometimes at a loss for words to describe your faith to others? Perhaps you need to have your tongue set free so that you may freely speak the truth.

respond to the coming of God's Kingdom in the here and now. Isaiah 11:1–9

So Jesus told us that God's Kingdom was here. But that was more than two thousand years ago. We might look around and wonder why it's taking so long for God's Kingdom to change the world.

Still Waiting for the Kingdom?

Jesus never said God's Kingdom in its fullness would be here overnight. Jesus said the Kingdom was like planting a seed. Matthew 13:1–43 A seed needs time to grow into a tree and produce good fruit. This made teaching about God's Kingdom hard for Jesus because many people wanted instant results. A lot of us are like that today, too. Those of us who are type A personalities should pay attention here.

The people of Jesus' time also expected the Messiah to be a strong leader, maybe even a king. Jesus wasn't a soldier or a king in this world. He led by words and example. He taught the people by telling stories called **parables.** These stories told people what the Kingdom of God was like. The stories were also meant to touch people's hearts and change the way they thought about God and each other. Luke 15:11–31

The parables of Jesus make us think even today. Are we ready to open our eyes, hear better and have new life in us? How important is the Kingdom of God to us? Matthew 13:44–46

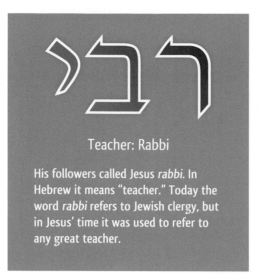

Teacher: Rabbi

His followers called Jesus *rabbi.* In Hebrew it means "teacher." Today the word *rabbi* refers to Jewish clergy, but in Jesus' time it was used to refer to any great teacher.

Not everyone then or now is ready to hear the words of Jesus and respond to them. Luke 8:4–15 The Kingdom of God is **countercultural** and difficult for most people to accept. The teachings of Jesus describe an upside-down world, one in which those things most treasured by the world are rejected by God. To the world we Christians are fools; our beliefs directly oppose what others feel is simple common sense or pragmatism, business as usual. 1 Corinthians 1:18–31 and 2:1–16

Jesus didn't come to gain power on Earth. He came to show us who God is and how God wants us to live. Jesus showed us the power of God through his miracles and taught things that challenge everyone who hears them to make changes in their lives.

The Promises of Jesus Are the Real Thing

Jesus promised that those who do see and listen well will have lives filled with happiness no matter who you are, what you've done, or where you find yourself. God is always with us through the person of Jesus—and where God is present, love is present also. Now Jesus did not say our happiness will be without suffering. In fact he pretty much guaranteed that following him will cause suffering and persecution. But he also promised a joy that will transcend all suffering on his behalf, foolishness that will overcome the wisdom of the world, weakness that will overpower the strong. 1 Corinthians 1:18–25

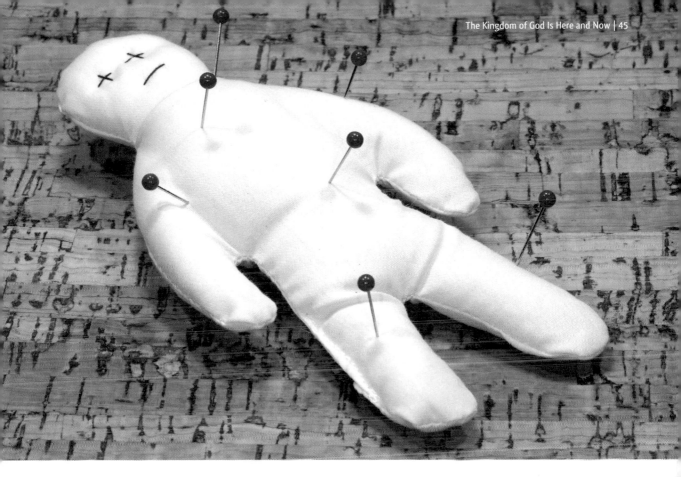

AN EYE FOR AN EYE

I've heard we should seek "an eye for an eye" because it's in the Bible.

People of the ancient world felt that if someone harmed you or stole from you, you were entitled to kill that person. The Torah forbade that, setting up a system of compensation for personal injury that allowed only commensurate retribution. Exodus 21:12–32 Today we still hear these words, "An eye for an eye."[3] Red with anger, some shout, "It's in the Bible!" And it is. Jesus, however, took the limits on revenge to another level.

One of the hardest things about the teachings of Jesus is how they can turn the world upside down and challenge us to look at things in a totally different way.

Jesus was well aware of this ancient tradition of limited retribution. It was part of his Jewish heritage. But in his Sermon on the Mount Jesus said this: "You have heard it said: 'An eye for an eye and a tooth for a tooth.' But I say to you, offer no resistance to one who is evil. When someone strikes you on [your] right cheek, turn the other one to him as well." Matthew 5:38–42

Christ continually challenges us to overcome our human inclinations for the sake of the Kingdom of God. It may be hard for us today to hear the words of Christ and follow them without fail. To be a follower of Christ doesn't mean we get it perfect every time. It means we keep trying to hear him and live his words.

....
3   *If you like to throw around Latin phrases, this eye-for-an-eye business is called* lex talionis.

The upside-down world of the Beatitudes

People began to follow Jesus everywhere. He was saying things that were different, and many people came to hear this new teacher and make up their own minds about what he had to say.

One day Jesus went into the countryside to teach his followers. There were a lot of people gathered around him, so he sat down among them and began to teach them.

This is the setting for the scripture passage known as the Sermon on the Mount. In it Jesus gives us an idea of what the Kingdom of God looks like. Matthew 5, 6, and 7

The most important part of the Sermon on the Mount is a series of nine statements Jesus made describing how we should live. Each of these statements begins with the word *blessed*, so they're called the Beatitudes (from the Latin word *beatus*, "blessed"):

> Blessed are the poor in spirit, for theirs is the kingdom of heaven.
> Blessed are those who mourn, for they will be comforted.
> Blessed are the meek, for they will inherit the earth.[4]
> Blessed are those who hunger and thirst for righteousness,[5] for they will be filled.
> Blessed are the merciful, for they will receive mercy.
> Blessed are the pure of heart, for they will see God.
> Blessed are the peacemakers, for they will be called children of God.

> Blessed are those who are persecuted for righteousness' sake, for theirs is the kingdom of heaven.
> Blessed are you when people revile you and persecute you and utter all kinds of evil against you falsely on my account. Rejoice and be glad, for your reward is great in heaven.
> (Matthew 5:3-11)

The Beatitudes describe the ultimate countercultural way of life. It's Jesus' way of life and the way God wants us all to live. If it were easy to follow the Beatitudes, everybody would be doing it. They depict an attitude in direct opposition to everything the world holds as true: Don't cry, be happy. The strong will inherit the earth. The rich are the most important. All these assumptions of worldly "wisdom" and more are shattered by the Beatitudes.

These statements of Jesus are at the heart of our Christian identity. The Beatitudes show us Jesus' love for the people and give us a guide for the Christian life.

People talk a lot about the Ten Commandments.[6] Some say the Commandments describe how a Christian should live. But the Commandments are the bare minimum. Do you really want to stand before Jesus on the last day and say, "Um, well, I never killed anyone…"? The Beatitudes, however, show us the positive ideal of the Christian life. Paul VI called the Beatitudes the *Magna Carta* of the Kingdom of God.

Jesus calls us all to new life in him, and the Beatitudes bless us and give us all hope as we make an effort to live life in Christ. The Beatitudes show us true happiness is not found in riches, fame, power, or any material thing. True happiness can only be found in healthy relationships with each other and with God.

---

4   The word *meek* as used here does not mean the kind of person who's afraid of his or her own shadow. You know the type. Rather, the scriptural concept of being meek is to be gentle hearted, one who is unassuming, undemanding—the kind of person who doesn't try to buy fifty things in the ten-items-or-less checkout at the supermarket. The "earth" is the Kingdom of God.

5   In the Hebrew tradition Jesus lived by, the words *righteousness* and *justice* are interchangeable.

---

6   For example, some people are always trying to put up the Ten Commandments in secular places. But are the Ten Commandments placed in such a prominent place in their own church, or even in their hearts? When faced with such a proposal to post the Ten Commandments in public buildings, the lone Jewish member of one state legislature said, "The Lord gave the Ten Commandments to my people, and he does not need the assistance of the Tennessee General Assembly in promulgating them."

backstory

PETER

Peter and Jesus were close friends. Peter was impetuous and outspoken and often didn't get it. Yet Jesus always showed great patience with Peter, despite his sometimes fumbling attempts to understand the teachings of Jesus.

One of the great stories of Peter's doubt was when Jesus invited him to walk on water. After a few steps, Peter's faith failed, and he began to sink. One can almost imagine Jesus laughing gently as he pulled Peter from the water. (See Matthew 14:22–33.)

When the Romans arrested Jesus, Peter three times denied publicly he had ever met Jesus before. He hid himself as Jesus died. Most of us would feel betrayed if our friend abandoned us like that. But Jesus not only forgave Peter, he made him first among the Apostles.

At times it seemed Peter was a quivering mass of doubt and fear. Yet Peter became the first bishop of Rome, the leader of the Church, and he too eventually was sentenced to the death penalty for his faith. Jesus never gave up on Peter, and he will never give up on us either. Jesus knows our human limitations yet loves us all the same. If he can make a guy like Peter head of the Church, imagine what he can do with you!

profiler

Sing to the **LORD** a new song,
his praise in the assembly of the faithful.

God Always Wins

THE LIFE, DEATH, AND RESURRECTION OF JESUS

Jesus began his ministry with drama. In his hometown synagogue, he read from the Book of Isaiah where it speaks of freeing prisoners, giving sight to the blind, and lifting oppression. He said he'd do all these things, and for three years, he became a celebrity as he did all this and more. It seemed to many that Israel would finally be freed from Roman occupation, Jesus would be their new king, and everybody would live happily ever after!

But things didn't work out exactly that way.

Even when Jesus began his public ministry at the synagogue in Nazareth, some people were so upset about what he said they tried to kill him. Luke 4:14–30 People in his home town dissed him. Matthew 13:54–58

This negative reaction continued to badger Jesus. Even as crowds followed him, some people never did like him. And every way they could, they tried to get him.

But Jesus wasn't afraid of them. He never changed what he said or did just to suit them. He kept on teaching the people, and they believed in him. He had a job to do, and nothing would stop him! Jesus understood how the world works. He knew that if powerful people wanted him dead, eventually they'd get their way. But he also knew that God's plan comes first. Jesus knew no matter what his enemies did to him, God would win in the end. So he always spoke truth to power. Luke 11:37–54

Good News for All People

Jesus always said he came to bring us Good News. The word *gospel* is an Old English word that means "good news."

What is the Good News? That we can be free from **sin**, fear, death, and doubt. Whenever he would cure someone, Jesus would say, "Your faith has healed you." Jesus wasn't performing magic tricks. He was showing people that faith had real power they couldn't even imagine. Jesus was always teaching us faith: faith in the love and mercy of God, faith in our ability to do great things for God and others, faith in what Jesus taught about how to live our lives.

Jesus Is Sentenced to the Death Penalty

For three years, Jesus went all over teaching people how to live by faith. But his greatest lesson was still to come. 1 Corinthians 1:18–25

You see, Jesus also came to teach us how to be servants of all. And the way he would teach us was to become the **Suffering Servant**. He would undergo great pain and a horrible death to show us how deep his love for everybody is. Isaiah 52:13–15 and 53:1–12 In many ways, his message to us is this: Love hurts.

Things were getting pretty bad. The enemies of Jesus had swung into high gear. Jesus knew it was only a matter of time before they got him. So he planned a special celebration of the Jewish feast of **Passover**, his **Last Supper**, with his friends. At dinner, he washed the feet of his disciples to show them they had to be **servants** of all people. He talked to them about his hopes for them. Then he went with them to pray in the nearby Garden of Gethsemane. He knew one of his disciples had slipped out during dinner to turn him in. While Jesus was praying, Roman soldiers came to arrest him. They tortured him and the next day they executed him after a fixed trial. John 13–19

But the death of Jesus was beautiful, even as it was terrible to watch. Jesus died out of love, and with his death—and the big surprise to follow—our relationship with God changed. Hebrews 9:11–14 We were no longer slaves to sin but could call God Father and Jesus our brother. Eternal happiness was now available to all people, past, present, and future.[1] We have witnessed the most perfect form of love, and we are called to live that love in our own lives. Romans 5:1–11

....

1   *Remember: God's not limited by our reality of time. So those who had served God and others before the time of Jesus shared in his victory.*

The Big Surprise

The followers of Jesus were grief stricken and terrified. When Jesus had been arrested, nearly all of them scampered off to hide, abandoning him. Not only had the Romans killed Jesus, but now they might come after them, too. His followers didn't know what to do. They laid low out of fear.

But on the third day, an amazing thing happened. The body of Jesus was gone from the tomb. Luke 23:50–56 and 24:1–12 Then people began seeing him alive in different places. Luke 24:13–49

God had won after all! Jesus had talked to his disciples before about resurrection, but they hadn't understood. Matthew 16:21–23 They now began to understand that Jesus was the first to rise from the dead, and all of us would one day rise too. The resurrection was God's proof that Jesus was his Son and that we should believe what Jesus taught us. Jesus is the Master of life and death. Death has no power over him. It has no power over us as his followers. 1 Corinthians 15:50–57

We Are Resurrection People

God always wins. That's one thing we learn from the life, death, and resurrection of Jesus. No matter who is against us, God is always for us, and his plan will always prevail. Some people see good and evil as equal enemies, always fighting, never sure which side will win. But as Christians we know differently.

Good is stronger than evil. Good will always win in the end, even when it looks like evil has the upper hand. Romans 8:28–39

Is death beautiful?

To the world, death is pretty much considered the worst thing that can happen to you. But for Christians, death is not an end, but a beginning.

In horror movies, death is depicted as the ultimate evil. Demons, psychos, zombies, monsters, and evil spirits kill people in these movies. This scares us, because supposedly dying is the worst thing that can happen to us. After all, isn't death the ultimate downer?

But there are worse things than death. Living a completely selfish life, for example. Being tortured. Going your whole life without experiencing the love of God. Living your life vicariously through the celebrities you read about in *People*. These are just a few examples.

The Christian doesn't fear death. For Christians, the experience of death is often something very beautiful. Perhaps you've experienced the death of someone who was a strong Christian. As sad as you were, you had to admit death was something good

ANTI-SEMITISM

What about those people who say we should hate the Jews for killing Jesus?

News flash: The *Romans* killed Jesus! So, by the same reasoning, you might as well hate all Italians. Yes, some leaders of the Jewish people did oppose Jesus and conspired to turn him over to the Romans. Yet many Jews honored him as a great teacher. If a people can be held responsible for the actions of their leaders, we Americans have much to answer for!

Jesus was a Jew, as were his mother and all his first followers. We must also remember Jesus went willingly to his death out of love for us. As Jesus' death offers redemption to all of us, all of us as well are responsible for his death.

The idiotic idea that the Jews killed Jesus has been responsible for atrocities throughout history. It's also led to distrust and hatred of the Jewish people, a sin we call "anti-Semitism."

Even today there are people who accuse the Jews of all kinds of wild conspiracies, like controlling all the world's money, or trying to get rid of Christianity. All these rumors are *lies*.

We should always respect the Jewish people. They gave us our scripture and were the first to teach that there is only one God. Many of our Christian beliefs, liturgical practices, and customs come from the Jews. We owe them a lot!

הללויה

Praise the Lord: *Hallelujah*

The word *Alleluia* comes from the Hebrew word *hallelujah*, which means "Praise the Lord." Christians use "Alleluia" as an expression of joy and celebration, especially to welcome the Gospel and at Easter.

in the media

for that person. He or she was peaceful and maybe even looking forward to death.

This is the concept of Christian death. It involves a great act of trust and love of God. The dying person realizes he or she is going to God, and this isn't a scary feeling, but a happy one.

Of course, there's a difference between death and the process of dying. It's natural to fear a long and painful process of dying, even for Christians. No one wants to endure months of agony. But for

the Christian, that moment of giving up earthly life for something better is very special.

Why can Christian death be called beautiful? Because the dying person knows, without a doubt, that he or she will be happy forever and that one day God will raise up his or her body. We're told that when we die "every tear will be wiped away." We'll be released from sickness, loneliness,

backstory

addiction, poverty, injustice—whatever has made our lives painful.

When a Christian dies, we remember especially the life, death, and resurrection of Jesus. It was the incarnation that opened for us the possibility of a wonderful new existence.

It's wrenching to lose someone we love. We wish that person could always stay with us because we like having him or her around. A little part of us dies with them, and our life may never be the same.

But we have the consolation of hope that we'll see them again. They will not be as we last see them, sick and in pain. They will be happy, as will we, enjoying their company forever in the presence of God.

And that's something to look forward to.

For a long time, people thought Mary Magdalene was a prostitute, though scripture never says this. Not so much. She was always a faithful follower of Jesus. Eastern Christians call her "Equal to the Apostles."

When Jesus was arrested, most of the men abandoned Jesus. They hid as he was dying. But Mary Magdalene was right there with Jesus to the end. She stood by the cross and watched him die. She wasn't afraid others would see her there.

Mary and some other women were the first to learn Jesus had risen from the dead. They told the men, but the men wouldn't believe the women. They had to see for themselves. Mary wasn't upset about the doubt of the men. She knew she was right.

Mary Magdalene was a great follower of Jesus. She never abandoned him. She was the first to see Jesus after the resurrection. She went on to teach many people about Jesus for the rest of her life.

MARY MAGDALENE

profile

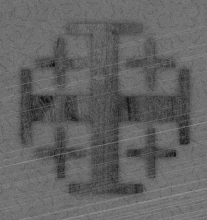

a JERUSALEM cross

The LORD knows our thoughts,
that they are but an empty breath.

We Don't Choose God; God Chooses Us

GRACE, FREE WILL, AND SIN

We don't call all the shots. God alone is all powerful. For some, that title may seem like God controls everything. And it's true that God keeps an eye on all Creation. God set the entire universe into motion; he created everything from nothing. When we grasp that concept, if we can, that certainly credits God with a lot of power and might. But at the same time, God created humans to choose him freely. And therein lay all our problems, but also something wonderful.

The Book of Genesis tells us God saw all Creation as good. Genesis 1 Wouldn't it be natural for anyone who made something as spectacular as the universe to look at it and know it was good? And it's by the **grace** of God that all things are kept in existence. All creation is constantly in the mind of God. Psalm 104

Grace Is a Free Gift of God

The last and greatest thing God created was the human person. Of all Creation, God has a special love for us. In fact we're made in God's own image. Humans are the only beings in God's Creation who have the ability to know God. Maybe you've heard of grace,[1] a share in God's life. It's grace that allows us to enter into a relationship with God. Grace can also be explained as God's love given to us, a love we can feel when our relationship with God is right. Isaiah 55:1–13

When you're looking beyond yourself, maybe for something bigger, maybe to find your purpose in life, that's a good example of God's grace moving your mind and heart in the direction of knowing the Truth. This inner need we have to know where we came from and where we're going is God's Spirit working within us. And like faith, grace is a free gift. We don't earn grace; God freely gives it. Ephesians 2:1–10

Freedom: Gift or Curse?

So God is all powerful. OK. We also know God is all loving. And God loves us because God made us in his own image to share divine life. (We can see most clearly in the person of Jesus what God thinks of all humans.) Humans have both the ability and the choice to love or not to love.

One thing God isn't? All demanding. God gives us the choice to love or not to love, and that includes loving or not loving God. This choice all people are given is called **free will**. So by God's grace, we are

---

1   Oh, come on now! Certainly you've at least heard of it in that wonderful song "Amazing Grace." That song is a beautiful meditation on the nature of grace, which finds us in our blindness and misery and lifts us up to new life in faith, hope, and love. Grace really is amazing! When you consider that this song was written by a former slave trader, that gives us a powerful perspective on grace!

ven the freedom and power to choose to know and love God.[2] Galatians 4:1–9

Love therefore is an act of will. You can't touch it or examine it on a table. We come to know someone loves us by what they have done or want to do for us. God has done everything for us. He has given us life on earth and the gift of eternal life after we leave this world.

And Here's the Part about Sin

When through our free will we choose to love God, we enter into a relationship with him. When we choose not to love God and all that God has done for us we sin. Sin, then, is really a conscious choice not to love. Note that we say "conscious" and "choice." You can't sin if you're not aware that an act (or a failure to act[3]) is a sin, or if you haven't freely consented to it. Romans 6:1–23

The Ten Commandments tell us something about sin. Certainly, choosing to turn our backs on a God who created us in his image and loves us enough to share eternal life with us is a serious offense. We also learn from Jesus about sins of not acting. Matthew 25:31–46

Knowing what's sinful isn't rocket science. In fact, God even gave each of us an internal compass[4] to guide us, called a **conscience**. It's the law God has written in your heart. Romans 2:12–16 The **Second Vatican Council** (Vatican II) called the conscience "the most secret core and sanctuary of a person. There he is alone with God, whose

voice echoes in his depths."[5] We cannot ignore our conscience. Deuteronomy 30:11–14

This internal compass can get out of whack if we don't maintain it. As Moe Szyslak, sage of Springfield, observed, "I've done stuff I'm not proud of. And the stuff I am proud of is disgusting." It's up to each one of us to know God more intimately so that our sense of good and bad will be authentic. We do this by reading and reflecting on scripture, praying, listening to our bishops, and above all getting to know Jesus, the Way, the Truth, and the Life. Jesus is God in the flesh, and everything Jesus says and does tells us something about who God is, how God wants us to respond to him and each other, and where God wants us to be when our life on Earth is over.

We must avoid being overly concerned about sinning by accident,[6] or dwelling on past sins after we've been forgiven. And there are gradations of sin; some are more serious than others. Stealing a candy bar from Wal-Mart isn't as bad as neglecting the poor, for example.

The key to overcoming sin isn't keeping lists of rules and checking them twice, but to let ourselves be infused with love. As Paul wrote, "Love does no evil to the neighbor; hence love is the fulfillment of the law" (Romans 13:10).

Falling in Love and Just Plain Falling

Being a Christian means more than just being baptized. Being a Christian means getting to know the Father through the Son in the Holy Spirit. Being a Christian means falling in love with God. Being a Christian means making choices to love God and people everywhere in God's world. Being a Christian is also knowing that when we sin or make bad choices God is always there to invite us back into relationship with him. Luke 19:1–10 While we live, it's never too late to return to God. Matthew 20:1–16

To be a Christian is to live in a way that's so different people notice your goodness without you having to tell them how good you are! Being a Christian is accepting the gift of God's grace, freely choosing to love, and wanting to share the Good News of God's love with everyone you meet in one way or another. 1 Corinthians 2

2   You could apply what Homer Simpson said about alcohol to our free will: "The cause of and solution to all our problems."

3   Yes, not doing something can be a sin. We call these "sins of omission." One example is passing an injured person without stopping to help. Sins of omission are the most common way we sin.

4   If you're of a scientific bent, you might like to think of conscience as more of a gyroscope than a compass. It doesn't just show direction; it helps to keep you in balance.

5   This quote is from section 16 of the Council's Pastoral Constitution on the Church in the Modern World, also called Gaudium et Spes. This may be a good time to point out that official Roman documents are called by the first few words of the Latin version. So gaudium et spes means "joy and hope," which are the first words of this document and also a good way of looking at our role in the world!

6   The fear of sinning by accident is called "scrupulosity," and for some unfortunate people it's a huge problem.

backstory

The struggle between good and evil

No doubt you've seen cartoons in which a person trying to make a decision is being pulled in two directions by a tiny angel on one shoulder and a tiny devil on the other. This can make for some entertaining comedy, but it's not the way we Christians view good and evil.

Today we also hear some people, even high government officials, describe "us" as good and "them" as evil. Wars are sold as fights between good and evil. We may hear someone accused of a crime described as "pure evil." None of these is a Christian way to look at good and evil.

First of all, the belief that good and evil are equal is a tired old idea called "dualism." It's been expressed by groups such as the Gnostics, Manicheans, and the Cathars. (Even though these groups believed the material world was evil and humans were spirits trapped in an evil world, they

still believed that good would ultimately triumph.) We have a special word for this idea of good and evil being equal: *heresy!* Evil is the absence of good, so it can never approach equality with good. The little angel and the little devil in cartoons make these two concepts seem roughly equal, and that's wrong, because good is a far more powerful force.

Second, people are created good. We know that in Genesis God created humanity in his own image and likeness, and he found all his Creation good. So no person can be evil. They may do evil things, but that doesn't mean they stop being inherently good, capable of conversion, worthy of salvation in God's eyes, and at all times loved by God.

Despite the goodness of Creation and the goodness of every human being, it's still true that the disobedience of our first parents brought evil into the world. We experience this evil at the hands of others and through "natural evils" such as sickness and death, the result of our fallen state. And while evil remains the absence of good, that doesn't mean evil is just "smoke and mirrors."

Evil can become manifest through the material world, for example, in the very real evil of nuclear weapons.

It is the wonderful nature of God always to pull good from evil. Our Christian tradition can even encourage us to be in awe of how God did this from the beginning. In the Easter Proclamation sung by the deacon at the Easter Vigil, we hear of God pulling triumph from tragedy in response to the very first sin of disobedience: "O happy fault, O necessary sin of Adam, which gained for us so great a Redeemer!"

The good that supplants evil may not always be readily apparent to us. But we should trust that God will do this in God's own time. In our own lives, we may recognize such occasions when grace has filled the empty void of evil to work marvelous things.

Consider the legendary Catholic African-American singer Ethel Waters, conceived by the rape of her impoverished thirteen-year-old mother. What good could come of such an evil act? And yet Waters flourished, becoming an influential member of the Harlem Renaissance in the 1920s. Imagine her singing "Stormy Weather" at the Cotton Club, art and beauty arising from such terror.

Some may see good and evil engaged in an eternal knock-down-drag-out fight. But we know good will always win out. In your own life, never call the victory for evil, because good will arrive victorious, maybe when you least expect it.

PUNISHMENT ON EARTH

Does God punish us on Earth?

We call God our Father. This sounds like a parent-child relationship for sure. Parents take care of their children, and part of that responsibility is discipline. Every child sooner or later is punished for something he or she does that Mom or Dad didn't like. Maybe our parents even said something like, "If you do that, God will punish you." While our parents may have been well meaning, God isn't out to punish us.

In fact any punishment we may feel on Earth, as it relates to God, is probably from the fact that we've moved away from God on our own. In moving away from that perfect Lover, the one who give us all the best things, we leave ourselves open to feeling a loss. But it's not God punishing us, rather we are punishing ourselves.

We say God is perfect Love. How can perfect Love be the one to punish? So one has to wonder about those who say that disasters, epidemics, and wars are punishment from God. Who is this God they're talking about, and where did they find him?

Natural disasters and other catastrophes are not evidence of the punishment of God. For example, your authors live in Southern California, with full knowledge that one day a huge earthquake will strike, perhaps killing hundreds and destroying cities. Shall we then blame God? *We* chose to live here.

In such situations, God weeps along with all those who are afflicted; God does not cause suffering of any kind. Our God is compassionate and merciful. Ezekiel 18:25–32

μαρτυρία

Witness: *Martyria*

The Greek word *martyria* means "witness." This is the witness we are all called to give by living the Gospel. From this word we also get our English word *martyr,* someone whose witness results in death.

profile

DIETRICH BONHOEFFER

Dietrich Bonhoeffer was a Lutheran pastor who spoke out against the co-opting of Christianity by the Nazis. The Nazis even created the office of a *Reichsbischof*, a "Reich Bishop" who coordinated the surrender of Christianity to the state, setting up a new form of Christianity that fit in with what the government wanted. Dietrich and his friends set up a radical Christian community that rejected the state-worship of the government-dominated Church and the Aryan Christian movement.

Dietrich's most famous book, *The Cost of Discipleship*, was a plea to abandon the "cheap grace" of habits and rule following that so many Christians accept. He called for acceptance of the "costly grace" of true discipleship.

His call to a radical Christian life is a legacy that has transcended the Lutheran tradition and spread to all other Churches.

Seeking this costly grace, Dietrich became involved in a plan to kill Hitler and save the German people. He was discovered and put in prison, where he continued to write on the Christian life. He was given the death penalty and executed in 1945.

Dietrich is an example of a Christian martyr. He was willing to risk his own life to save the lives of others—a follower of the costly grace that's not confined within the doors of a church building, but empowers the believer to accomplish great things for God and others.

11

Come, O children, listen to me;
I will teach you the fear of the LORD.

PSALM 34:11

How We Show Respect to God
THE GREAT COMMANDMENT AND THE TEN COMMANDMENTS 1–3

Relationships are not one-sided. God is our loving Father who watches over us and cares for us. In return, God asks that we love him, honor him and follow his Law. If we truly seek a relationship with God, we must respond to his love. There were many rules about how to honor God, but Jesus boiled them all down to one: "You shall love the Lord your God with all your heart, and with all your soul and with all your mind and with all your strength."

This was the first part of a teaching of Jesus we call "the **Great Commandment**."[1] Mark 12:28–34 Jesus wanted to cut through the clutter and get to the root of what we owe God. By explaining our duty to God in this way, Jesus wanted to show that just following rules isn't enough. Checking off the requirements isn't what God wants of us. He wants us to follow his law out of love for him, not as something forced on us.

The **Ten Commandments** are rules we should follow not just because we're told to or threatened with punishment if we don't, but because they were given to us by God and we come to truly believe they're best for us and for those around us. In the first three commandments we get down to the details of how we show our love for God. Psalm 27

The Commandments of Wonder and Awe

After Moses led the Israelites out of slavery in Egypt, God gave to Moses ten basic laws for the people to live by. Deuteronomy 5 These are the Ten Commandments.[2]

The first three Commandments (or the first four, depending on how you number them[3]) deal with how we honor God above everything else.

1. I am the Lord, your God, who brought you out of the land of Egypt, that place of slavery. You shall have no other gods besides me. You shall not make idols for yourselves.... You shall not bow down and worship them.

1 Note that in proclaiming this Law, Jesus begins with the ancient Jewish invocation, the Shema: "Hear O Israel; the LORD is our God, the LORD alone!"—"Shema Yisrael, Adonai Eloheinu, Adonai Echad!" (Deuteronomy 6:4)

2 A fancy way of referring to the Ten Commandments is the Greek word Decalogue, which means "ten words." You can use this word in college essays to look like you know what you're talking about.

3 Yes, Christians have different ways of numbering the Ten Commandments. What Roman Catholics and Lutherans consider the First Commandment is often broken into two by other Christians, who then combine what Roman Catholics and Lutherans consider the Ninth and Tenth.

The First Commandment is the most important: God must be the center of our lives.[4]

Idols were statues of false gods that people used to worship. The worship of idols is called **idolatry**. Maybe we don't carve idols out of stone and worship them much today, but we do worship other things or make them more important in our lives than God.

Money, fame, power, sports, sex, drugs, possessions, nationalism, and war are all examples of things—idols—we sometimes make more important than God in our lives. The world tells us constantly through commercials and other ways that these are the most important things in life. Example: There's a TV show that tells people fame is the most important thing in life. It's even called *American Idol*! And don't forget the most popular idol of all: ourselves, the false god named "Me."

We must always avoid making anything more important than (or equal to) God. Jesus reminds us, "For where your treasure is, there your heart will be also" (Matthew 6:21).

2. You shall not take the name of the Lord, your God, in vain.

Maybe when you were a kid someone told you this Commandment meant that you could not "cuss." Maybe your grandma still reminds you of this![5]

We should respect God's name[6] in everyday life. But probably God isn't so concerned about what you say when you hit your finger with a hammer. Using God's name "in vain" means to use it wrongly.

The most offensive way to use the name of God is to use it for **evil**. Some people will say, "God wants me to kill you," or "God says it's OK to discriminate against you." People will say God wants us to go to war, or God hates some group. One group of "Christians" is notorious for waving picket signs that say, "God hates fags." These would be the same people who'll condemn you if you blurt out, "God, that hurts!" when you stub your toe. But who's *really* taking God's name in vain?

Of course, God doesn't hate anyone, and God doesn't bless any evil some people may propose against others. To use God's name to bless evil is a serious offense against God. That's truly taking God's name "in vain" and is called **blasphemy**.

3. Remember to keep the Sabbath day as the Lord commanded you.

Ancient Jewish law forbids any work on Saturday (*Shabbat*, the Sabbath) out of respect to God and to allow time to worship God. The Christian Sabbath is **Sunday** because that's the day Jesus rose from the dead. It's a day sacred to God. We follow the Third Commandment when we set aside Sunday for God. We try not to make it "just another day." If possible, we don't work. We gather together with our Christian community to celebrate Mass. If we are unable to attend Mass, we should try to find another way to honor God or learn more about him on the Lord's Day. It's not enough to set aside one hour on Sunday to worship God; the entire day belongs to God.[7]

----

4 Many spiritual writers believe the First Commandment is the one most frequently violated today! Who would've guessed? Something to think about.

5 Those earthy four-letter words Eric Cartman favors as conversational Tabasco are often thought to be violations of this Commandment, but they're not. This Commandment has to do with respect for God, not social propriety.

6 OK, the word God isn't technically God's name. You got us there. But since we rarely use his revealed name, use of the word God is considered the same thing.

7 Following ancient Jewish custom, Catholics celebrate the Lord's Day beginning at dusk on Saturday, just as Jews celebrate Shabbat (Sabbath) starting Friday evening. That's why we have Sunday Mass on Saturday evening. All our feasts begin at dusk on the day preceding the feast. So the principal celebration of our holiest day, Easter, begins at dusk on Holy Saturday.

AMERICAN EXCEPTIONALISM

My dad says America is God's chosen nation to do his will on Earth. Is that true?

Your dad's comment is a common idea in the United States. We call it "American exceptionalism." According to this idea, God prefers the United States to other nations, blesses our form of government and its policies, and gives superior virtue to Americans. We often see it in phrases such as "God and Country," which put the nation on the same level as God. We also see this idea expressed when people refer to the flag as "sacred" or talk about "desecrating the flag."

Sometimes we hear people say the United States is special because we honor the family, but other cultures do as well. When we meticulously record and honor the deaths of American military but refer to unknown numbers of others killed in war merely as "collateral damage," we fall prey to this extreme form of nationalism.

God does not prefer any nation over others. That's why in Catholic funerals a flag isn't allowed on the casket while it's in the church—the casket is covered with a white cloth (a "pall") to symbolize baptism, which is more important than nationality. And while we may display an American flag outside a church building, in the narthex (vestibule), or in the main assembly area, it should not be regularly displayed in the altar area (sanctuary), which is reserved for sacred objects and symbols. The flag is not a sacred object.

There's nothing wrong with being patriotic. But we must realize there's a danger of excess. That's when patriotism becomes nationalism. American exceptionalism is an extreme form of nationalism that comes dangerously close to worship of the state, which of course is against the First Commandment. Suggesting that God blesses any evil we may do as a nation is blasphemy, a sin against the Second Commandment.

It's true that the United States has been blessed with abundance and affluence. But that's not a sign God loves us more than others. It really means we have a greater responsibility to share our gifts with the poor among us and in other nations. Paul VI warned, "Nationalism isolates people from their true good."

in the media

Afraid of God?

There's a very ancient and beautiful idea that doesn't sound so inviting in modern English: *Fear of the Lord.*

That's too bad. This old-fashioned way of putting it can make people think we should be afraid of God. That's not what it means.

"Fear of the Lord" uses an older English meaning of fear: awe.

We use *fear* this way in our everyday language sometimes even today. When we say "I'm afraid of you!" it means that person has it going on. *Fearsome* also means "great." So when we speak of the "Fear of the Lord," we mean a sense of wonder and awe at the power and love of God. We're not afraid of God. We're amazed by God.

And how could we not be amazed by God? God has made such a beautiful universe for us to live in. He's given us not only his own love but the love of other people. He's made each of us beautiful and awesome in our own way.

Many of the psalms express wonder at everything God has done for us. Psalm 139 expresses this very beautifully.

Read this psalm to get a good sense of being in awe of God. One of its most famous parts talks about the wonder of God we see in ourselves:

For it was you who formed my inward parts;
you knit me together in my mother's womb.
I praise you, for I am fearfully and wonderfully made.
Wonderful are your works;...
(Psalm 139:13–14)

Maybe there were times when you had a powerful awareness of how awesome God is. For many people, it's when they first hold their newborn child. At that point, many people have said, "I was overcome with the awareness of God," or "I was blown away to think that God gave me this perfect child to care for."

How do you know when you have an experience of awe at God? You'll know. It can make you feel on top of the world with joy or overcome with grief at the sufferings of others. It can make you cry just thinking about how God has blessed you. Perhaps you will be blown away by a feeling of intense gratitude to people who've helped you out of love. Maybe it's that moment after reading some part of scripture when you're just quiet and let the words play out in your head. That's the awe we express after hearing a reading at Mass: "The Word of the Lord! Thanks be to God!"

Our God is an awesome God! He's not frightening; he is to be loved and adored for all he has done for us!

"The fear of the Lord is the beginning of knowledge" (Proverbs 1:7).

backstory

From the time of Jesus' death and resurrection until nearly three hundred years later, it was illegal in the Roman Empire to be a Christian. Because the Roman Empire covered nearly the entire world known by the early Christians, that basically meant Christianity was illegal everywhere.

Christianity was illegal because everybody was required to worship the state gods of Rome. The punishment for not worshipping these gods was death.

But even the death penalty couldn't keep people from honoring only God and the message of Jesus. Thousands and thousands of people became Christians and led hidden lives. Many of them were discovered, and they were tortured and executed in very horrible ways.

Yet the more the politicians killed Christians, the more the regular people were impressed by their faith. Because of the example of the martyrs, more and more people became Christians. They didn't care they might be executed.

"The blood of martyrs is the seed of the Faith." This is an old Christian saying. It's always been true. Even today, right now, somewhere a Christian is suffering or dying for his or her faith. And someone watching may be inspired.

THE ROMAN MARTYRS

profile

He judges the world with righteousness;
he judges the peoples with equity.

PSALM 9:8

How We Act Justly toward Others

THE GREAT COMMANDMENT AND THE TEN COMMANDMENTS 4–10

We can be so self-centered. "Looking out for Number One" often means harming others to get our own way. But when God becomes "Number One" in our lives, we see our relationships with other people in an entirely new way. True love of God always means love of other people. It means God's justice fills us and flows out from us to others. That's what Jesus was getting at when he said, "You shall love your neighbor as yourself."

This is the second part of a teaching of Jesus we call "the Great Commandment." Mark 12:28–34 He also said, "Treat others as you would like them to treat you." This teaching is called the Golden Rule (Matthew 7:12). The Great Commandment and the **Golden Rule** sum up the second part of the Ten Commandments. 1 John 2:7–11

The Commandments of Justice

The second part of the Ten Commandments, Commandments 4–10 (or 5–10, depending on how you number them) deal with how we treat each other. These Commandments are all related to justice.[1] Psalm 19

4. Honor your father and your mother.

When you were a kid, it was important to obey your parents. There were good reasons why they didn't let you chase your kickball out into

the street or jump off the roof while playing Superman.

As adults, other authorities take the place of our parents. We must follow secular laws (assuming they follow God's Law) because these laws are made for the good of everybody in society.

As we get older, we still have a duty toward our parents because of everything they did for us. We must love them, respect them, and if necessary care for them.

5. You shall not kill.

People are always looking for exceptions to this rule. They're always coming up with reasons why they think it's OK to kill someone. "She was stealing from me!" "He killed my friend!" "She disobeyed God!" "He's not born yet!" "She's in pain!" None of these are reasons to kill someone. God's law is very clear. The only exception for Christians is self-defense or the defense of another. And that's only a last resort in the face of immediate danger to life. Sometimes people make war seem glorious and noble, but war is never

---

1 There are teachings drawn from these Commandments that don't have to do with justice to others, but our focus here is on justice.

holy; it is never good. It's always evil, because at its root it's mass murder.[2] When faced with someone proposing yet another reason for an exception to the rule against taking human life, we must remember the basic premise: that every human is made in the image of God, that God gives life, and only God can take it.[3]

6. You shall not commit adultery.

Adultery is having sex with someone who's married to someone else. It is clearly against the law of God. It's unjust because of how it damages the marriage bond. Other ways of having sex besides adultery can cause injustice. Often sex outside marriage leaves a woman alone to care for a child with great hardship to her and the child. Sex outside marriage can lead to deep feelings of hurt when one of the people "moves on" because there was no long-term commitment. Sex outside marriage might cause a woman to think of abortion as a solution to an unwanted pregnancy. Some people think this Commandment only spoils the fun, but there are good reasons for it when you think about it in terms of justice.

7. You shall not steal.

Taking another person's possessions is a crime against justice because that person worked for those things. He or she may even need them to survive. Not only individuals but even societies can break this Commandment when they take away land or opportunity from poor people. We Christians realize the right to private property isn't absolute. God has given us food, for example, so that all might live. If a rich person hoards food while a poor person starves, the poor person may take what he or she really needs to survive. That person would really be taking what is his or hers,

with a sincere understanding of justice. Justice also requires **restitution** when one has stolen something. The stolen goods must be returned, replaced, or paid for by the person who took them.

8. You shall not bear dishonest witness against your neighbor.

We have a duty in justice to be truthful to each other. If everybody lied, society would fall apart. Because this Commandment is rooted in justice, it might not apply when people seek the truth from you to use in unjust ways. For example, if an angry man with a gun were to ask you where your sister is, you don't have to tell the truth. We also don't have to tell the truth when it involves a trivial matter when the truth will only hurt someone. An example is that dreaded question: "Do you think this dress makes me look fat?" A really bad form of lying is when we do it swearing in God's name; that's called "**perjury**." If we destroy or damage another person's reputation through stating or spreading falsehood (as often happens in gossip), that also requires restitution in justice.

9. You shall not covet your neighbor's spouse.
10. You shall not covet anything that belongs to your neighbor.

To *covet* means to wish something was yours. That's not to say you can't see your cousin's new 60-inch plasma TV and think, "Dude, that's sweet. I wish I had one of those!" Coveting is when you see his new 60-inch plasma TV and think, "What a jerk. He doesn't deserve that TV as much as I do." Then you get all worked up and leave because you're so envious. That's coveting. It may even get so bad you're glad when the TV is broken. Or even worse, you break it "just to teach him a lesson." As you can see, being upset at someone else's good fortune can have very serious results that are not just. And if it's a serious offense against justice to covet another's possessions, imagine how much worse it is to covet another's spouse! It can only lead to heartache for all involved.

....

2   Hey, some will say, what about the "just war"? This is a principle for deciding when a nation may engage in war for reasons of self-defense. Applying the principles of "just war" doesn't make a particular war good; it only means that it may be an exception to the rule against the evil of war when there is no other choice. There's more about this in the glossary.

3   You still don't think so? Go back and read the Commandment again.

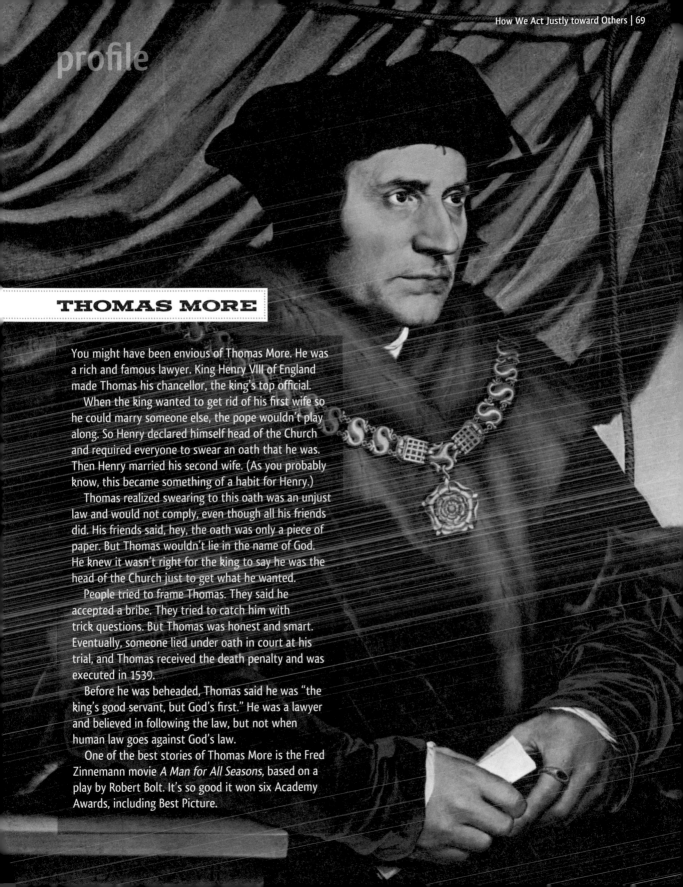

profile

THOMAS MORE

You might have been envious of Thomas More. He was a rich and famous lawyer. King Henry VIII of England made Thomas his chancellor, the king's top official.

When the king wanted to get rid of his first wife so he could marry someone else, the pope wouldn't play along. So Henry declared himself head of the Church and required everyone to swear an oath that he was. Then Henry married his second wife. (As you probably know, this became something of a habit for Henry.)

Thomas realized swearing to this oath was an unjust law and would not comply, even though all his friends did. His friends said, hey, the oath was only a piece of paper. But Thomas wouldn't lie in the name of God. He knew it wasn't right for the king to say he was the head of the Church just to get what he wanted.

People tried to frame Thomas. They said he accepted a bribe. They tried to catch him with trick questions. But Thomas was honest and smart. Eventually, someone lied under oath in court at his trial, and Thomas received the death penalty and was executed in 1539.

Before he was beheaded, Thomas said he was "the king's good servant, but God's first." He was a lawyer and believed in following the law, but not when human law goes against God's law.

One of the best stories of Thomas More is the Fred Zinnemann movie *A Man for All Seasons*, based on a play by Robert Bolt. It's so good it won six Academy Awards, including Best Picture.

HALL OF JUSTICE

God's justice system

Justice is a word we hear used in a lot of different ways. Most often we hear it used to refer to society's system of laws. People refer to "the justice system" when they talk about courts and lawyers and police. This would account for about half our TV series: you know, the ones that aren't about doctors.

But God's justice is different from human justice. Human laws are supposed to follow God's laws of justice. Often they do. But a lot of times they don't.

One of the main differences between human laws and God's justice is the element of mercy. God is always merciful and ready to forgive those who seek to be reunited with him. Human laws rarely allow for mercy.

And while human laws are not perfect, God's law is eternally perfect. For example, while rich people and big corporations pay for laws that make them richer at the expense of poor people, God's laws see all people as equal. Isaiah 10:1–4 To God, Bill Gates and a poor child starving to death are both of infinite value.

As Christians, we must take God's approach.

God's approach to justice is universal. It's the same for everybody. God's justice is above all human laws. Just following human laws does not always mean we are following God's Law. In fact, if a human law goes against God's Law, as Christians we must not obey the human law. For example, in Nazi Germany it was against the law to hide a Jew in your home. But God's Law requires us to protect those others are trying to kill. So many Christians broke the human law to save lives.

Because God's justice is universal, it doesn't take into account national boundaries. For example, God has provided sufficient food for the whole

backstory

world to be well fed. But rich countries hoard and waste food while poor countries don't have enough to eat. God demands that food be shared equally among all his children. Luke 16:19–31

When we share with those who have less than we do, we're not just being good guys. We shouldn't congratulate ourselves on our virtue. We're merely sharing what's due that person in justice. A great bishop, John Chrysostom,[4] once said that if I have two coats and my neighbor has none, I am a thief.

Human laws often favor the wealthy, but God's Law favors the poor. Psalm 10 Worldly wisdom says if you are trampled upon, the only way out is to become a trampler. But God requires us to stand up for and help the poor and other people society disdains: immigrants, gays and lesbians, the disabled, the elderly, and everyone we shudder to share space with. Human laws that favor the rich and the respectable are opposed to God's law. Micah 6:9–11

All true justice is based on respecting all people. Why? Because each of us is made in the image of God. But you already knew that.

....

4   *John Chrysostom was a fourth-century bishop of Constantinople (today's Istanbul). "Chrysostom" wasn't his last name; it's a Greek nickname that means "golden mouth." He was a great preacher who challenged his people to the point that he was twice run out of town. Once he was walking with a friend who saw a poor barefoot man and wondered, "Where are his shoes?" John replied, "His shoes are in your closet, gathering dust!"*

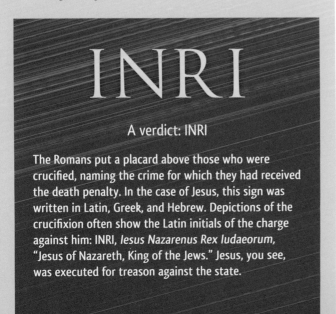

INRI

A verdict: INRI

The Romans put a placard above those who were crucified, naming the crime for which they had received the death penalty. In the case of Jesus, this sign was written in Latin, Greek, and Hebrew. Depictions of the crucifixion often show the Latin initials of the charge against him: INRI, *Iesus Nazarenus Rex Iudaeorum*, "Jesus of Nazareth, King of the Jews." Jesus, you see, was executed for treason against the state.

What should a Christian think of the death penalty?

It's clear God does not permit us to kill one another. It's forbidden by the Fifth Commandment: "You shall not kill."

In Christian tradition, there's an exception to this rule. It's self-defense. If someone comes at me to kill me, I have the right to protect my life. I can wound or even kill the attacker if that's *the only way* to stop him or her. I can also defend another person in the same kind of situation. It's important to realize that self-defense is a right, not an obligation.

Some claim capital punishment is a kind of self-defense. Maybe that was true in ancient times, when there were no secure prisons and someone likely to kill again had to be executed to keep society safe. That's the only justification our Christian tradition allows for capital punishment. But self-defense is not a valid reason for executing people today in the United States, where we have secure prisons.

Some say the death penalty is a matter of justice: "An eye for an eye." But Jesus taught us not to follow this law. Matthew 5:38–42 Jesus was totally against any kind of revenge.

People also claim the death penalty "brings closure" to the families of those who are killed. But Jesus taught us love is expressed not in revenge, but in forgiveness. Only forgiveness can bring "closure." Others say the death penalty deters crime, but this claim is unproven, and more important, it's not one of the criteria our Christian tradition uses to evaluate the morality of the death penalty.

Over the centuries Roman Catholic teaching on the death penalty has developed as society has found more certain ways to protect citizens from those who would threaten them. As practiced in the United States, the death penalty is not compatible with current Catholic teaching.

in the media

13

Open to me the gates of righteousness,
that I may enter through them
and give thanks to the LORD.

Psalm 118:19

We Are Made for Glory

HEAVEN AND HELL

Death isn't a popular dinner topic. In our American culture, we even have euphemisms for death, like "passed away," to avoid even saying the word. But everyone dies—of this we are sure. Think of those last six minutes of the final episode of *Six Feet Under*, where you see how each family member will die. It's so wrenching, yet at the same time somehow beautiful. Now, what happens to us after our natural life ends can be more a matter of dispute. For the Christian, our faith tells us death isn't the end. It's more like a window into eternity. We go to be with God, as God intended for each of us from the very beginning of all Creation.

In the Roman tradition, these are the words spoken to those near death by a priest or deacon who's there to pray with them as they die, words that speak of what we believe is about to happen:

Go forth, Christian soul, from this world
  in the name of God the Almighty Father,
  who created you,
in the name of Jesus Christ, the Son of the
  living God,
  who suffered for you,
in the name of the Holy Spirit
  who was poured out upon you.
Go forth faithful Christian...
  May you return to your Creator
  who formed you from the dust of the earth.
May holy Mary, the angels, and all the saints
  come to meet you as you go forth from this life....
May you see your redeemer face to face.

Eternity Begins with Our Choices in Life

God allows us to choose for ourselves how we'll spend eternity. We make choices every day. During our lives, we're free to choose to live with God or to live outside God's love. When we die, the time to choose is over. We Christians believe that some time after death we see Jesus face to face, for he is the final judge of all humanity. At that moment, each of us sees our entire life before us and compares our life and our choices with what God expected of us while we were on earth. The final judgment involves us, in the presence of Jesus, realizing how we experienced heaven (selflessness) or hell (selfishness) in our life, and whether we chose to continue our way of living.

Our Final Destination: Heaven

Because our immortal soul is a share in God's divine life, the soul has a desire to return to God.

The state where our soul finds perfect rest we call "heaven." Heaven is being in perfect happiness forever, enjoying the love of God and others. In heaven we'll be reunited with those who have gone before us. We'll be in the true presence of God, and this will be satisfying in ways that we cannot now even dream about. Revelation 7:9-17

Perhaps you've tried to imagine what heaven is like. It's impossible for us to understand. Heaven isn't like what we see in movies and TV, with clouds and harps. That would be kind of lame, don't you think? It's way better than anything you can ever think of. Paul puts it like this: "No eye has seen, nor ear heard, nor the human heart conceived, what God has prepared for those who love him" (1 Corinthians 2:9).

Choosing Ourselves over God

Here comes the part that frightens us. We've all seen pictures of a place called **hell**. We think of fire, thirst, torture, darkness, schlepping big rocks, yada, yada, yada. That's kid stuff. Hell isn't devils with pitchforks and fire. Still, the idea of hell is scary. It becomes less scary if we realize God does not want anyone in hell![1]

We talked about choices. God allows us to choose. We don't have to be perfect to go to heaven. If that were the case, no one would be there except God and the **angels**. While we try to live our lives as Jesus taught us, we all fail sooner or later. But we don't give up, we get up. And try, try again. We try to live with God's love in our

hearts each day of our lives. If we sincerely try, we are indeed invited to the heavenly banquet.

But back to choices. Jesus did warn us it's possible to separate ourselves from God's love, even though God will never turn his back on us. Romans 8:28-39 It's possible some people are so selfish they would prefer spending eternity wrapped up in themselves instead of being with God. Such people would have spent their lives thinking only of themselves, so God permits them to remain that way forever. It's their choice to be that way. That's hell. It's not God's choice to put people there; it's their own. Nobody knows if a lot of people choose this way to spend eternity, but some theologians think it's very few, if any.

Moved by a deep consciousness of God's mercy for those who are not yet ready for heaven, Roman Catholics hold out the possibility at death of an honest pain of realization at judgment of how we have disappointed God in our lives. This pain of remorse is intense but purifying and followed by entry into eternal joy.[2] We who are living can even help our loved ones through this process by prayer.

Christian Hope Is Our Calling

The hope of the Christian is the promise of resurrection and life with God, not fear of hell. Still, in the end it's all about choices. God allows us to make those choices and be in charge of our own destinies. The choices we make should be out of love, not fear. 1 Thessalonians 4:13-18

---

1 Now some people think we need to talk a lot about hell to scare people into "being good." That says more about their own motivations in life than it does about a loving God.

2 Some of us were taught that people could spend "years" in a "place" called purgatory. Of course, that's wrong, because there's no time or space in eternity. Still, we Roman Catholics use the word purgatory to describe this process of purification.

A to Z: *Alpha* and *omega*

The first and last letters of the Greek alphabet, *alpha* and *omega,* are used to refer to Christ. The deeper meaning is that all things begin and end with and in Jesus Christ. Also used with lower case letters:

profile

JOSEPH BERNARDIN

Joseph Bernardin was archbishop of Chicago and a cardinal. Joseph worked hard for social justice. He was known as a man of great compassion.

One time a man falsely accused Joseph of molesting him. This young man later admitted that his accusations were false, made because he was angry at Church leaders. Joseph visited his accuser, who was dying of AIDS, and forgave him. The accuser was reconciled with his Catholic heritage and died in peace.

Joseph was a great teacher of what's important in life. When he found out he was dying from cancer, he set an example of how to die. He visited other cancer patients. He consoled his friends who were in grief that he was dying. He told the people of Chicago about how he was facing death with great hope. In his last days, Joseph even wrote a book called *The Gift of Peace* about how to face suffering and death. (It's a great gift for someone you know who's sick.)

When Joseph died in 1996, the people of Chicago were moved because of what he taught them about life and death. More than 10,000 people stood along the road to honor him as his body was taken to be buried.

How to be happy

Everyone wants to be happy. Just think of all the books written about how to live a happier, fuller life.

Amazon.com lists some 75,000 self-help books (compared to about 30,000 on Catholicism). Clearly, the desire for happiness commands a strong market. Self-help books may help some of us to be happier, but unless they deal with our relationship with God, that happiness will be short-lived.

There's nothing wrong with wanting to be happy. God gives us the desire to be happy. And we can only be truly happy when we are close to God and the things of God. Some have called this need for happiness "the God-shaped hole" in our hearts.

Augustine, a great saint, put it this way: "How is it, then, that I seek you, Lord? Since in seeking you, my God, I seek a happy life, let me seek you so that my soul may live, for my body draws life from my soul and my soul draws life from you."

We long to be happy by being close to and filled with the things of God. Other things may give us a measure of contentment, or fun, or momentary pleasure. But there's no other way to be truly happy except with God.

It's a breakthrough when we finally realize what will make us happy. When we seek out the things of God we no longer place our hopes of happiness in big houses, nice cars, money, prestige, celebrity, and all the other things that are in and of the world. Not that it's always wrong to have these things, not at all. It's just not right to think anything like them will bring us true happiness. Maybe you've seen people chasing these things all their lives and yet never being satisfied, never looking happy. Maybe you recognize some of that in yourself?

Hope is a Christian virtue. It has a lot to do with being happy. In times of our greatest troubles, it's hope that keeps us from being discouraged. Hope lets us know we are never alone. Hope whispers to us that God has something bigger and better in mind for us.

backstory

God created the human person to live a full life here on Earth and discover the things that truly make us happy and fulfilled. That's why he gave us the simple pleasures of life. And God wants us to enjoy the happiness we find in this life and be with him forever in the happiness of heaven.

"Our hearts were made for thee, O Lord, and restless ever will they be, until they rest in thee."

That's another bit of wisdom from Augustine. Next time you find yourself a little down, find a quiet place where you can connect with God. When you do connect, you'll find happiness even if your problems don't all go away. In that place you'll know happiness as the gift it is from the God who loves you more than you can ever comprehend.

GHOSTS AND MEDIUMS

Is it OK for a Christian to believe in ghosts and mediums?

Some people read the Hebrew Testament and say you can't believe in ghosts. Leviticus 19:31, 20:6, and 20:27 But Christian tradition takes no stand on whether ghosts exist.

There are lots of laws in the Book of Leviticus. For example, Leviticus says if we shave our face or get a haircut, we're breaking God's law. How do we know what rules to follow and what rules can be changed? The Book of Leviticus isn't exactly a handy guide to everyday life.

Everything has a place and time. The laws given to the Israelites were meant to remind them of the relationship God wanted to have with them. They had to live and act in a way that was different from those who worshipped false gods.

Today many believe that mediums have helped find lost people or buried bodies. Of course, there are some who claim to talk to the dead, but only for a lot of money. There are scammers in all areas of life, even in the Church! Still, the fact that some are in it for the money shouldn't discount the apparent benefits some claim to receive from those who claim paranormal abilities. We Christians don't have a simple answer to such phenomena.

Answer this question: "Who is my God?" Do you know and love God as Jesus taught us? If you answer yes, then you don't worship ghosts or mediums. You're just open to the possibility they exist but have no power over you or anyone else!

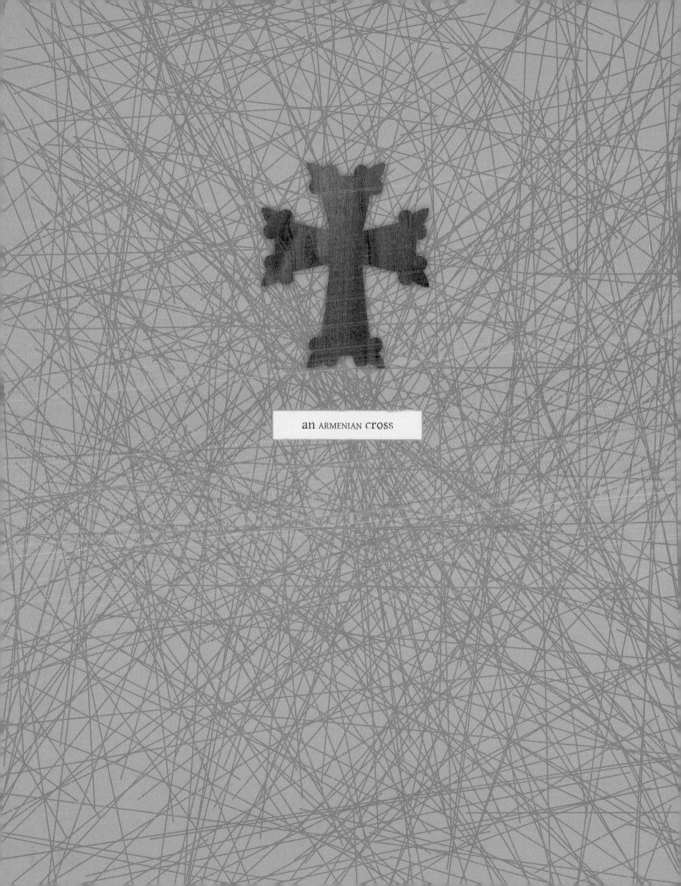

an ARMENIAN cross

14

O Give thanks to the LORD, for he is good;
his steadfast love endures forever!

Psalm 118:1

God Invites Us to Conversation

PRAYER

Can a person relate but not communicate? No way! All relationships involve communication. You couldn't have a relationship with your spouse or a friend if you didn't have conversations. Even our relationships with pets are based on communication, even if it's only interpretations of meows, barks, and body language. Because God desires a relationship with us, he also desires a lifelong conversation with us. This conversation is one of the heart, where nothing is held back, where desires and dreams are shared, where wonder and love are exchanged in total openness.

God himself is a community of love, the Trinity. In this dynamic and eternal sharing of love, we find a pattern for us to imitate in our own relationship with God. We don't initiate **prayer** by ourselves. It's a response to the eternal loving call of God's Spirit to be in relationship with us, individually and as a community.

Most of us are familiar with the kind of prayer where we ask something of God. We call this form of prayer **petitionary** or **intercessory** prayer. To those who don't understand prayer, it's considered only an individual act of selfish desire: "Gimme!" And it may be that even a lot of Christians never really get beyond the idea of prayer as a wish list. They think prayer is mojo to get stuff they

want.[1] But because prayer is a conversation, it also involves responding to God and involving ourselves with the needs of others. And just as we often share quiet times with friends and family, prayer can involve merely being in the presence of God, enjoying each other's company.

So there are different forms of prayer: intercession (or petition), **thanksgiving**, **praise** (or **adoration**), and **union**.

God: Not So Much a Big Candy Machine in the Sky

In April 2002, as John Paul II lay dying, the media showed how they don't get the idea of prayer. Even as it became clear the pope had refused medical

....

1   *An example of this magical way of thinking are those prayers people leave in your parish church that promise special power: "Be careful what you pray for, because this prayer has never been known to fail!" Such promises are a grave distortion of true prayer, reducing God to a robot who responds to incantations and rituals to deliver what you want. It's voodoo cake with Catholic frosting.*

treatment, reporters said dramatically that he was "fighting for his life." Because, of course, they knew no other way to approach death. And as St. Peter's Square filled with people praying, they opined that these people were all "praying for a miracle," even as many of the people there explained they were thanking God for the life of John Paul and uniting themselves with him in a peaceful death. The reporters could find no way to explain why people were praying except to assume they were asking God for something specific, like a miracle.

There's nothing wrong in asking God for something in prayer. In fact, we should always do this. Even though we may not know what is best, God understands our fundamental need and hears us, even if our prayer may be imperfect. Matthew 7:7–11 But at the root of every prayer of intercession must be an acknowledgment that God knows what's best for us. This is the aspect of trust that's basic to every authentic relationship. We may ask for a new cobalt blue Benz convertible with bird's-eye maple interior trim. But God may give us the gift of learning more about our neighbors and time to read the newspaper by riding the subway. Either way, we still get to our job in the morning and home at night, and isn't that what we really need? Matthew 7:25–34

And while we frequently ask for things like money to pay the bills, a new house, or good health, there are other less tangible things we could be asking for: forgiveness, humility, patience, wisdom, faith, and compassion, to name just a few qualities that'll last us beyond the next Visa bill! Wisdom 7:7–12

When we ask God for something—be honest— isn't it usually something for ourselves? When we step outside that first ring of concern, we probably pray for our family and friends. But as Christians, we have a priestly dignity by baptism to pray for people we don't even know. Open the newspaper or turn on CNN; you'll discover many reasons to pray, and many people who are more in need than we are. Can we set aside our own needs for a moment to pray for theirs? If so, we may even find ourselves praying for our enemies! Shocking, but true!

Would It Kill You to Say "Thank you" Every Now and Then?

God has already given us so much more than we could ever ask for. For the Christian, the most frequent prayer should be one of thanksgiving. Each Sunday, we gather to celebrate the **Eucharist**, a word that means "thanksgiving." Our highest and deepest form of prayer as a community is giving thanks.[2]

What do we give God thanks for? If we listed all the reasons here, it would fill this book and hundreds of additional volumes. To start with, how about thanking God for answering our prayers in wonderful ways that had nothing to do with the ridiculous wish lists we originally presented to him? Then, of course, there are the basic things, like life, love, and the world around us. There's the relationship God offers us, faith, the gift of his Son, and the wisdom provided by his Spirit. There is no end to God's gifts, and so there should be no end to our thankfulness for those gifts.

A Never-Ending Song

Aside from whatever we ask of God or what he has already given us, God also deserves praise simply because God is God. The prayer of praise isn't kissing up to God so we can get what we want. It's pure and simple in its essence. It's a spontaneous, heartfelt celebration of God, whose name is "I Am Who Am." This form of prayer is also a conversation with God, because our hearts respond with joy to God's revelation of himself to us.

Quality Time with God

One of the purest forms of conversation with God is the prayer of union. In this form of prayer, above all we listen, so it's usually relatively unstructured and doesn't use established words. 1 Samuel 3:1–10 It's a mistake to think the prayer of union is simply waiting for omens, signs, or secrets from God. When we enter into union with God,

---

2 A beautiful way of living in thanksgiving is to thank God for every meal before we eat. You don't need a memorized formula. A simple, silent, and sincere "Thank you" will do just fine.

we have no preset expectations. We simply place ourselves in the presence of God and enjoy the loving embrace of God. Many people begin such a session with a reading of scripture and then just sit and let the Word speak to them. This practice is called **lectio divina** (Latin for "divine reading"). There are many other approaches to the prayer of union, many of them described by the great **saints** throughout history. 1 Kings 19: 11–13

Prayer: The Greatest Hits Collection

Would you find it helpful to see a collection of prayers of every kind, for every need and mood? Hey, what do you know, it's already existed for thousands of years! It's called the Book of Psalms. Prayers of petition, thanksgiving, and praise are there, expressed in anger, joy, exultation, despair, and every other human emotion. If the tone of a psalm doesn't fit your attitude at that moment, try praying that psalm in the name of someone who's experiencing that feeling. And who knows, maybe somewhere someone else is doing just that for you.

ST. TERESA OF ÁVILA

Teresa of Ávila was a smart, driven woman who stood up to men who tried to "keep her in her place." She faced down the Inquisition. A tireless reformer of the Church, she's one of our greatest teachers of prayer. Teresa's *Autobiography* is among the treasures of Spanish literature. She founded dozens of Carmelite communities, where she was known to have a good time, dancing with her sisters while playing a tambourine.

Teresa was a mystic. She described the various stages of the prayer of union with God. One of her most famous analogies of prayer in her autobiography was a walled garden where one went to walk with God. She expanded this analogy to describe four stages of prayer as ways to water that garden to make it beautiful for our time with God. In another book, *The Interior Castle,* she talked about different approaches to prayer as seven different rooms in a heavenly palace.

Teresa's experience of prayer was ecstatic and emotional. Those who witnessed her praying were struck by the intensity of her union with God. But here's Teresa's gift to us: she didn't consider this kind of prayer something only for famous saints. Her works invite us all to practice mystical prayer, and she guides us on the path to that ideal. She believed firmly that the prayer of union with God was not just for a few, but for anybody to experience.

TERESA OF ÁVILA

profile

The Lord's Prayer

By now you may have noticed your authors have a certain impatience with using archaic terms when we talk about God. So you can imagine how we feel when we use archaic language to talk *to* God!

But we don't make the rules. Somewhere along the line, the decision was made to use archaic language when we pray the Lord's Prayer in English. This isn't the case in all other languages; English is an exception. Now, we're not saying we should use modern English in this prayer, because that would cause rioting in our cities; burning cars would line our streets and armed bands would roam our neighborhoods. Well, maybe not, but some people would get bent out of shape and waste a lot of time arguing about it.

Our use of archaic English can at times obscure the profound meaning of this prayer. So let's take a look at it in a modern paraphrase (we assume you already know the traditional version):

Our Father in heaven,
may your name be held holy by everyone.
May your Kingdom be as present in our lives as it
  is present in heaven,
and in the same way may your will be done here
  and now.
Give us whatever we need today,
and forgive us our sins,
even as we forgive those who sin against us.
Do not let us give in to temptation,
and keep us safe from evil.

The version used by Roman Catholics ends here; other Christians add a final proclamation of praise: *For the Kingdom, the power and the glory are yours, now and forever.*[3] *Amen!*

....

3   *Why don't Roman Catholics include this doxology? Because historically there's been disagreement among scholars as to whether this was always a part of the Lord's Prayer. In the Roman liturgy, this issue has been addressed by including this doxology but separating it from the main part of the prayer with an introduction, which seems a neat compromise. If you're praying with other Christians, don't purse your lips and remain silent for this part; go ahead and say it! It's a beautiful proclamation! The traditional form is "For thine is the kingdom, the power, and the glory, for ever and ever."*

backstory

God's Mercy: *Hesed*

The Hebrew word *hesed* refers to God's mercy, his steadfast love, or loving-kindness (used as a single word).

The most revolutionary aspect of this prayer is the naming of God as Father. This would've been shocking to people in Jesus' day, maybe even more shocking than saying this prayer in modern English would be to some today. That's why in the Mass, one of the invitations to this prayer proclaims' "We dare to say..." Jesus brought a new way of relating to God as Father. He used the Aramaic word *Abba* to express this relationship. Now sit down, Dancing Queen, it's not a Swedish pop group, nor is it pronounced like one. *Abba* (AH-buh) translates not just as Father, but even "Daddy" or "Da-da." That's how intimate it's meant to be. Romans 8:14–17 Note also that we call on *Our* Father, not *My* Father, because we are saved as a community.

For those who read Shakespeare in *Cliff's Notes*: The word *thy* goes back to the days when English had an intimate way to address people, as many other languages do today. *Thou*, *thee*, *thy*, and *thine* were the way to address loved ones; everybody else was *you*.

The Lord's Prayer, then, is a tender and intimate expression of our total trust and dependence on God, who cares for us with loving-kindness. It's a model prayer because it comes from a place of humility (we acknowledge our faults and admit our tendency toward evil) and makes reference to the will of God, who is all knowing and must sometimes laugh a little at our own idea of what's best for us.

The prayer also makes reference to our need to forgive others. In this way we become more like our Father, who is willing to forgive us, no matter what we do. Matthew 6:9–15

"Lord, teach us to pray," the disciples asked Jesus. He responded by giving us this prayer. It's become the favorite prayer of Christians not only because we received it from Jesus, but also because by praying it we learn how to pray in our own words as well. Luke 11:1–4

THE PROSPERITY GOSPEL

I couldn't sleep last night, so I turned on the TV. A preacher was saying God would give me a new car if I mailed the preacher a check for $100. Do they take Visa?

Yes, they take Visa, but you won't get a new car. The televangelist you saw was all about something called the "prosperity gospel." It says we can make God give us material things if we pray hard enough and send money to certain rich people.

The prosperity gospel is a new idea popularized by television preachers on networks like TBN and broadcast throughout the world masquerading as authentic Christianity. Many uneducated people fall for this scam; they may send in thousands of dollars they can't afford in the hopes they'll rise out of poverty. You won't get a new car, but you can bet the televangelist will. There are even stories of people who gave their life savings to these preachers in the hope that a loved one would be cured of terminal illness. Some even continued to "have faith" to the end of the funeral, certain their loved one would emerge from the coffin because they gave all their money to a televangelist.

When we ask God for something, we should always realize God knows what's best. Especially in praying for a cure, we should remember that everybody must die sometime. To claim that God can be manipulated and formed to our own will for money perhaps says more about our own priorities and approach to life than it does about God.

The prosperity gospel is a shameful distortion of Christianity and the beauty of prayer. Those who use it to "spread the Gospel" are only infecting the world with American consumerism served up as Christianity. This can only ruin lives and endanger faith. 1 Timothy 6:3–10

First donation to a televangelist: $250. Airfare to his healing service: $700. Additional donations: $1,500.

Trust in God to give us what we need: priceless.

in the media

Lead me in the path of your commandments,
for I delight in it.

PSALM 119:35

Following in the Footsteps of Jesus

DISCIPLESHIP

Did Jesus do doublespeak? He said, "My yoke is easy and my burden is light." Yet Jesus also said that following him means to take up our own cross every day. Which path of Jesus is the real one, the easy way or the hard way? Paradoxically, both promises of Jesus are true. Following Jesus means to enter into the upside-down Kingdom of God, where things the world thinks are difficult become easy, and things the world thinks are easy become difficult.

The ongoing work of **conversion** is key to understanding **discipleship**. By conversion, we don't mean becoming a Christian, or joining the Catholic Church in the way this word is sometimes used. As some have said, there are plenty of Catholics; what we need are more disciples!

Conversion is a lifelong process of allowing ourselves to be shaped to the person of Jesus Christ for the glory of the Father by the power of the Holy Spirit. Matthew 10:34–39 There's no day when our conversion is complete; those who believe that are only fooling themselves. How many "respectable" Christians might be outraged if you were to suggest they're in need of conversion? Yet that's what we all need. Colossians 1:9–14

The Right Kind of Heartburn

In the story of Jesus meeting the disciples[1] on the road to Emmaus after the resurrection, one of them says after the encounter, "Were not our hearts burning within while he was talking to us?" Luke 24:13–31 This is the radical response of faith to him who tells us, "I came to bring fire to the earth, and how I wish it were already kindled!" (Luke 12:49). Hearing the Good News is the first step to discipleship; we can't begin conversion until we have accepted the Good News and made it our own so that it will form us from within. In this way, we're set free from mere external conformity to the rules. We're remade by the Spirit to live the Gospel more faithfully. 2 Corinthians 4:7–18

This living faith isn't static. It guides us to an ever deeper and higher relationship with God, a greater conformity to the person of Jesus, an

---

1 *The disciples in this story are usually depicted in art as two men. But the Gospel only tells us that one of them, Cleopas, was a man. The other disciple isn't named and could well have been a woman. Just one example of how we can always see something new when we read scripture without relying on previous assumptions of what's in it.*

awareness of the Spirit in our lives, and a new way of relating to others.

Someone whose faith life has remained static for many years isn't engaged in the process of conversion necessary for the disciple. That's what we call "dead faith." Some people can live their entire lives as Christians on autopilot, never growing in their faith, perhaps even with a faith that hasn't changed since their childhood. The danger of dead faith is that individuals adhere externally to the basics of the Christian life out of social conformity while adopting views and practices incompatible with the teachings of Jesus. They go to Mass, they recite prayers, but these practices have become mere habits. Their daily activities, their desires, their political beliefs are not affected by the Gospel. Isaiah 29:13–16

Faith Seeks Understanding

So faith is alive and dynamic, not passive. The mind is also involved in an adult faith. The adult disciple struggles with some aspects of following Jesus. A living faith doesn't guarantee immediate acceptance of all his teachings. At times they're difficult to understand or apply in our daily lives. But the grace of ongoing conversion enables us to gradually integrate more and more of the teachings of Jesus into our lives and to follow him more closely. As the song from the musical *Godspell*[2] puts it, "Day by day, O dear Lord, three things I pray: to see thee more clearly, love thee

....

2   *Godspell is an old English variant of* Gospel, *which of course as you already know means "Good News."*

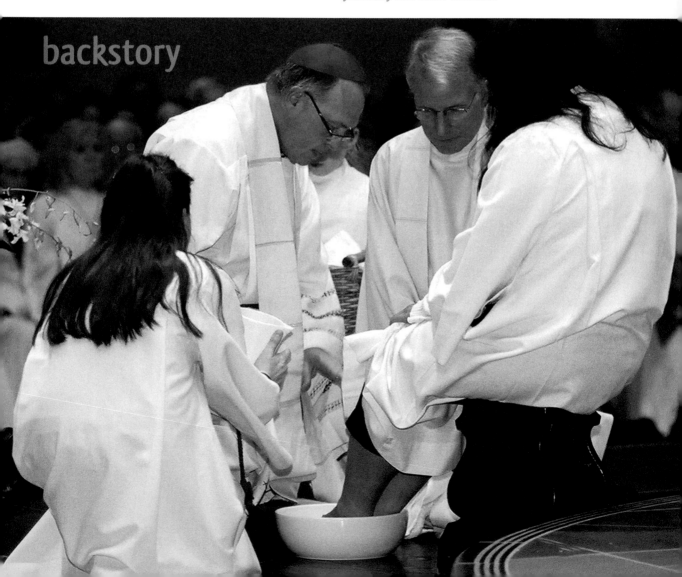

backstory

more dearly, follow thee more nearly, day by day."
2 Corinthians 6:1–12

You might notice that some people, perhaps sometimes even yourself, begin with a given belief and then look to scripture to validate that view. For example, some people may want to start a war, and then they look for Christian teaching they think will justify it. It's like Stephen Colbert has said: "Reality has become a commodity." For the disciple, all aspects of life begin with and end in the Good News. The Gospel becomes a lens through which the disciple views the world, evaluating all things first by the Gospel, rather than the backward way of looking to the Gospel to validate what we already want to believe. Matthew 13:44–46

Discipleship Is Viral

Through our ongoing process of conversion we follow Jesus, the Way, more closely. We realize our faith compels us to reach out to others. James 1:19–27 It's like a centrifuge spreading the love of God outward from us. We cannot love God without loving our neighbor. 1 John 4:7–21 The disciple reaches out to others in justice, shows concern for the outcast, and freely shares his or her faith with others in appropriate ways that are always characterized by gentleness and humility. James 3:1–18 The argumentative, self-important Christian is of use to no one but stand-up comedians and cynical politicians.

Service is standard procedure, not an option

Volunteerism is a secular concept that implies the volunteer is doing something more than is required out of his or her own personal virtue. Such people may be rewarded for their efforts with society's highest honors. That's not the Christian idea of service.

Central to the life of discipleship is service. For the Christian, service, or ministry, isn't an optional add-on to the life of faith. It's a part of our baptismal responsibility, an essential aspect of a living faith.

Christianity isn't just a prescribed set of dos and don'ts and elaborate rituals. It's a way of life that must embrace service to others. Jesus emphasized service throughout his teaching ministry. At the Last Supper, he washed the feet of his disciples in a dramatic ritual to stress the importance of service. John 13:1–17 There are some teachings Jesus offered as options for those called to a particular ministry or way of life, but foregoing service wasn't one of these options. Philippians 3:1–18

The Church today is a sleeping tiger. Imagine how the world would change if all Christians were to take their responsibility of service to heart. It would be a revolution of earth-shaking dimension. It would be the Kingdom of God built in our time. Matthew 5:1–16

But we're not called to wait until every Christian finally springs into action. We're called to begin building that Kingdom here and now with our own lives, through service. Each of us, in our own way and within the parameters of our own daily lives, is called to live our discipleship through service. Sometimes you hear Christians say, "The Church should do such-and-such." News flash: You are the Church. If you begin doing that very thing, the Church will be doing it. When you act to address issues of justice and compassion, it's the Church acting. You don't need a bishop marching in front of you to do something as the Church.

In some ways, we're hobbled today by old-fashioned ideas of how the Church works. It wasn't long ago that Catholics assumed clergy and religious (those in religious orders) were the ones who did all ministry. Lay Catholics as a rule didn't feed the poor or minister to the suffering. They went to Mass, said their rosary alone, and on occasion might give some money to the priest for the poor. This model of Church life has been called "pray, pay, and obey." It was almost entirely passive.

Those were the days when seminaries and convents were bursting at the seams, so even as the Christian laity abdicated their responsibility of service to priests and nuns, a lot of important work was still being done. Today, however, a positive aspect of having fewer priests and religious is a growing realization that we're all called to service. Service isn't something optional or something to be pushed off onto the clergy alone. Not a few people have pointed out that even if the seminaries and convents were full again, we must never go back to the days when clergy and religious did everything and laypeople did little. Of course, we haven't entirely emerged from that model of Church life. As one person in such a parish once remarked, "Go to Mass and say your prayers. That's all that's needed." Jesus would disagree. Vociferously. Mark 4:1-20

Consider this: While we worry about the "priest shortage" and pray earnestly for more priests, God sends us more deacons and inspires more laypeople to greater involvement in the life of the Church. Does God just not get it, or is God telling us something? Some say it's our fault we don't have more priests because we're not praying hard enough. Is that really how prayer works?

Discipleship also involves stewardship, the assuming of responsibility for the welfare of the Church, society, and the environment by sharing of time, treasure, and talent. As the Church, we all have the responsibility to support and be involved in our common ministries such as shelters, schools, food pantries, ministry to prisoners, and all the good works in our community and even the world.

"Preach the Gospel always. If necessary, use words." This is the timeless advice we receive from Francis of Assisi, who together with his best friend Clare followed the command of God to reform the Church. Those who strive to true discipleship can learn much from them.

Francis was born into a rich family, but he was eager to discern the will of God for his life. He wound up renouncing his family's wealth and lived a poor life relying on what food others would give him. He was ordained a deacon but refused to be ordained a priest.

One day while praying in a ruined chapel, he heard a voice tell him, "Rebuild my Church." He gathered friends together and rebuilt that chapel, and they set about rebuilding other churches. It wasn't until later Francis realized God wasn't calling him to restore buildings, but the Body of Christ. He called bishops to account. He refused ecclesiastical honors. He engaged in dialogue with Muslim leaders.

With Clare as his ally, he began preaching reform throughout the area. Together they welcomed thousands of men and women into their movement. By the example of the simple life of Francis, Clare, and their followers, Christians were moved to reexamine their own lives and how closely they followed the teachings of Jesus.

The joyful simplicity of Francis extends even to our own age. He's one of the most popular of the saints, honored by Christians of every tradition and even people of other faiths. His example still teaches us how to be disciples.

THE MEETING OF ST. FRANCIS AND ST. CLARE

FRANCIS & CLARE OF ASSISI

profile

THE ENVIRONMENT AND ANIMAL RIGHTS

The Bible says God put humans in charge of the world. Doesn't that mean we can do whatever we want to with it?

It's true God put humans in charge of the Earth and all its creatures. Genesis 1:28–31 Some people take this to mean there's no moral aspect to pollution, greenhouse gases, deforestation, extermination of species, depletion of ocean life, global warming, or other environmental issues. As long as it enriches some, these people say, it's all fair game.

Most Christian Churches today, however, disagree with that idea. Roman Catholics, among others, believe the idea of stewardship should form our approach to the environment.

In his parables, Jesus told stories about stewards. Matthew 25:14–30 In these stories, the stewards were held accountable for what they were placed in charge of. In the same way, we're placed as stewards over the Earth, to protect it and use it responsibly. We don't have the right to change nature as God has established it. We may take only what we need while passing on the beauty and resources of Creation to future generations.

John Paul II and Bartholomew, the Orthodox patriarch, made a joint statement that said, "Christians and all other believers have a specific role to play in proclaiming moral values and in educating people in ecological awareness, which is none other than responsibility towards self, towards others, towards creation."

In the same way, animals are part of the Earth God has given us. They're a wondrous and beautiful part of Creation. God permits us to use animals for food and other legitimate uses, such as carrying burdens, but we must do so responsibly and with respect to animals. We must honor their nature, by which they give glory to God by their simple existence. Animals have an inherent dignity and way of life that's in total conformity to the will of God. We shouldn't kill animals merely for amusement or cause them any unnecessary pain or discomfort. Experience has shown that those who enjoy causing pain to animals frequently act that way toward humans.

ἰχθύς

A fish: *Ichthys*

The most ancient of all Christian symbols is a fish. Early disciples would use this symbol as a secret code to identify themselves to each other. The Greek word *ichthys* means "fish." In Greek, it's an acronym for "Jesus Christ, Son of God, Savior."

in the media

16

Unless the LORD builds the house,
those who build it labor in vain.

PSALM 127:1

We Are the Body of Christ

THE CHURCH

"I will not leave you orphans." Jesus made this promise to all his disciples. When Jesus gave us the mission to go out to all the world and proclaim the Good News, he entrusted this band of believers to the Holy Spirit, who he promised would come to guide us. And in order for Jesus' command to be carried out, it was necessary that a community be established to carry out the mission. The Church, therefore, is a community living in the Holy Spirit, born in the fire of Pentecost.

The Church exists to **evangelize**. That's the mission Jesus entrusted to us as his final words in the **Synoptic**[1] Gospels:

> Go therefore and make disciples of all nations, **baptizing** them in the name of the Father and of the Son and of the Holy Spirit, and teaching them to obey everything that I have commanded you. And remember, I am with you always, to the end of the age. (Matthew 28:19–20)

The Church Doesn't Have a Mission; the Mission Has a Church

The mission given us by Jesus preceded the founding of the Church on Pentecost, "the birthday of the Church." Acts of the Apostles 2:1–41 That mission is evangelization, the preaching of the Good News to the whole world. And yet it's clear from the example of Jesus that preaching the Good News isn't merely a verbal or intellectual process. Luke 4:18–19 The mission Jesus gave us can't be accomplished by random individuals acting on their own. It's a transforming call that involves an entire community and each individual believer. The Greek word *ekklesia,* from which we get the word *church,* means "convocation." We're a people gathered from every nation by the Holy Spirit to serve the Father through Jesus Christ.

The visible Church exists on different levels. The primary level is the local Church, the community of Christians gathered around a bishop,[2] the diocese. The bishop guides the local Church, ensuring unity. In turn, each diocese is in communion with all other dioceses, making up the larger, universal Church.

Even as we describe these various ways we live as Church, we must remember the Church isn't merely a visible institution, like an earthly corporation. As the Body of Christ, the Church is

---

1 Fancy word of Greek origin for the Gospels of Matthew, Mark, and Luke. Sorry, John! Synoptic ("with one eye") means these three Gospels have roughly the same structure and content.

2 Archbishops, primates, metropolitans, patriarchs, eparchs, auxiliary bishops, coadjutor bishops, popes: whatever fancy titles they may have, they're still simply bishops.

both human and divine. We can clearly see the human institution, flawed and in need of reform. But the divine reality transcends institutional boundaries. As the Church, we are neither club nor corporation, but a worldwide movement or revolution guided by the Holy Spirit for the glory of the Father through the life of Jesus,[3] a movement embracing and advancing truths that stand in opposition to much of what the world values.

One, Holy, Catholic, and Apostolic

In the Nicene Creed, we proclaim our faith in the "one, holy, catholic and apostolic Church." Through this description,[4] we can more clearly understand how we as the Church carry out our mission not as an institution, but as a worldwide movement.

The Church is one. As Paul explained, there is "one Lord, one faith, one baptism." Ephesians 4:1–16 When you were baptized, you were baptized into the Body of Christ, not a particular earthly institution. This one baptism, recognized by all Christians despite our current divisions, remains a precious reminder of our past unity, a promise of the unity to come, and a present fact that witnesses to the power of the Holy Spirit in our lives today.

Unity is the essence of the Church. Even as Christians are divided, there's more that unites us than divides us. In unity, there will always be diversity. As Catholics, we believe this unity and diversity is compatible in full communion with one another through our communion with our own bishop and through him with the Bishop of Rome, the pope.

The Church is holy. Because we are the Body of Christ, the Church is holy. We are "a chosen race, a royal priesthood, a holy nation, God's own people, in order that you may proclaim the mighty acts

of him who called you out of darkness into his marvelous light." 1 Peter 2:1-10

Although as individual members of the Church, we may fall short of holiness, we still know that if we strive in grace to follow the teachings of Jesus we believe in as the Church, we will advance in holiness.

All Christians individually are sinners, and as the institutional Church we have sinned before and will sin again as a community. Yet despite these blemishes, the soul of the Church—our mission and the life promised by the head of the Church, Jesus Christ—remains holy. The essential holiness of the Church remains intact, despite all we've done individually and institutionally to neglect our mission or even advance evil in the name of the Church.

The Church is catholic. The word *catholic* means "all embracing" or "universal." So when we speak of the Church as being catholic, we don't equate it with the human institution called the Catholic Church.[5] The universal nature of the Church is present in the local Church as well as the worldwide Church because our mission is to the whole world. As the popular saying goes, Christians "think globally and act locally."

As a universal Church, we're not limited by national or ethnic considerations, although we do embrace diverse cultures. So it would be a mistake to think of the Church merely as a Western institution. Whenever we as the Church present ourselves as too closely aligned with a particular nation or culture, we've failed in our mission. Only by refusing to be aligned exclusively with any culture, nation, or ethnicity or even any particular liturgical tradition can we, the Church, be truly catholic. As someone once said, *catholic* means "Here comes everybody!"

The Church is apostolic. We're an apostolic community because our faith was handed on to us by the Twelve and we're guided today by their successors, the bishops. The Apostles were given the mission of evangelization by Jesus. They fulfilled that mission by going out into the entire

---

3 Christianity isn't a "religion of the book" like other religions whose precepts are derived primarily from a written scripture; the source of our faith life is the person of Jesus Christ.

4 Also called the "four marks of the Church."

---

5 Although we do say that the universal Church "subsists" in the Catholic Church.

known world and passing on what they'd learned. The Apostles became leaders of far-flung Christian communities that were all united in a common Faith.

In the same way today, thousands of local Churches gathered around their own bishop are joined together into the larger universal Church. In each of these local Churches, the bishop safeguards and passes on what we've learned from the Apostles and Christians who've gone before us.

The Pilgrim Church

As a community that engages every culture and people of the Earth, we often talk about the Pilgrim Church. Our engagement with the world is a two-way dynamic. Even as the people of the world learn from us as the Church, we also learn something in every land and culture we're present in. You can't go on vacation to another place without learning something about the people there and the ways they do things that are different from yours. In the same way, we, the Church, learn something new in every age and in every place from the people we evangelize, even as they learn from us the saving truth of the Gospel.

CHRISTIAN NATION

Is the United States a "Christian nation"?

In its early years, many people called the new republic a "Christian nation." However, this definition of Christianity didn't include Catholics, and our country's actions and values have often fallen far short of the teachings of Jesus.

While we're often told the United States has always provided freedom of religion, Catholics were usually specifically excluded from this "freedom." In most states, Catholics were forbidden to vote or own property because we weren't considered "real Christians." It wasn't uncommon for Catholic churches to be burned or for priests and nuns to be murdered by lynch mobs. As a "Christian nation," Americans felt they should rid themselves of Catholics. Catholics were thought to be traitors because they were in communion with a "foreign power": the Bishop of Rome.[6] The Ku Klux Klan lobbied—successfully in some places—to outlaw Catholic schools.

The election of John F. Kennedy as president in 1960 was a turning point in many Americans' view of Catholics. But anti-Catholicism remains strong among Christian fundamentalists, who consider themselves the only true Christians. Now that there are nearly 70 million of us Catholics here, that complicates things for those who'd like to see us all leave.

These fundamentalists are the ones who want to make the United States into a "Christian nation" like it was before. It's not clear what would become of Catholics, Orthodox, Anglicans, other Protestants, Jews, Muslims, or other people of faith in the fundamentalist theocracy they propose.

We must work to form our nation's policies according to Christian principles such as peace, prizing diversity, generosity to poor nations, concern for the outcast, economic justice, and other such vital teachings of Jesus. But these are not the Christian values espoused by many of those who desire a "Christian nation." They claim to defend Christian morality with vocal opposition to bad language[7] on television, while they turn a blind eye to violence, intolerance, greed, and injustice. Matthew 7:1–5

6 *The word papist was—and sometimes still is—used as a derogatory way to refer to Catholics because we honor our connection to the pope as a sign of Catholic unity. Example: In 1854, Pius IX contributed a stone for the construction of the Washington Monument as a gesture of solidarity with Americans. The stone was thrown into the Potomac River by an anti-Catholic mob.*

7 *"Proper" society views certain words as grave and shocking sins when used in certain situations, even though the words themselves are not sins. However, out of respect for the human person, we use Christian restraint, avoiding such words in a situation where someone may be offended or when they are meant to hurt.*

in the media

Christianity is wounded and divided

The Church is one in the eyes of God. But we can't help but notice there exist many Christian traditions. In many cases we believe different things and have different practices. It's important to keep perspective, though. Christians of whatever tradition must acknowledge we have much more in common than we have differences.

Christianity is divided on Earth. That's a sad fact we must admit. There's no Church that's blameless in the ways Christianity came to be divided. In some cases there were sincere disagreements on how certain teachings were to be understood, but in most cases minor theological disagreements became amplified through worldly considerations such as ethnicity, nationalism, language, political intrigue, misunderstandings, bureaucracy, rigidity, factionalism, and yes, even money. Those who claim any particular division among Christians was due to one side being totally right and the other being totally wrong are almost always engaging in dramatic oversimplification.

For nearly a thousand years, Christianity existed as a worldwide communion that embraced a great diversity in theology, liturgy, and cultures. One major distinction in attitudes and approaches was between the East and the West. The Eastern Church tended to have a more mystical understanding of theology, characterized by wisdom. The Western Church tended to be more analytical, trying to explain theology in minute detail with an emphasis on reason. Together, these two approaches—wisdom and reason—complement each other. John Paul II described this synergy between the East and the West as the "two lungs" of the Church. Without each other, it's more difficult to breathe the breath of the Holy Spirit.

But as some insisted on uniformity over diversity, relations between the East and West became strained over centuries, complicated by geographic, linguistic, and cultural differences and political considerations.[8] The rift grew wider until both sides had to admit they no longer were in communion with each other.[9] In this way, Orthodoxy and Catholicism became separated communions. For a few hundred years, various efforts at unity were attempted and failed.

Then, in the sixteenth century, many Western Christians found they could no longer tolerate the widespread corruption that had become common in the Western Church. Many clergy were addicted to power and wealth and had little concern for the people. The Church was thought of as consisting of clergy who performed rituals apart from the people, who were not allowed to participate. The papacy was ensnared in the traps of wealth and power.

....

8   *The Oriental Orthodox Churches (Armenians, Copts, Ethiopians, Syrians, and Antiochians) and the Assyrian Church had drifted apart from the other Eastern Churches (today called Eastern Orthodox) and the West around the sixth century due largely to factors of geographic isolation.*

9   *The generally accepted low point of this gradual growing apart was in 1054, when the pope and the patriarch of Constantinople issued mutual excommunications. These excommunications were lifted with mutual apologies in 1965 by Pope Paul VI and Ecumenical Patriarch Athenagoras I.*

backstory

Council (1962–65) called by John XXIII. The defensive Counter-Reformation came to a dramatic end. Christians began to look instead at everything we share in common and to find ways through dialogue to address the differences. Protestant communities began to heal old rifts between themselves. Many merged, and these larger bodies began talks with Catholics to find a way to restore the lost unity of Christianity.

The stated aim of the ecumenical movement is the full, visible unity of all Christians in our lifetimes. This is the unity we believe Jesus wishes for all his followers. Unity won't be uniformity. As Benedict XVI said, unity will be "neither absorption nor fusion, but respect for the multiform fullness of the Church." It will be a convergence embracing the positive aspects of each tradition that has emerged while still allowing all Christians to gather around one Eucharistic table, to receive the Body and Blood of Christ from each other. All Christians, Catholics included, are required to pray and work for that coming day of unity in diversity. As Ecumenical Patriarch Bartholomew, the leader of Orthodoxy, has noted:

> It is commonly recognised that the times in which we live today bring with them serious challenges to the Christian Church. The rapid advance of science with the ethical dilemmas they create; the ecological crisis with its alarming consequences for the natural environment; the domination of technology which accompanies and sustains tendencies of globalisation at the expense of cultural diversity; the social and economic injustice that widens the gap between rich and poor countries and people; the discriminating attitude towards minorities; the outbreak of unjust wars; and, above all, the use of religion as a means of national and racial conflict—all these call the Christian Churches to reconsider their theological and pastoral priorities and place their confessional differences in a new light. The quest for Christian unity appears to be imperative in the present circumstances.

The invention of printing allowed the Reformers to express their outrage at this corruption and reach large numbers of people. Unfortunately, rather than hearing these concerns and acting upon them, the hierarchy became rigid and chose instead to reaffirm the status quo.[10]

The cause for reform (the Reformation) then became entangled in nationalism and politics, with disastrous results. Some Christians began setting up their own communities outside of communion with Rome.

The Council of Trent (1545–63) was convened to try to heal these divisions by launching internal reforms, but it was too late. The cow had already left the barn. The Western Church was now divided among Catholics, Anglicans, and Protestants (those who protested). For hundreds of years following this split, each of these traditions defined itself against the others, concentrating on real—or more often imagined—differences rather than what they had in common. In Roman Catholicism, this period was called the "Counter-Reformation."

In the twentieth century, the beginnings of a movement toward unity called "ecumenism" received a huge boost from the Second Vatican

---

10   In 2000, John Paul II made a formal public apology for the sins of the Roman Church that contributed to the division of Christianity.

JOHN XXIII

"We are not on Earth as museum-keepers, but to cultivate a flourishing garden of life and to prepare for a glorious future." These words of John XXIII about the Church marked his life and his brief ministry as pope—only five years.

As papal nuncio (ambassador) to Turkey, he saved thousands of Jews during the Holocaust by giving them fake Vatican passports. After his career in the Vatican diplomatic service, he became archbishop of Venice before being elected pope.

A joyful, rotund man with a mischievous sense of humor (when asked how many people work in the Vatican, he said, "About half"), John shocked the world by declaring he would call a council of the Church, a gathering of the bishops of the world. The Council, he said, would open the windows of the Church to the modern world. Protestants, Anglicans, and Orthodox would be invited.

Powerful Vatican bureaucrats tried to derail the Second Vatican Council every way they could. But in the end, the Council called for wide-ranging reforms in the Church and issued a series of earth-shaking documents to the Church and the world at large that gave new life to a Church many considered defensive and stuck in the past. Even though John died before the end of the Council, the bishops were so moved by his spirit of openness and love that they continued to approach things as he had.

John earned the love of Jewish people when he removed texts in the liturgy that were considered anti-Semitic. He won the love of other Christians by reaching out to them and including them in the Council. He's known as "Good Pope John" not only to Catholics; Anglicans and some Protestant Churches honor him in their liturgical calendars.

A Monogram of Christ: *Chi Rho*

The first two letters of the Greek word *Christos* ("anointed"), *chi* (X) and *rho* (P), are often combined in an ancient symbol for Christ. Another Greek abbreviation is IC XC (*inta sigma, chi sigma*), for Jesus Christ, often used in Icons. You may also see these letters (usually with a cross): IC XC NIKA, which means in Greek: "Jesus Christ is victorious!" You can also see the *chi* used as an abbreviation for Christ in "Xmas" for "Christmas."

profile

Satisfy us in the morning with your steadfast love,
so that we may rejoice and be glad all our days.

PSALM 90:14

We Are Each Called to Serve

CHURCH MINISTRIES AND ROLES

In a film, the stars get top billing. They're the ones we think of first when we talk about a movie. But the movie can't be made only with those actors who get the top billing. In fact, the actors are the least responsible for the film being made. Producers, directors, special effects experts, cinematographers, camera people, lighting technicians, and hundreds of other people are needed to make a film. In a similar way, people often think of the Church as the highly visible pope and bishops, maybe also priests and occasionally deacons—the clergy. But the Church, the People of God, consists of all those who are baptized, and each Christian has a role to play.

Not long ago, it was common for people to refer to lay Catholics being guided by "the Church," as though the Church were something separate and distinct from the laity. Many people still talk this way today.

John Henry Newman was once trying to explain the dignity of the laity to an especially obnoxious bishop. "The laity?" the bishop snorted. "Who are they?" Newman replied, "Well, your Grace, the Church would look pretty foolish without them." Mark 10:35–45

And the Church *would* look ridiculous if it were made up only of clergy. It'd be just a Bollywood costume extravaganza. But each Christian has an individual role to play in the Church, according to his or her state in life. That's what we mean when we say the Church is hierarchical: not that some are better than others, but that each person has a role. 1 Corinthians 12:12–31 Christianity isn't a spectator sport; everybody gets to play.

The Initiated (That would be you)

The term *lay* is often used in secular society to refer to someone who doesn't understand what's going on, someone without specialized knowledge. So you might say to a lawyer: "Can you put that in layman's terms?" But in the Church, the word *lay* comes from the Greek word *laios*, which means "initiated." So laypeople are fully initiated into the knowledge necessary to be a member of the Church. Yes, some laypeople know more than others, but you could say the same thing about the clergy. 1 Corinthians 12:1–11

To the **laity** belong all those dignities and duties common to all Christians baptized as priests, prophets, and kings (or queens). You are called to live the Beatitudes and to serve others. Matthew 25:31–45 The laity are called to holiness. You are to be fully involved in the ministry of the Church, evangelizing the world and offering prayer through full, conscious, active participation in the **liturgy**. The laity are to be involved in the governance of the Church by serving on finance councils and parish councils. You also have the right and the duty to make your needs known to pastors and bishops.

The laity also have a role separate from the clergy that belongs only to them: to be involved in secular affairs in a way that advances peace and justice in society. That's why clergy generally can't run for public office—because it's the special role of the laity to transform society.

Incorporating aspects of the lives of both laity and clergy are the members of religious[1] communities, people who live what is called a **consecrated life**. These are women and men (sisters and brothers) who live their lives according to poverty, chastity, and obedience in a common life as a radical response to Jesus, who invites us to leave everything behind to follow him. Matthew 19:16–30

The Servants

In the earliest days of the Church, a bishop led each community of believers. As the numbers of Christians increased, the bishops found they could not do everything. So we read in scripture that the Apostles ordained the first seven deacons to help them serve the poor and hungry.[2] Acts of the Apostles 6:1–7 One of these first deacons, Stephen, became the first Christian martyr. Acts of the Apostles 6:8–15 and 7:1–60 Around the end of the first millennium, for reasons that are unclear, permanent deacons became less common in the Western Church, although the Eastern Church has always had them. The diaconate became a

ceremonial step along the way to becoming a priest. The Second Vatican Council restored the permanent diaconate in the Roman Church.

The deacon has three ministries of service. By the ministry of the Word, the deacon preaches, teaches and proclaims the Gospel at liturgy. By the ministry of the Altar, the deacon has certain duties during liturgy. By the ministry of Love, the deacon has a responsibility to serve the outcast, to help the Christian community serve the outcast, and to welcome the outcast into the Christian community. The deacon is ordained for social justice. In addition to the threefold ministry, deacons also preside at baptisms, marriages, funerals, and other liturgical and devotional rites.[3]

The Leaders of Worship

Some time after the bishops in the early Church delegated authority to deacons to serve the poor, it became apparent that the bishops could not preside at every celebration of the Eucharist, as was the custom to that point. So the bishops ordained presbyters[4] to preside in their place at community celebrations of the Eucharist. The presbyter, or priest, is ordained to preach the Gospel, build up the Christian community, and preside at Eucharist.

At various points in our history, bishops also delegated to presbyters the power to reconcile sinners to God and the community, to anoint those who are sick, and to give the anointing that calls down the Holy Spirit on adults who are initiated into the Church at the Easter Vigil (or, in the Eastern tradition, on all who are baptized). Like bishops and deacons in the West, priests are also

1 *This use of the word* religious *is different from our usual use of the term. It means these communities live by a rule, or guide to common life. That's why ordained members of these communities are also sometimes called "regular clergy" in that they follow a rule, or* regula *in Latin, to distinguish them from diocesan, or "secular clergy," who do not take vows.*

2 *In fact, the word* deacon *comes from the Greek word* diakonos, *which means "servant." You may often hear a term used in the Church:* diakonia, *which means "service." Adjective: diaconal.*

3 *While Catholics, Orthodox, and Anglicans all share a belief in the three clerical orders of bishop, presbyter, and deacon, Lutherans do not consider deacons ordained clergy. Other Protestant traditions have varying understandings of these three terms. In the Roman Church, most deacons are married, maintain their own homes, and make their livings by secular professions.*

4 *We get the English word* priest *from the Greek word* presbyter, *which means "elder." Adjective: presbyteral.*

ordinary ministers[5] of baptism and preside at marriages.

Some priests also have the title of pastor,[6] which means they have the responsibility to care for a Church (parish) by providing everything necessary for that community to live the Christian life. Often this may include acting in an administrative role, but paying the bills and hiring the custodian isn't part of the essential role of the pastor. Many pastors have found a new freedom to be better priests by having laypeople take over the administration of parishes, allowing pastors to concentrate on their presbyteral duties.

The Shepherds

The presbyter and the deacon are the helpers of the bishop.[7] All their ministry comes from the bishop; without him they cannot minister.[8] This is because we're an apostolic Church. The bishops are the successors of the Apostles, and that's the basis of authority in the Church.

The bishop is the source of unity for the local Church. His ministry is often described as teaching, governing, and sanctifying. Catholics, Orthodox, and Anglicans believe the ministry of the bishop is essential because he's our link to the Apostles. In each diocese, the bishop is the chief teacher, the chief priest, the chief liturgist, the chief shepherd.[9] It's his responsibility to provide faithful teaching, to ensure that each community (parish) has a priest to celebrate the Eucharist with them, to ensure order and unity among the clergy and the laity, and financial support of communities and ministries to the poor and outcast.

As you can imagine, the job of a bishop is no cakewalk. Leading the Church is a lot like herding cats. And if you think it's hard leading a diocese, imagine the job of the Bishop of Rome, the pope.

The Servant of the Servants of God

As the successor of the Apostle Peter,[10] a part of the pope's job is to ensure unity among all Catholics. This involves trying to reach some level of consensus among 1.3 billion people of every nation, culture, socioeconomic status, and educational level. At times, we in the United States especially may become impatient because we think the pope isn't addressing something we feel is important. But the pope isn't thinking only of the United States.[11] His concern has to be for the whole world.

The pope isn't someone who becomes a living saint upon election. He's no better than anyone just because he's pope, nor are his prayers more powerful than yours. But he does have a job you don't have, and one you wouldn't want if you're smart.

The pope has wide-ranging authority in directing the Church. Still, he does not issue day-

---

5   While bishops, priests, and deacons are the ordinary ministers of baptism, anyone can baptize in case of emergency or where no clergy are available by pouring water over the head while saying, "I baptize you in the name of the Father, and of the Son, and of the Holy Spirit." The bishop can also give a layperson authority to regularly baptize in some circumstances.

6   More Latin: this word means "shepherd."

7   Bishop: from the Greek episkopos, meaning "overseer." Adjective: episcopal.

8   In fact, priests and deacons must have written permission from the bishop, called "faculties," to do anything. The validity of some sacraments even depends upon whether the priest or deacon presiding has faculties from the bishop.

9   The symbols of the bishop's office are the cathedra (his chair in the cathedral) and his pastoral staff (also called a crosier). A cathedral isn't just any big church, but is the mother church of a diocese, literally "the church with the chair." The pastoral staff represents a shepherd's crook.

10   Peter received his authority as head of the Apostles from Jesus himself. See Matthew 16:13–20.

11   Example: We may be annoyed when we think the Vatican isn't sufficiently interested in the status of women. And we may have a point. But the Vatican's priorities on women's rights may be preventing people from killing infants who are girls or defending the rights of girls to education in developing nations. We Americans are not the center of the universe.

to-day directives to every Catholic.[12] Some think the Roman Church is like a corporation with the pope as CEO and bishops as branch managers receiving orders from those "above" them and handing down orders to those "below" them.[13] This idea is wrong.

The pope's communion is primarily with the bishops, who each have full authority over their dioceses; the clergy and laity of each diocese have communion with the pope through their bishop. The Church is a communion of communions. As the ultimate sign of unity, the Bishop of Rome governs largely by listening—or at least should. The widely misunderstood concept of **infallibility** means that the pope, upon **discerning** that a teaching on faith or morals is already believed by the Catholics of the world, defines it to be true. More about this later.

Because he is the successor of Peter, the pope's role in the Church is sometimes called the "Petrine Ministry." While many non–Catholic Churches accept in theory the idea of a Petrine Ministry, they differ on some details of theology and practice as to how this primacy should work. These disconnects are a source of ecumenical dialogue to see if consensus can be reached for unity or if it's possible to adapt the everyday workings of the papacy[14] in a way that would meet the needs of all Christians.

....

12   This erroneous idea is called "ultramontanism," a term derived from a Latin phrase meaning "from beyond the mountains," because its adherents ignore their own bishop to give primary allegiance to the pope.

13   The common but erroneous idea that the pope delegates authority to the bishops was specifically denied by Vatican II in Lumen Gentium.

14   Remember, the papacy involves more than the pope. It also includes officials, called "the curia." Some non-Catholic Churches have more of a problem with the curia than with the idea of a pope. So one ecumenical consideration is that, because the curia isn't divinely mandated, how can it be reformed to address these concerns? This whole package of pope and curia is called "the Holy See" (see is another word for diocese).

The Good News

OK, so by now you've read several references to "the Good News" in this book. Maybe it's time we took a moment to look at this central concept of Christianity. If we're to go out into the world and proclaim the Good News, seems like we should know what it is.

As you know, "Good News" is what the word *Gospel* means. But the Gospel, or the Good News, isn't confined to what's written in Matthew, Mark, Luke, and John.

When Jesus began his public ministry in the synagogue at Nazareth, he read from the Book of Isaiah to state what his work would be:

> *The Spirit of the Lord is upon me,*
> *because he has anointed me*
> *to bring good news to the poor.*
> *He has sent me to proclaim release to the*
> *captives*
> *and recovery of sight to the blind,*
> *to let the oppressed go free,*
> *and to proclaim the year of the Lord's favor.*
> (Luke 4:18–19)

And after reading these words from the scroll, he said to the people there, "Today this scripture has been fulfilled in your hearing" (Luke 4:21).

This was an audacious claim. Now it's certainly true that Jesus did all this and more in a literal sense during his life through his teaching and miracles. And recovery of sight to the blind, for example, was certainly good news if you were a blind person who could now see.

But in a deeper sense, this passage from Isaiah was chosen by Jesus to describe the Good News he was bringing for all people. He'd not only bring sight to a few people who were physically blind but would open our eyes to what's true and important for our lives. He'd not only bring good news to the poor but would show all of us the poverty of our spirits that causes an endless cycle of victimization by the

backstory

powerful, even if we're the powerful. He'd set the oppressed free by showing us how to do it. He'd proclaim liberty to us who are captive to sin, fear, and doubt. He'd proclaim a new era marked by a new relationship between God and humanity by his saving life, death, and resurrection.

And these are only a few ways to read this passage. No doubt you can discover more facets of this passage for your own life, ways you experience the Good News of Jesus Christ.

The essential truth of the Good News is freedom. That's the heart of the Gospel. The world is scared that by embracing the Good News it will lose freedom and have to give up many things it holds important. But the Good News is that the "freedom" of the world is slavery and can be escaped. The Good News is that by releasing our hold on these things that are ultimately worthless, we can receive better things and have a better life, both here on Earth and after we die. Benedict XVI said, "If we let Christ into our lives, we lose nothing, nothing, absolutely nothing of what makes life free, beautiful and great."

By its unredeemed nature, the world is fearful of the Gospel because the Gospel comforts the afflicted and afflicts the comfortable. The world, while attracted to the Gospel, doubts there's anything better than the way things are: the powerful trampling the powerless, the single-minded pursuit of wealth and celebrity, the reliance on violence to deal with its problems, the worship of self and state. In response to this doubt, the Good News offers faith: faith that the truth will set us free.

κήρυγμα

The Proclamation: *Kerygma*

The Greek word *kerygma* is used to describe the joyful proclamation of the Good News, the essence of Jesus' teachings that sets us free.

CLERICAL ABUSE

We were always taught to put our faith in priests, so I could no longer be a Catholic when I learned our pastor had molested a child.

We don't really know why so many priests abused children. Many who claim to know are operating from preexisting agendas, such as homophobia.[15] Whatever the causes, it's clear that a clericalist[16] culture is responsible for allowing the situation to develop into a full-blown crisis of horrifying scale.

You're right to be appalled at what happened in your parish. There's no excuse for it. Aside from the terrible reality, many people of good will have lost their faith over this matter. And that's a shame, because it doesn't have to be that way.

Many of us were taught the priest was a sort of superhuman arbiter between God and humanity, and that "Father is always right." Someone once said to me the priest was the outlet that enabled her to plug into God. For such people, the priest *was* the Church.

It fell upon the bishops then to deal with these situations individually. Some bishops, it's true, did act to protect the institutional Church. Failure to understand the nature of the illness caused many bishops to believe it was curable (a belief also shared in the past by some mental health professionals). Most bishops looked at these priests simply as people in need of repentance.

Looking back, it's tempting to assume there was a vast cover-up. But can we assume the bishops understood the complexity of the problem and how to deal with it back in the 1950s? Still, the sheer scale of the clerical abuse crisis shows what can happen when the Church becomes synonymous with the clergy. Dedicated and active lay involvement will help avoid clerical misconduct in the future and keep the Church focused on our mission instead of centered on the clergy. If not, we're in for other crises involving other issues.

....

15   *Your authors tend to think it was a deficient seminary approach to dealing with sex that resulted in a stunted sexuality, but we're not experts.*

16   *"Clericalism" is the false assumption that the Church is made up of clergy, or that clergy are superior to laity.*

in the media

Teresa was born in Albania and joined a teaching order of nuns. But upon reflection, she knew she didn't connect with their mission of teaching children of the affluent. She was convinced she was called to serve the poorest of the poor. So she went to Kolkata (the current name of the city once called Calcutta) and began picking up people she found dying in the streets, caring for them in an abandoned Hindu temple.

Teresa began to attract others who wanted to share in this ministry to those she called "Christ in the distressing disguise of the poor." This small band of women would grow to an international community of thousands serving the destitute, those with AIDS, lepers, orphans, and other outcasts of society in several hundred centers around the world.

She was an outspoken advocate for the outcast, fighting governments and bishops alike to bring compassion to the streets of the world's cities, winning a Nobel Peace Prize along the way.

When she died in 1997, this humble but focused woman was given an official state funeral by the Hindu nation of India and was mourned by people of all faiths.

She wrote that her work began by helping one person, then one more, then another. We can do as she did, she said, by helping "just one, just one." Teresa's vast community of some 5,000 religious and 100,000 lay helpers is eloquent testimony that the work of the Church isn't confined to the clergy.

TERESA OF KOLKATA

profile

I cry to you, O LORD; I say, You are my refuge,
my portion in the land of the living.

The Lord Hears the Cry of the Poor

SOCIAL JUSTICE

The widow, the orphan, and the alien. They're mentioned 375 times in scripture. For Jews and Christians, the widow, the orphan, and the alien (immigrant) represent all those whom polite society considers outcast and unworthy of concern. So why do we put so much emphasis on our rituals and so little on serving the outcast? We'll argue till the cows come home on whether a chalice should be gold or glass, and who may clean it, while our parish ignores hungry people huddled on our church steps. And yet both the Hebrew Testament and the New Testament make it clear: God's priority is the poor.

The prophet Amos gives us these words from the Lord:

I hate, I despise your festivals,
  and I take no delight in your solemn assemblies.
Even though you offer me your burnt offerings
and grain offerings[1]
  I will not accept them;
and the offerings of well-being of your fatted animals
  I will not look upon.
Take away from me the noise of your songs;
  I will not listen to the melody of your harps.
But let justice roll down like the waters,
  and righteousness like an ever-flowing stream.
(Amos 5:21–24)

Again and again, the prophets of the Hebrew Testament, the Apostles, the Fathers of the Church,[2] the great saints and even Jesus himself, no less, have implored us to stop concentrating on the silly trappings of religion and to put a priority on the poor and outcast among us. Matthew 23

The passages from our ancient tradition are too numerous to mention here fully; they would take volumes. This rich tradition of compassion, more comprehensive than any other single topic in our tradition, is called "social justice," and we can't be good Christians without dealing with it. Too often, we concentrate on ritual and correct belief while neglecting our duty to the poor and outcast. James 2:1-7

---

1 Burnt and grain offerings: gifts given to God at Temple ceremonies.

2 The Fathers of the Church are those early writers from apostolic times and immediately thereafter whose teachings have been considered authoritative by Christians throughout our history. The study of the writings of the Fathers is called "patrology" or "patristics."

Back to the Beginning

To understand the basis for social justice, we go back to the first words of scripture, the Book of Genesis (1:27). There we're told God made humanity in his own image. For the Christian, this is the foundational truth of human dignity and the basis of our interaction with each other. Even as each of us harbors a spark of the divine, so we all share equally in this dignity.

Among the first stories of human interaction in scripture is the murder of Abel by his brother, Cain. It was the first injustice between two persons. Genesis 4:1–16 Cain's cop-out was to distance himself from Abel's well-being—"Am I my brother's keeper?"—the first instance of a question we hear often even today. To this question scripture gives a resounding "Yes" over the millennia. We are our responsible for our brothers and sisters. Luke 10:29–37 As Homer Simpson might say, "D'oh!"

Throughout the Hebrew Testament, we hear especially from the prophets of our duty toward others, especially the **anawim**, those who are so desperate that they rely on God—and by extension his people—to escape misery and certain death. Sirach 4:1–10 These are the widow, the orphan, and the alien,[3] those without the protection of a property-owning male in a hand-to-mouth nomadic culture, those who would die unless the people were required to share with them some of their own meager resources. Seven of the Ten Commandments deal with how we act in justice toward our neighbor, and in Hebrew the word for *righteousness* is synonymous with *justice*. James 2:1–13

In his account of final judgment, Jesus didn't consider religious observance or correct belief as defining characteristics of those who are saved, but rather how we treat the least among us. Matthew 25:31-46

The Kingdom of God Is the Rule of Justice

Throughout Christian history, we as the Church have become ever more aware of how our responsibility toward others is rooted in justice. From the earliest times, the Fathers of the Church taught that when we give to the poor, we're not acting through personal virtue ("charity" in the secular sense of the word) but are giving to that person what's owed to him or her in justice.

With the Industrial Revolution, new affronts to justice arose. Leo XIII[4] put the language of justice into words for a new age: all people have the fundamental right to dignity and a means to provide for themselves and their families. Employees may not be exploited as a means of profit. Workers have the right to organize to improve their working conditions. Governments, too, are required to practice justice, ensure human dignity and freedom of belief, and enact laws for the common good rather than for the benefit of the powerful.

Just as individuals may sin, a society may also engage in **social sin**. Social sin is when a society embraces injustice as public policy or becomes so accustomed to injustice it no longer sees its structures as an affront to human dignity.

A clear example of social sin is slavery. The United States not only had laws sanctioning slavery but had become so dependent upon it we couldn't see the basic humanity of the people producing our food, our clothing, or building our homes and public buildings.[5] The evil fruits of this

---

3   Those who question the Church's advocacy on behalf of immigrants should consider hundreds of passages in scripture that require welcome, just treatment, and compassion for immigrants. This isn't something we just came up with recently. It's not merely a political issue. It's a justice issue that falls squarely within the Church's purview.

4   Leo's teachings were in the encyclical Rerum Novarum in 1891, the first social justice encyclical. Since then, for more than a hundred years, just about every pope through John Paul II (except John Paul I, who was pope for only a month and didn't get a chance to write much of anything) has issued at least one social justice encyclical, making social justice the single most common theme of all papal encyclicals. (An encyclical is a letter from the pope to the whole Church.)

5   For example, such monuments to freedom as the White House and the U.S. Capitol were built with slave labor.

social sin are with us still today as we struggle with the sin of racism.

Any form of social sin perverts the social order and often leads to greater evils such as war. Paul VI said, "If you want peace, work for justice."

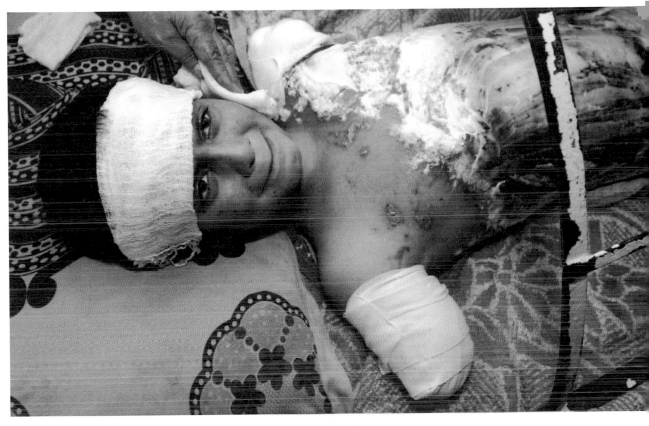

WAR AND PEACE

What are the chances for ending war in today's world?

First, let's be clear that peace is not the absence of war. War is the absence of peace. This isn't a trivial point.

Peace is the state of justice, harmony, tolerance, mutual respect, compassion, and love—all the things implied in the ancient Hebrew concept of *shalom*. This is what we mean when at Mass we say to each other, "Peace be with you." So where there's injustice, strife, intolerance, disrespect, vengeance, and hate, we shouldn't be surprised when people begin large-scale killing of each other.

In such situations, governments or militias may be convinced to stop killing people for a while through political means consisting of carrots and sticks, but such a "cessation of hostilities" isn't a long-term solution. Blind, selfish human nature will continue to wage war, thinking it can engage in injustice to get what it wants, whether oil, land, religious advantage, or whatever else is coveted.

The only way to avoid war is to establish peace. True peace will never erupt into war, because all wars are caused by injustice, whether on the part of those who attack or those who are attacked. There's no lack of people eager to justify war and make it seem noble. But at the root of their arguments is always a need to perpetuate injustice through brutal force, unless they're fighting off a foreign invader in their own streets.

Politically expedient solutions to end war will always fail because they do not take into account God's plan for peace. James 3:13–18

The prophets and their message to us

Ever go by a homeless person holding a sign that says something like, "Will work for food" or "Homeless, PLEASE HELP, God Bless." What if any feelings does that encounter bring up in you? Do you wonder if they're for real, or just out to grab a few coins, that maybe begging is their primary profession?

Some say, "If I give them anything they'll go spend it on cigarettes and alcohol, so I'm doing them a favor by passing by." Seeing another person in need and taking stock of our motivation to help, as baptized Christians who are required to do so, tells us a lot about our readiness to respond to the Gospel and follow Jesus. Isaiah 58:1–14

It's a common mistake to read the prophetic books of the Hebrew Testament and look at the prophets as fortunetellers who predict future events. This wasn't the reason God chose them to speak out. The prophets talked about the present and warned what would happen if present needs in the community were not attended to with true justice. Those who had a lot were told by the prophets to share their wealth with those in need. The prophets were not popular people! Isaiah 10:1–4

The Hebrew prophets tell us this today. If you want to measure the true level of justice in the land (or any society) take a look at those most in need. Today we would have to look at those suffering with AIDS, children with no parents or homes to live in, the homeless on our streets, all our citizens and immigrants among us who live in an affluent society but exist well below the poverty level and cannot provide the basic necessities for themselves and their families. We need to think of our senior citizens in homes or facilities with no one to visit them, those in prison. Can you think of any others, maybe even members of your own family? And then look at how we (you and me) care for these people, who are God's People. Justice present in our society is measured by how those most in need are assisted and made whole again.

This isn't a task left solely for our government, although elected officials should be held accountable to act on behalf of those who elected them. This work is for each one of us. We must care for others who have little or nothing. And we do this because Christ did it and we claim to be followers of Christ.

At the conclusion of every liturgy we are dismissed to go out in to our world...and not just for coffee and donuts!

Vatican II challenged every Catholic not to just "go to Mass on Sunday," but to embrace a life of service, and that service is directed to those most in need. If we fail to roll up our sleeves and with the resources we have make a difference in the lives of the least of our sisters and brothers, then we simply fail as Christians.

Now is the time for us to examine our own personal commitment to prophetic justice. Are you filled with compassion that moves you into action or are you leaving this work to someone else, like "the Church," to take care of "them"? But remember, you are the Church.

Perhaps worth even more soul searching: Have you heard the cry of the poor or have you become so busy in trying to accumulate personal wealth and status that you forgot what your prophetic call as a Christian should compel you to do? In quiet, pray about this. The voice of God will no doubt move your heart with compassion and from compassion to action! The Lord hears the cry of the poor, and one day he may ask us if we did too!

Beloved of God: *Anawim*

The Hebrew word *anawim* refers to the poor and outcast, those who are so desperate they rely in a special way on the protection of God.

backstory

profile

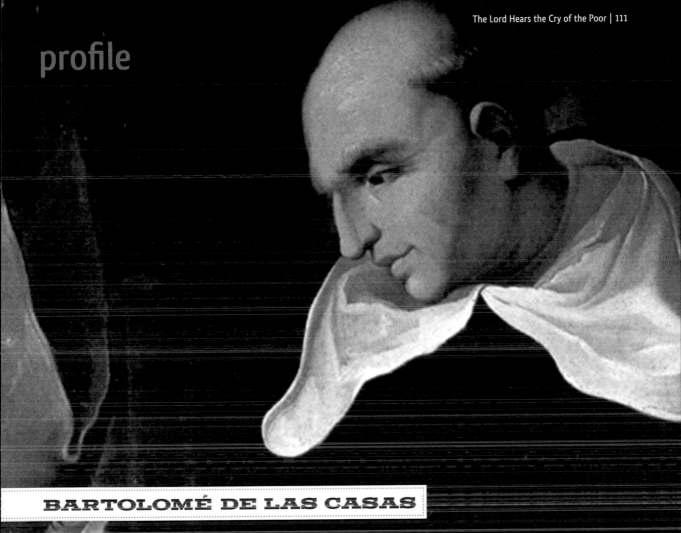

BARTOLOMÉ DE LAS CASAS

Less than twenty years after the famous voyage of Columbus, a young Bartolomé de las Casas was ordained a priest and returned to the Americas to live with his father. A former participant in the notorious *encomienda* system of Spanish slavery, Bartolomé freed his slaves. He became a vocal critic of this cruel and vicious system that resulted in the deaths of hundreds of thousands of indigenous people.

For a while, Bartolomé tried political methods to end slavery in Spain's colonies, but was bitterly disappointed in the results. So he wrote *The Devastation of the Indies*, one of the best-sellers of the time, which described in excruciating detail the sufferings of the indigenous peoples at the hands of the heartless *encomienda* masters. As a result of the book's impact, King Charles V of Spain outlawed slavery.

Bartolomé was made Bishop of Chiapas in today's Mexico and charged with enforcement of the new law. This didn't make him the most popular guy in New Spain. Even the clergy, themselves slaveholders, refused to obey him.

Fleeing the New World for his life, he returned to Spain, where he spent his remaining years in theological debates to prove the indigenous peoples of the Americas were, in fact, human. One result of his tireless efforts (he lived to be eighty-two) was a 1537 papal document by Paul III denouncing slavery.

Where others saw only instruments of profit to be exploited, Bartolomé saw beautiful and noble human beings and a magnificent culture being systematically plundered. His example is one we desperately need today.

19

Will you not revive us again,
so that your people may rejoice in you?

PSALM 85:6

We Have Died to Sin and Risen to a New Life

THE SACRAMENTS OF INITIATION: BAPTISM, CONFIRMATION, AND EUCHARIST

Do you believe? That's the question asked of us as we're initiated into the Christian faith. At baptism, adults are asked to profess their Faith in the tenets of the Creed, and parents and godparents respond on behalf of the infant. At **confirmation**, we proclaim again our baptismal assent so we may receive wisdom and be strengthened in our Faith. And as we approach the Eucharist, we're called to believe what faith teaches but our eyes cannot see. These three sacraments set us apart from the world, transforming individuals into a community. We become God's own people, born to new life by faith.

A **sacrament** is an act by which God shares his life with us through the material things of this world and other people. The ultimate revelation of God, Jesus Christ, is the Father's sacrament to the world. In turn, Jesus made us, the Church, the sacrament of his love for the world to bring all people to the Father through the Holy Spirit. There are many ways God works sacramentally in our lives, but when we talk about "the sacraments," we refer to the seven liturgical sacraments.

Through the sacraments of **initiation**, we participate in the mystery of Christ's life, death, and resurrection. We share in the divinity of Christ, who shared in our humanity. Because we're invited to share in his divinity, that includes an invitation to share in the life of the Trinity: the Lover, the Beloved, and the Union of Love they share among them.

This call to partake in the divine life is so amazing the Eastern Church refers to its fulfillment as **divinization**, or **deification**. We

can actually become like God! All the sacraments impart this share in the divine life (grace) through simple material things—water, olive oil, bread, wine, another person's hands—and words. This is the sacramental worldview: that God works wonders through the good things of Creation, here and now. It's one of the essential hallmarks of our Christian Faith.

It All Begins with Baptism

"Do you not know," Paul asks us, "that all of us who have been baptized into Christ Jesus were baptized into his death?" Romans 6 Strange as it may seem to think of this as we see a newborn baby at the font, baptism begins with death, because without death there can be no resurrection. The ancient ritual act of **immersion** in water symbolizes burial by going under the water and resurrection by coming out of the water. The power of this symbolism is why baptism by immersion is now the preferred method in the

Roman Catholic Church, although baptism by pouring over the head is still OK but not ideal.[1]

In the early Church, only adults were baptized, and then only at Easter Vigil. This ancient practice of identifying those who wished to be baptized as **catechumens** was restored by the Second Vatican Council with the **Rite of Christian Initiation of Adults** (or **RCIA**, as you may hear it called in your parish).

Early in our history, Christians recognized the value of raising children in a community of faith from the start, and the decision was made to baptize infants so they could benefit from the example of the community through their childhood and beyond.

In baptism, we become members of the Body of Christ, the worldwide movement we know as Christianity, regardless of the Christian tradition we belong to. Those who choose one tradition over the one they were raised in are not re-baptized; most Christian traditions recognize baptism as celebrated by each other.[2] Baptism is a once-in-a-lifetime event. John 3:1-21

In baptism we assume the three dignities of the Christian: priest, prophet, and king (or queen). With the baptismal priesthood we take on the responsibility of praying for the whole world. Our prophetic dignity requires us to see injustice in our world and to take up the cause of those who are oppressed. Our royal dignity empowers us to work for a just society. These three roles of the Christian are underscored in the anointing

with Chrism,[3] a remnant of the ancient rite of coronation. In baptism, we're freed from the slavery to sin we inherit from humanity's first parents[4] and become a new creation in Christ. In fact, the effect of baptism is so extreme that those who receive it as adults are forgiven all the sins of their past lives.

Completing Our Baptism

Confirmation (called **chrismation** in the Eastern Church) is an anointing that calls down the Holy Spirit. It was originally a part of the rite of initiation that in the West was reserved to the bishop. As the number of Christians grew, it took years for the bishop to arrive in a town and complete baptism with this anointing.

In the Eastern Church, chrismation is celebrated when an infant is baptized (and also receives his or her first communion as an infant). In some places, Roman Catholic children are confirmed before they receive communion for the first time, which retains the ancient progression of baptism →confirmation →Eucharist. In the United States, this progression is retained in the Rite of Christian Initiation of Adults, but those baptized as infants in most U.S. dioceses receive communion for the first time as children before receiving confirmation from the bishop as teenagers.[5] Like baptism, confirmation is received only once.

Whatever the sequence, confirmation is a completion of baptism, and its effect is to bring

1 Following the Second Vatican Council, the ritual acts of the sacraments and other rites were restored to their original form after centuries of creeping minimalism. The richness of these signs was restored instead of doing only the minimum required.

2 So we are not baptized Catholic or Orthodox or Anglican or Protestant; we are baptized into the Body of Christ according to one of these traditions.

3 Chrism is olive oil mixed with perfume. Along with the Oil of Catechumens and the Oil of the Sick, it is blessed by the bishop in the cathedral during Holy Week each year and distributed to the parishes of the diocese to be used in the celebration of the sacraments in that parish until Holy Week of the next year. You can see these oils displayed in your church in a cabinet called an "ambry," the oil vessels designated by Latin initials: SC = Sacred Chrism, OC = Oil of Catechumens, OI = Oil of the Sick.

4 The sin of our first parents is called "original sin," transmitted to all of us as an inclination to not always choose to do what is good. It is the cause of ignorance, suffering, injustice, and death.

5 Are you confused yet? The difference in how and when various cultures celebrate these sacraments of initiation, even within the Catholic communion, is proof that unity is possible in diversity.

the recipient into the life of the Holy Spirit, who animates the Church. Through this sharing in the life of the Holy Spirit, we're drawn more closely into the life of the Trinity. The meaning of the word *confirmation* is a strengthening, and that's what this sacrament does. It strengthens our bond with Christ, the Church, and our Christian mission by anointing with Chrism and the invocation "Receive the Holy Spirit." [6]

The Body of Christ Receives the Body of Christ

The initiation of the Christian culminates in the Eucharist. In the early Church, only the baptized were allowed to even witness this act, much less receive the Body of Christ. "The doors, the doors," the deacon would cry, as the church doors were shut to keep this sacred mystery hidden from the uninitiated. That's why Holy Communion is restricted to baptized Christians.[7]

We take a closer look at the Eucharist later. But participation in the Eucharist, with its climax of the people eating and drinking the Body and Blood of Jesus, is the ultimate act of every Christian, the fulfillment each week of an ongoing initiation into lifelong conversion that doesn't end until we die and are initiated into eternity. By receiving the Body of Christ, we become the Body of Christ, over and over again. We conform ourselves more closely to the Risen Lord and take that new life into the world.

....

6   You may have heard that confirmation makes you a "soldier of Christ." But Christians are not militaristic, so we have to be careful in using such analogies.

7   Intercommunion is a term that refers to Christians of one tradition receiving Holy Communion in another. While all twenty-three Catholic Churches have intercommunion among them, formal intercommunion with other Churches is limited, although there are instances where other Christians can receive communion in a Catholic church—and vice versa.

We are saved as a community

All humans long for community. We seek connection to others because we are social beings. From the beginning, God did not create a single human, but two, so our social nature is established by God.

Many secular communities exist for various purposes. There are towns and cities and nations that come into being for the purpose of forming an ordered society. There are communities of common bonds that exist among people of various ethnicities, nationalities, tribes, languages, sexual orientation, ideology, profession, and avocation.

Dorothy Day eloquently expressed our desire for a connection to others based in our common Faith: "We have all known the long loneliness, and we have learned that the only solution is love and that love comes with community."

The Church exists as a community of baptized people called to bring the Good News to every person and transform the world. In every place, we gather around a bishop to form the People of God, a community of sinners struggling toward holiness and justice. We look beyond the confines of our local Church, expanding our community to embrace all the other local Churches around the world, solidifying that unity through the ministry of the Bishop of Rome, the Servant of the Servants of God.

As in any community, living with each other in the Church presents a challenge that's not insignificant. Because everybody is welcome in the Church, we're often called to live, love, and learn with people we might not mix with in our secular life. This requires a focus on discerning the various gifts we all bring to the Church and putting those gifts to work for the benefit of all.

At times, this discernment may show we're doing something we don't have the gifts for. That'll require that we give up that role to someone who has the necessary gifts to do it well. And our personal gifts may evolve or change over time, so we must listen carefully for the guidance of the Spirit.

Living as a Christian community also means we respect the roles established by hierarchy, "the order of the holy people." Laity should not infringe on the roles of the ordained, and the ordained should not infringe on the roles of the laity. Priests should not infringe on the roles of deacons, and deacons should not infringe on the roles of priests. These roles may not be what we assume at first just because "that's the way we've always done it." Dialogue and reflection on our dignities and responsibilities can help us navigate the gray areas and discover new ways of respecting hierarchical roles while allowing the fullest possible involvement of all God's people.

Different communities have different ways of relating. Some communities are democratic. The Church, however, is not democratic. Neither are we monarchical. No other institution or movement on Earth is similar in organization to the Church.

The Church's hierarchical structure isn't intrinsically inferior to a democratic structure. You can have a democracy that's insensitive to the needs of the community, and you can have a hierarchical structure that's very sensitive to the community's needs. And vice versa. It's all in the attitude. If we find our hierarchical structure isn't working at some time, the solution is to find ways to make it more responsive, not to change the basic structure we received from apostolic times. The Church is always in need of reform,[8] but so are democracies.

Our way of relating to each other as a Church has lasted for more than two thousand years, longer than any form of secular government. At times, adjustments and changes—even radical changes—may be necessary to renew our community, but its essential form will always remain, a community undemocratic but focused on service, no matter what our role.

---

8 Here's another Latin phrase: ecclesia semper reformanda, "The Church is always in need of reform." If someone is shocked when you say this to them in English, drop the ancient Latin saying on them as the nuclear option. After all, if it's in Latin, it must be true!

backstory

BAPTISM BY IMMERSION

My cousin says I'm not really baptized because I wasn't fully immersed in water. Why is this so important to her?

Your cousin has a point. Baptism by immersion is a fuller and richer symbol of what happens at baptism. However, we respectfully disagree that the fuller symbolism is required to administer this sacrament.

We're no fans of minimalism in sacraments. But since the time of the early Church, it has been acknowledged that while people should be immersed at baptism, it is acceptable to at least pour water on the head of those to be baptized (called "baptism by infusion").

For hundreds of years, infusion was the standard way of administering baptism. During the Reformation, some Protestants insisted on full immersion as a requirement for valid baptism, but they were in the minority, even in the Protestant traditions.

Baptism by immersion is now the preferred form in all twenty-three Catholic Churches. But those who choose to continue baptizing by pouring water on the head still validly baptize according to apostolic tradition, even if the rite celebrated that way isn't the ideal. We must make allowances for those who are accustomed to baptism by pouring, whether because of nostalgia or habit or because their church building wasn't designed to accommodate the richer symbolism of immersion. All in good time.

in the media

An Italian Jesuit with a passion for spreading the Gospel and a true Renaissance man, Matteo Ricci (born 1552) dedicated his life to creative ways to reach out to the people of China. He immersed himself in their culture to present the Good News with an Asian face.

On his arrival in the East, he spoke not a word of Chinese. With great dedication, he learned the language and adapted himself and Christianity to the culture, dressing as a Confucian scholar and setting up a chapel in the style of a Chinese temple. He wrote books in Chinese explaining the Christian faith in traditional Chinese terminology, referring to God as the "Lord of Heaven," 天主 (*Tianzhu*), an existing term in that culture. He sought to integrate existing Chinese customs into the worship and prayer life of those he converted. He was successful in interesting many in Christianity.

Unfortunately, Vatican officials made a huge mistake. They insisted he present Christianity in China from a European standpoint, even requiring that he refer to God with the Latin word *Deus* rather than the Chinese term *Tianzhu*. This caused the Chinese to view Christianity as a foreign European concept, and the missionaries were expelled. The Vatican eventually admitted its error—350 years later. Matteo's approach to evangelization by inculturation was vindicated, but by that time Asia had been largely lost to Christianity.

The Chinese who encountered Matteo respected him and were eager to be initiated into the Christian faith when it was presented to them in the context of their own culture. From Matteo we can all learn to respect the integrity of Christianity while adapting its expression to new cultures and situations.

MATTEO RICCI

天主

God: The Lord of Heaven

The Chinese term *Tianzhu*, "the Lord of Heaven," was used by the great Jesuit missionary Matteo Ricci to evangelize the Chinese people.

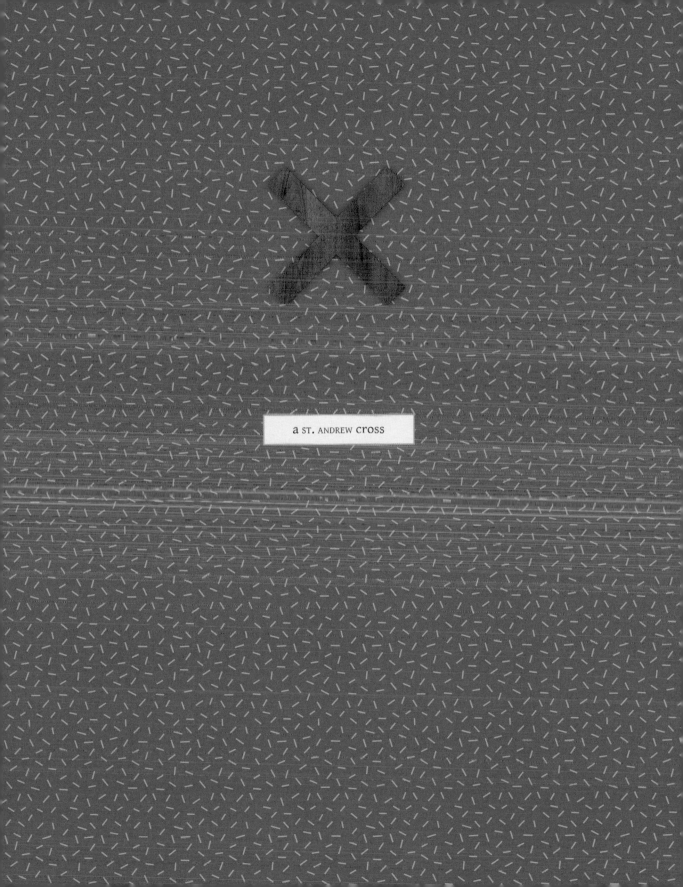

a ST. ANDREW cross

Your statutes have been my songs
wherever I make my home.

PSALM 119:54

God Calls Each of Us to Our Own Way of Life

THE SACRAMENTS OF VOCATION: MARRIAGE AND HOLY ORDERS

"What do you want to be?" A firefighter? A lawyer? An archaeologist? From the time we're very young, people start to ask us that question. We even wonder about it on our own before too long. Usually this question really means "What do you want to do?" rather than "What do you want to be?" Put this way, the question, at least at first, asks us what we are going to end up doing to earn a living. It's a natural question, no doubt, and one we answer over years of our lives. The answer can even change from time to time. But for God, being comes before doing.

The sacraments of vocation have more to do with the question, "What do I want to be?" Even after we figure out how we want to earn a living, the question of how to live our lives still remains unanswered.

For the Christian, this question is answered by responding to the call of our own baptism. How do I want to live my life, being true to myself, in response to all the unique gifts God has given to me?

The sacraments of vocation are **marriage** (sometimes called "**matrimony**") and **holy orders**. And while we'll discuss each of these, at the outset let's agree that there can be other vocations that are just as valid yet may not be sacramental. There are those who never marry, those in religious communities, those who are separated or divorced, and in today's world we must acknowledge families of various makeups. No matter what, every person is called to live his or her life in response to how God has made and called us.

A Union Stronger Than Blood

The Book of Genesis tells us the divine intention for a man and woman who choose to enter into marriage: "A man leaves his father and his mother and clings to his wife, and they become one flesh" (Genesis 2:24). We think a lot about blood relationships: our brothers and sisters and all those in our family. When a couple commits to marriage they create a union that is more powerful and stronger than any "blood" relationship. A new family is formed. The man and woman choose to bind themselves together exclusively for life, for their mutual benefit, for the raising of any children born from their union, and for the building up of the Christian community.[1]

In the Roman tradition, a priest or deacon usually witnesses the exchange of vows, but the couple marry themselves to each other by their words of commitment. In the Eastern Churches, it's the priest who administers the sacrament through the nuptial blessing. In both traditions, the couple must enter into marriage freely and with full knowledge of the vocation they're about to begin together. A period of preparation precedes the marriage, during which the couple come to understand how we, the Church, understand married life and the permanence of the commitment they will make. God enters the picture by giving the couple the grace they will need, through the sacrament, to live out their marriage vows for the rest of their lives.

Called to Serve the Christian Community

Jesus invited many men and women to be with him during his life and public ministry—the Seventy-Two. They learned from the Master and spread the Good News to others. From among these disciples, Jesus chose the Twelve to be his Apostles. After Jesus' death and resurrection, the Apostles began teaching the people and choosing their successors, conferring authority on them by the laying on of hands.

This laying on of hands, the sacrament of holy orders, sets aside some Christians for service as bishop, priest, or deacon. Through ordination, each assumes a particular type of service to others according to a specific place in the **hierarchy.** By the bishop's invocation of the Holy Spirit, God provides the grace necessary for these servants to live out their vocation faithfully.

Jesus is the Good Shepherd, the head of the Church. Bishops are called to serve the community as shepherds not by their own choice, but as others discern their gift for leadership. As a successor of the Apostles, the bishop stands in the place of Jesus himself as teacher, shepherd, priest, and servant. The ordination of a bishop confers on him the fullness of holy orders, which the bishop then shares with his helpers, the priests and deacons.

While a bishop is in charge of a diocese, by communion with all the bishops he helps to guide the whole Church. That's why a bishop must be ordained by at least three other bishops. It's a sign of his membership in the college of bishops.[2] So when the bishops work together, they're said to act **collegially**.

The bishop shares some of his authority with those whom God has called to be priests. By laying his hands upon him, the bishop confers on the priest a share in his ministry as high priest, serving in the image of Jesus who offered the perfect sacrifice of himself to the Father. The priest becomes the one who will assume the person of Christ at Eucharist, who will care for the good of the people in Christ's place, absolve sins by authority of the bishop and preach to all the Good News.

As the bishop shares his ministry with the priest, so he also shares it with his other helper, the deacon. The part of his authority he shares with the deacon is his ministry as a servant. As the deacon sits beside the bishop or priest and assists him at Eucharist, we're given a strong visual reminder that we Christians are all called to be servants. The ministry of the deacon is in the margins and gray areas, bridging the gap between the Church and the larger community as the voice of the Church to the outcast and the voice of the outcast to the Church.

---

1 *This community aspect of marriage is why Roman Catholics are married in church buildings: to emphasize that they take on a new role in the faith community. As lovely as a wedding on the beach may be for photos, it does not adequately communicate the context of marriage within the faith community. Some people even underscore this connection (and save a lot of money!) by being married simply at a regular Sunday Mass rather than with their own private extravaganza. Something to think about....*

---

2 *The word* college *doesn't mean they're taking classes, although good ordained ministers are always learning. It means they're part of a group. We also use this term in the United States when we refer to the "electoral college," those who gather together to choose the president.*

The ordained person has responded to a call from the Lord that lasts a lifetime. The clergy are challenged every day to live life in a way that models Christ in the world as shepherd (bishop), priest (presbyter), or servant (deacon). But ordination is no guarantee of holiness.

As with all Christians, the ordained minister, by entering into a life of prayer, contemplation, and action seeks to lead the faith community and grow in faith, hope, and love with all the People of God. Whether a member of the clergy or a layperson, all God's People working together live the real Christian vocation, namely bringing the Kingdom of God into the world as Christ challenged us to do.

Who Do You Want to Be?

The sacraments of matrimony and holy orders are two ways people respond to the questions, "What do I want to be?" and "How do I want to live?" As Christians, they give us a better way of looking at these questions: "Who does God want me to be?" and "How does God want me to live?" And in these questions each of us finds our true vocation.

Ignatius (Íñigo) was a Spanish nobleman, a soldier, and a player. In battle his leg was badly broken by a cannonball. He underwent a crude and painful operation to reset the leg so he'd look good in his tights and catch the ladies' eyes. They had a thing about men's legs back then.

While recovering and confined to bed, Ignatius read about Jesus and the saints, mainly because there were no novels in his family library. Ignatius underwent a conversion experience, and he gave up his military career for a life of study and prayer. He attracted a group of six like-minded friends around him, all of them students at the University of Paris. They called themselves the Society of Jesus; today we also call them Jesuits.

Ignatius and his band of close friends created a new form of religious life. It was so revolutionary he was investigated by the Inquisition. Their friendships kept them close even as they scattered around the world as missionaries and founders of universities. Far away from each other, their relationships continued to deepen through the exchange of hundreds of letters among them. Hundreds more joined the Society, inspired by the love that was so apparent among this band of brothers.

For Ignatius and his friends, it was very difficult to live so far apart from each other for so long. But their roots in healthy, strong relationships served them well wherever they went. They found new relationships rooted in service and cultivated them among every race, in every culture and place.

IGNATIUS OF LOYOLA

profile

Vocation is about relationships

"How's your love life?" That's how an Anglican priest I knew would slyly greet his friends. After a good laugh, he'd clarify, "You know, your love life with God and your neighbor!"

This wise priest knew a love life didn't just mean whether you'd had sex recently. He was making a point about the value of healthy relationships by taking a common phrase and turning it on its head.

Humans are the highest order of social animals. We do best when we are in healthy relationships. Our attitudes about our relationships, how we choose them, how we cherish them, what we are willing to do to make them work, all say something about who we are as people.

One important relationship we need to look at is our relationship with God. Jesus shows the depth of God's love for us. And it's just as important that we share that love with others.

Love is the binding force of any relationship, and we know God is the source of all love. So the first thing we must bring into any healthy relationship is love.

Some hear the words *love* and *relationship* and think they're only achieved in an intimate or sexual way. Love between husband and wife is this kind of love, but it's not the sum and substance of the relationship, as anyone who's married knows! The Christian is called to bring love into all his or her relationships: family, friends, coworkers—even that surly person at the DMV window.

Love brings with it the desire to serve. Real service is putting the needs of another before the needs of yourself. Answering God's call to your vocation will only make sense if we understand the call to love and serve.

It's a mistake to think only married people are called to live in relationship. Those who are ordained and celibate are also called to live lives of healthy relationships with others: to cultivate friendships, to be involved in the lives of those they serve.

Single people too are called to cultivate close relationships, as are religious within their communities and outside them.

For all of us, no matter what our vocation, the call to loving relationships always includes a call to serve. If you have a relationship with someone and you've never had to give up a little for that other person, or do something for them you'd rather not, you might want to think about the value of that relationship.

Vocation is a response. Responding to your call or vocation is the decision to live out your desire to love and serve in a public way, to proclaim the Good News. For married couples and those who are ordained, this public commitment to relationship is a sacrament, but the public nature of vocational relationships is true for all Christians. The character of those relationships should be driven by our need to be connected to others and our response to the teachings of Jesus.

backstory

CELIBACY

I don't understand why Catholic clergy are not allowed to be married.

First, we should make an important point: many Catholic clergy *are* married.

Most deacons are married, and some Roman priests who used to be Anglican priests or Protestant ministers are also married. In the Eastern Catholic Churches, both priests and deacons may marry before they're ordained.

That being said, a usual requirement for ordination to the diocesan priesthood in the Roman Church is that one make a promise of celibacy, that is, a promise not to marry in favor of single-hearted service to the Church. This promise of celibacy is different from the vow of chastity made by religious men and women. Vows are made to God; promises are made to the bishop. And celibacy isn't exactly the same as chastity.

It's clear from our Christian history that in every age, some men and women made a choice to forego the good of marriage for another good: to devote themselves to the Kingdom of God in a different (not better) way. This has always been the case and will always be the case.

Some people today wonder if celibacy for diocesan priests should be optional rather than mandatory. There are cases to be made either way, and no one can say we as a universal Church have yet arrived at consensus on this issue. Celibacy for diocesan priests is a matter of custom, not faith, so it can be changed any time. For the first thousand years of our history, some Roman diocesan clergy were married. For example, Patrick of Ireland was the son of a deacon and the grandson of a priest.

If a decision is ultimately made to again make celibacy optional for Roman diocesan priests, it must be made carefully and with wisdom. This wouldn't be just "doing away with celibacy." Even if diocesan priests were allowed to be married, celibacy would still be chosen by some diocesan priests, and those in religious communities would still follow the evangelical counsels of poverty, chastity, and obedience.

in the media

But I am lowly and in pain;
let your salvation, O God, protect me.

PSALM 69:29

God Heals Us

THE SACRAMENTS OF HEALING: RECONCILIATION AND ANOINTING OF THE SICK

Humans get hurt. Crisis and pain are part of our human story. When things are going well for us we don't often think about it, but sooner or later we're all faced with this reality in our lives. These tough times are challenging to all people, including people of faith. Everyone, deep inside, wants an answer to the question, "Why?"

Two significant themes are present in the ministry of Jesus: forgiveness and healing touch. Mark 5:21–43 Christ knew the burden and stress caused by pain, suffering, and even guilt from our own actions. Jesus knew it was impossible to live life in abundance weighed down by any form of illness or personal failing. That's why Christ promised us not a way out but a way through!

When we're sick, we want to be well. When we've offended someone, we want—no, need—to know we're forgiven. We need to be strong enough to forgive others as well. "Forgive us our trespasses as we forgive those who trespass against us." As Christians these words from the Lord's Prayer speak loudly to us.

We celebrate healing in two sacraments. Reconciliation or penance (sometimes called confession) provides forgiveness for those times we have failed our God, another, or ourselves. Isaiah 43:18–25 Anointing of the sick gives hope and consolation to those who are physically or emotionally ill.

A Challenge to Change

Christ constantly challenges us to change our lives. This process, which takes a lifetime, is called "conversion." It's the process of turning away from those things that are harmful and living more and more in the presence and grace of God. Along the way, no matter how great our efforts, we all fail. We all sin. 2 Corinthians 5 Yet in God's eyes, we are not what we do. That's what grace is all about.

Sin is never an individual thing; it's communal. In some way our own failings have an effect on those around us and on the community. For example, steal something and even if you don't get caught someone else will end up paying for the loss, perhaps in the form of higher prices down the line. We're social beings, and our interdependence exists on many levels we may not always be aware of.

The sacrament of reconciliation is celebrated by admitting our sins to a bishop or priest, who then gives us absolution.[1] You might ask why we confess

---

1 In the movies, they love to show people confessing sins kneeling in a dark box called a "confessional." We don't do that much anymore. Usually we sit down with the priest face to face in a welcoming environment. It's much easier to have a fruitful conversation that way. An anonymous option is generally provided for those who are not comfortable with face-to-face conversation. In the Eastern Church, confession is always face to face, with the priest laying his stole over the person confessing.

our sins to another person. After all, it's God who forgives, not the priest.

Sin is communal. Think of it as breaking a bond not only with God but with the community. The bishop or priest represents the Church and the community and reconciles us with God and with his people. As difficult as it may be to talk directly to the priest, hearing the words of absolution and knowing you've participated in the process of forgiveness is very powerful.[2] It's Christ himself who entrusted the ministry of reconciliation to the Church. John 20:19–23

Perhaps in this brief discussion of reconciliation it would help to consider the words of absolution we hear in this sacrament according to the Roman rite:

> God the Father of mercies,
> through the death and the resurrection of his Son
> has reconciled the world to himself
> and sent the Holy Spirit among us
> for the forgiveness of sins;
> through the ministry of the Church
> may God give you pardon and peace,
> and I absolve you from your sins
> in the name of the Father, and of the Son, and of
>   the Holy Spirit.

That kind of says it all, don't you think?

A New Dignity for Those Who Are Sick

In Jesus' day illness was seen as the outward sign of sin. It was assumed people who suffered did so because of some sinful action on their part or perhaps even on the part of their parents. John 9 Jesus had sincere compassion for all who were sick in any way. In fact he often identified with them. Jesus healed many from physical and mental illness, always asking those who were healed to believe in the power of God. John 11:1–44

Anointing of the sick has taken place from the earliest of times in the Church. James 5:13–15 The sacrament is celebrated by a bishop or priest who anoints a person on the head and hands with blessed oil.[3] It was once thought this sacrament was only for those in danger of death. You'd make that call to the priest at the last possible moment, and he would race to the bedside at any hour. That's not the way this sacrament should usually be celebrated.[4] It's anointing of the sick, not anointing of the dying. The proper rite for the dying is *viaticum*, the last time one receives the Eucharist.[5] Any Christian can be anointed when he or she has any life-threatening illness—and the sooner the better.

The sacrament celebrates the healing power of God and also the presence of Christ who identifies with us in our time of pain. It recognizes the nobility inherent in each person, even though sick, and imparts on them a new dignity in grace that transforms their suffering. It's God's awesome nature to turn bad things into good.

The purpose of this sacrament is healing and not curing. Yet God has allowed some to be cured

---

2   In the Roman rite, there are three forms of celebrating the sacrament of reconciliation: (1) private individual confession, (2) communal penance service with individual confession, and (3) communal penance service with general absolution—that is, no individual confession. This last option is rarely used in the United States; the second is probably the most popular; and the first was the only form prior to the Second Vatican Council.

3   This olive oil, blessed by the bishop at the cathedral during Holy Week, is the Oil of the Sick. In addition to the hands and head, other senses may be anointed, or other parts of the body as appropriate. For example, if the illness is cancer of the throat, the throat might be anointed.

4   Perhaps you once heard that a family member received the "last rites," meaning he or she was about to die any minute. The media love to use this term as a dramatic way of indicating imminent death. People call parishes asking for "last rites" without knowing what they are. Yet we shouldn't wait until a person is taking his or her last breath before calling a priest in a panic to celebrate anointing of the sick. It should be celebrated as often as necessary when the person and loved ones can actively participate in the rite, well before death is imminent—even months or years before. "Last rites" properly refers to the continuous celebration of reconciliation, anointing, and viaticum.

5   Viaticum is (you guessed it) a Latin term meaning "with you on the journey," and this is what is provided to the dying. If the dying person has not yet been anointed, he or she is anointed along with reception of viaticum and a final celebration of reconciliation if he or she so chooses.

after anointing. Still, most do not improve in their physical condition. This brings us to the question "Why?" all over again. Ultimately Christ's suffering led to his own death. Out of that tragic event a wonderful act of love brought salvation to everyone. We Christians believe in redemptive suffering. Just as Christ prevailed over suffering to give it meaning and purpose, so can we. Isaiah 5:3

Our earthly lives will eventually come to an end. The sacrament can't take away that inevitable fact. It can prepare us to transition from this world to the next where we'll meet God face to face. And in the end, what could be more healing and definite than that?

THE TRAPPISTS OF TIBHIRINE

profile

In a Muslim country, Algeria, a small community of French Trappists worked and prayed according to their ancient custom. Because their monastery was dedicated to Mary, and a statue of her overlooked the town of Tibhirine, the Muslim neighbors had great respect for the monks. They admired the monks' faithful prayer, something the townspeople did not see practiced by other Christians. The Trappists participated in the life of the town and provided much-needed medical care and food to all, free of cost. There was great peace in the village.

But in 1996 Algeria was torn by a bloody civil war. Fundamentalists sought to impose their own version of Islam on the people and to expel non-Muslims. One day, these terrorists came to Tibhirine and took seven monks hostage, making demands on the French government that

could not be met. Despite pleas from around the world and the intercession of their Muslim friends, the heads of the monks were discovered along a road nearly two months later.

The family of one of the monks, Christian de Chergé, made public a letter he'd written in anticipation of his death. His letter was a moving call to forgiveness, stating he had already forgiven anyone who might kill him. And he asked others not to seek revenge on his beloved Muslim brothers and sisters on his account. That, he said, would be too high a price to pay for his "gift" of martyrdom.

For Christian and the other Trappists of Tibhirine, nothing was unforgivable. In the face of terrorism, Christian's prayer was noble in its simplicity: "Lord, disarm them, and disarm me."

Does suffering have meaning?

All of us have witnessed suffering. Some in the lives of others, some in our own lives. If God cares for us so much, how can he allow such horrible suffering to exist in the world? That's a question asked by many.

No doubt the world can often seem like a very different place than the one promised to those who have faith. In fact, it's easy to have our faith shaken as we look at all the injustice, suffering, inequity, and senseless death in our world.

Jesus cured many but certainly not everyone he came across. It wasn't his mission to eliminate all suffering from the world. If you look at the cross it won't take you long to figure that one out. Christ cured some to show the power of God and the power of faith. And who wouldn't have faith when they receive a cure? Well, actually, Jesus cured ten lepers and only one came back with a "Thanks!" so even when cured not everyone can show gratitude. Luke 17:11-19

So let's go back to the cross and talk about the way suffering can be seen as part of the human condition rather than as a curse from God or some outside force.

Crucifixion was one of the most painful deaths one could endure.[6] God allowed his only Son to be put to death in that way. What good came from all that suffering? The suffering of Christ

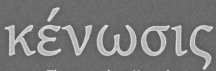

The emptying: *Kenosis*

The Greek work *kenosis* means the "pouring out" of oneself in compassion and service. It's used to describe the lifelong attitude of Jesus that culminated in his death. We're called to follow his example in renouncing selfishness and transforming pain by pouring ourselves out in service.

shows us, without a doubt, the love God has for all humankind. Jesus sacrificed himself in love as an offering for us all. This was a redemptive act. This act brought humanity closer to God after our first parents challenged God's plan and providence in primeval times.

Being human means being vulnerable to sickness and disease. Suffering cannot be avoided. Some are able to offer their suffering to God as their own redemptive act in a way similar to Christ. This requires a lot of faith and hope in the promises God has made to us and the certainty of our final destination, heaven.

Suffering in the world that's not part of the human condition—war, starvation, the inadequate living conditions of the poor in every country, and the like—is the kind of suffering that can be eliminated. This distinction is an important one, too, because all Christians are responsible for building the Kingdom of God, and in that Kingdom there's no room for injustice.

What are we doing to eliminate the kind of suffering that is brought about by those who refuse to see everyone as a child of God?

---

6   *Maybe you were taught as a child no death is worse than crucifixion. As awful as it was, we must admit human ingenuity has devised far worse ways to die. Just read the newspaper. When one of your authors once pointed this out in a homily, he was called a heretic! Yet the reality of even worse methods of torture does not diminish the death of Jesus. Crucifixion was "state of the art" in cruelty in his time.*

backstory

FAITH HEALERS

On television I saw what appeared to be miraculous cures by a preacher taking place on a stage. Was that for real?

We Christians totally believe in miracles. Jesus announced the Kingdon of God. One way he did this was to perform miracles, which were powerful signs of God's presence. Even today, there are many recorded instances of people being cured of life-threatening illnesses with no apparent scientific explanation.

Faith is a powerful thing. Recall that whenever Jesus would cure someone, he'd say, "Your faith has healed you." In some instances, people were healed or even raised from the dead due to the faith of another. We believe this dramatic intervention of God in human lives can happen here and now.

So even though there are many proven cases of "faith healers" staging fake cures and bilking people out of money, we hesitate to paint all faith healers with the same brush. Who are we to say God may not work in our lives in miraculous ways? His workings are too wondrous for us to close the door on any possibility.

Still, there are warning signs that a particular faith healer may not be on the up-and-up, and we should avoid getting caught up in hype. For example, do the "cures" last? Is there any solicitation of money connected with the "miracle service"? Do the "cures" appear to generate great wealth for the "healer"?

Another thought: The miracles of Jesus were always for the benefit of more people than the one cured. Is the supposed miracle for one person's private benefit, or does the community somehow benefit by increased faith and witness to God? What's the message that accompanies the cure? Is it compatible with the teachings of Jesus, or is it rooted in selfishness?

It's absolutely possible for people to be healed by faith. But we're a bit concerned when supposed cures become not so much a show of faith, but just a show.

I will give thanks to you, O Lord, among the peoples;
I will sing praises to you among the nations.

PSALM 57:9

Our Celebration Knows No End

THE LITURGY

Celebrations always involve a feast. In every culture, an occasion of great joy is marked with a festive meal, and it's no different for Christians. In the earliest days we gathered each Sunday to celebrate the resurrection of Jesus with a communal meal. But it was more than a simple meal. After everyone had eaten their fill, a ceremonial climax to the feast involved readings from the scriptures and offering, breaking, and sharing bread and wine, as Jesus did at the Last Supper. This ceremonial act of praise and thanksgiving became the defining hallmark of the early Christians, an act we continue to this day in response to our common baptismal priesthood.

This act of thanksgiving, or *eucharistia* in Greek, is sacred because it continues the saving work of Jesus in our own day. Through the celebration of the Eucharist, Jesus becomes present in our midst in mysterious ways, ways we can only partially understand. This is his great gift to us, given at the Last Supper. There he both celebrated the deliverance of the Jews from the Egyptians with Passover and prepared to deliver the world from sin by the marvelous events that would occur over the next three days. Psalm 149

The Work of the People

Liturgy is the public prayer of the Church. It includes the celebration of the sacraments, the **Liturgy of the Hours,** and the liturgical calendar. All these things make real in our own time the saving acts of God from **Advent** through the end of **ordinary time** each year. The greatest and highest form of liturgy is the Eucharist, also called the Mass or Divine Liturgy.[1] Because the Eucharist is the highest form of liturgy, we often refer to it simply as "the liturgy." It's the source and summit of Christian life.

Not too long ago, people in the Roman Catholic Church[2] thought only the priest celebrated the liturgy and the people simply attended as reverent spectators. This passive idea was reflected in everyday language: the priest "said Mass" and the people "heard Mass." But the word *liturgy* comes from the Greek word *leitourgia*, which means "the work of the people." So we all celebrate liturgy by

....

1 *There are other names for the Eucharist in various traditions. The Armenians call it* Badarak. *Chaldean and Assyrian Christians call it* Qurbana. *Both of these terms mean "offering."*

2 *Because the historical language of the Roman Catholic Church is Latin, it is also sometimes called the Latin Church, and its way of doing liturgy is called the Latin rite.*

our full, conscious, and active participation, whether in the assembly, as liturgical ministers (lectors, altar servers, extraordinary ministers of holy communion, cantors, ushers, greeters, musicians, and so on), as deacons, priests, or bishops.

εὐχαριστία

Thanksgiving: *Eucharistia*

The Greek word *eucharistia* means "thanksgiving." It is the greatest act of the Christian community, where we offer to God our highest form of praise.

Jesus, Present in the Assembly and the Word of God

Because of everything God has done for us, we give him thanks and praise. And because God has done great things for us not just as individuals, but as a community, we gather as a community to do that. Furthermore, because we are Christians, we gather to praise and thank God in the way Jesus told us to, by "the breaking of the bread," as this act has been called from our earliest days. As we gather together in the Eucharistic assembly, Jesus becomes present in *the first of four ways*: in us, the Body of Christ gathered to pray as one. "For where two or three are gathered in my name, I am in there among them" (Matthew 18:20).

After acknowledging our faults and asking forgiveness, Matthew 5:21–24 we then experience Jesus as the Word of God by hearing the scripture proclaimed, the *second* way in which Jesus becomes present in the Eucharist. This first major part of the Eucharist, called the "Liturgy of the Word," is modeled after the ancient synagogue service the first Christians were familiar with. We first hear a lector (reader) read from the Hebrew Testament, we sing a psalm, and hear a reading from the New Testament.[3] Then, with the joyful singing of "Alleluia," we rise to hear the proclamation of the Gospel by the deacon, for standing is the ancient Christian posture of respect. In the Eastern

Church, the deacon alludes to what we are about to hear: "Wisdom! Let us attend!"

The **homily** (sometimes called a "sermon") is an integral part of the liturgy, not a "break" in the ritual. It's when the bishop, priest, or deacon teaches the assembly from the readings we just heard. We profess together the faith we hold in common with all Christians—those alive today and those who have gone before us—and the deacon leads us in our priestly duty to pray for the whole world. This concludes the Liturgy of the Word. Nehemiah 8:1–12

Jesus, Present in the Priest and the Sacrament of the Altar

As we begin the Liturgy of the Eucharist, the catechumens (adults preparing for baptism at the Easter Vigil) are dismissed; they leave to continue their learning. The altar is prepared and the people bring forward gifts: bread, wine, financial support for the Church, and offerings for the poor.

The bishop or priest approaches the altar, and acting in "the person of Christ" (this is the *third* way Jesus is present in the Eucharist, are you keeping track?), he offers bread and wine to the Father[4] and begins the Eucharistic Prayer, or *anaphora*, the central act of praise and thanksgiving. He recounts the saving works of God throughout human history, calls down the Holy Spirit upon the bread and wine,[5] and pronounces the words of Jesus at the Last Supper.[6] Mark 14:22–26 He then recalls the saving power of the life,

---

3   The readings are meant to be heard, not read, by the people. So put down that missalette and listen carefully to the proclamation of the Word. God's word is meant to be heard; it's not time for private reading. Some Christian liturgical traditions have only one reading before the Gospel.

4   In the Roman liturgy, you may not be able to hear the offertory prayers on Sunday because there's generally music at that time, but they're remarkably similar to prayers offered by Jews over bread and wine at Shabbat dinner every Friday night.

5   The calling down of the Holy Spirit is called the epiklesis, Greek for "invocation."

6   This "institution narrative" (the words that instituted the Eucharist) is also called the "consecration." The words of institution are not present in all Eucharistic prayers.

death, resurrection, and ascension of Jesus[7] before ending with the remembrance of all the Church, living and dead.

The assembly concludes the Eucharistic Prayer with the Great Amen, giving their assent to something wonderful and mysterious that has just occurred. Jesus Christ, true God and true human, has become fully present in his Risen Body under the appearance of bread and wine. This is the *fourth* and greatest way Jesus is present in the Eucharist. We stand in the living presence of Christ himself, who here among us has continued his saving, sacrificial death and resurrection before our own eyes, and pray the prayer he taught us. At the deacon's invitation, we offer a sign of peace to each other before we joyfully approach the holy table to receive our Lord and brother under the appearances of bread and wine. John 6:22–69

After receiving communion, our physical connection to Jesus and a sign of our unity with one another, the remaining Eucharistic bread is set aside in the **tabernacle** to be brought to the sick, the dying, and the homebound. The deacon then sends us out into the world to bear fruit of the wonder we have just experienced, to "go in peace."

John Paul II reminds us liturgy must bear fruit in service as we go out the church doors: "We cannot delude ourselves: by our mutual love and, in particular, by our concern for those in need we will be recognized as true followers of Christ. This will be the criterion by which the authenticity of our Eucharistic celebrations is judged." 1 Corinthians 11:17–34

Every Hour of the Day, Every Day of the Year

In addition to the Eucharist, we also celebrate liturgy in the Liturgy of the Hours,[8] an ancient method of praying the psalms at set times throughout the day. This is the prayer known from the beautiful medieval Books of Hours used by those who prayed it. While we may be most familiar with this form of prayer today from its monastic observance, any Christian is encouraged to make it part of his or her daily prayer life.

And for all of us, the seasons of the Church year are also liturgy, reminding us through months and days of the events of salvation history, the mysteries of our Faith, the lives of the saints, and events in the life of Jesus and Mary. The liturgical year begins with Advent and continues through the Christmas Season (which is after Christmas, not before as retailers would have you believe), Lent, Easter Season, and Ordinary Time.[9] Each season has a color associated with it. The calendar isn't merely a remembrance of past historical events and people, but a way to make them real in our own lives.

Although we live our lives in time and space, liturgy expands our horizons, bringing us into the reality of God and giving us a glimpse of eternity in the here and now. No wonder liturgy is often said to bring heaven to Earth.

....

8 You may also hear it called "The Divine Office," because it is the duty (Latin: officium) of religious and clergy to pray it daily. The book used for the Liturgy of the Hours is sometimes called a "breviary."

9 In some Christian traditions, the Sundays of Ordinary Time (during which we count the Sundays outside Advent, Christmas Season, Lent, and Easter Season in "ordinal" numbers) are counted "After Pentecost."

....

7 This part is called the anamnesis, Greek for "memorial," by which these acts are both remembered and made real again.

We love to celebrate and we celebrate to love

There was a time when the priest, with his back to the people, would mutter quickly to himself in Latin: *"Cantate Domino canticum novum."* Today, we might be more likely during Mass to sing with a contemporary beat—"Sing to the Lord a new song!"—which is what the priest was saying in a language we could neither hear nor understand.

These two examples represent different approaches to celebration we've had in the Roman rite throughout our Christian history. They exist in a certain tension, which isn't entirely bad, because ideally they serve to balance each other.

Back before the Second Vatican Council, the way Mass was celebrated (at least in the United States) was a somber, quiet rite centered on the actions of the priest and emphasizing the fact that Eucharist is a sacrifice. After the Council, the celebration of Mass was more participatory, often emphasizing the fact that Mass is a celebratory banquet.

Of course, both of these approaches are correct. The Mass is both a sacrifice offered at an altar and a meal celebrated around a table. It's a mistake to emphasize one exclusively at the expense of the other. Yet it was common in the years before the Council to put too much emphasis on sacrifice, and after the Council some put too much emphasis on meal.

When too much emphasis is placed on one aspect of the Eucharist, there's liturgical weirdness. Before the Council, these problems included a loss of the sense of community, clericalism, and a dour, private devotional atmosphere at Mass. Some issues after the Council include lack of time for silence, an attitude that is too casual, and a lack of understanding of the priest's proper role.

Just mentioning the fact that bad habits existed before or after the Council will infuriate some people. Polarization in the Church, as in the larger society, means some people want to see everything in black and white. One side complains, "You people, you're just happy-clappy hippies!" The other retorts, "Oh yeah? Well you're God's Frozen People!" Then they start hurling hymnals at each other. The fact remains there were liturgical problems prior to the Council, which is why the bishops at the Council made reform of the liturgy their first priority. And there are liturgical problems after the Council.

Central to the balance of these two attitudes and the discovery of a happy medium is the understanding that we come together on Sunday to celebrate. Is the first example of the priest muttering something alone in Latin too little of a celebratory attitude? Probably. Is juggling at Mass too much of a celebratory attitude? Probably.

It helps if we realize the reforms of the Council did not just come out of nowhere. The process of liturgical reform had been going on for about a hundred years before the Council, in small but incremental ways. For example, just before the Council, people followed an English translation of the Latin Mass in a book called a "hand missal." But it wasn't until the 1900s that the people were even allowed to have an English translation—or any language—available to them. Before that, if you didn't know Latin, you were just out of luck. The hand missal was a liturgical innovation.

The reform of the Council that made the Eucharist available in a language we could understand was initially a shock to some, but it became one of the most popular and visible reforms of the Council. Use of the language of the people was not something new. In the early centuries Christians worshipped in their everyday language, and this was always the case in the Churches of the East. The introduction of Latin was a change from the previous use of Greek as fewer people understood Greek, speaking Latin as their everyday language. Liturgical reform is not a new idea!

Today we have what some call "liturgy wars," with different factions campaigning for various changes and declaring victory when they get their way. But at the Eucharist we are called to join together in a celebration. If our Sunday liturgy winds up polarizing instead of uniting, then we have some thinking to do about how we can have a truly authentic celebration.

backstory

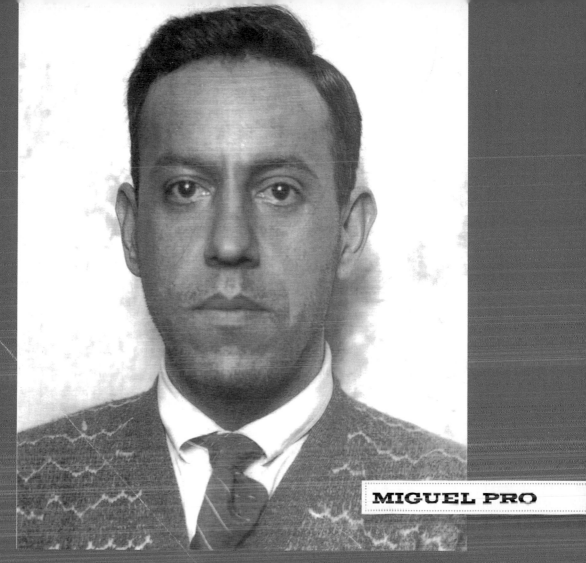

MIGUEL PRO

Because we know Mexico today as a Catholic country, it might surprise you to know Catholicism was outlawed in that nation early in the twentieth century. It was in this environment that Miguel Pro became a Jesuit priest after some years away from the Church. Utilizing a variety of disguises that ranged from an affluent, well-dressed man to a beggar, he ministered to the people in secret, celebrating the Eucharist and the sacraments.

Miguel didn't only celebrate the liturgy; he also gave equal time to serving the poor and outcast of Mexico City by taking up collections of food and clothing for those in need. He was a friend of homeless people and prostitutes. This was the authentic fruit of his celebration of liturgy.

Finally discovered and arrested in 1927, Miguel received the death penalty and was executed. After praying, he stood before the firing squad with his arms outstretched in the form of a cross and proclaimed *"¡Viva Cristo Rey!"*—"Hooray for Christ the King!" In an attempt to discourage the practice of the Faith, the government took photographs of Miguel's execution and published them in newspapers. But as is so often the case, they had the exact opposite effect, strengthening the faith of the people. Twenty thousand people risked arrest to attend his funeral.

When their grand and historic church buildings were closed, the people of Mexico City found a way to celebrate liturgy with Miguel in auto repair shops, alleys, and homes. Miguel's witness should shame us when we become engrossed in the external trappings and minutiae of liturgy.

profile

CHRISTMAS CONSUMERISM

Sometimes I get so exhausted by the buildup to Christmas that it just leaves me tired and glad it's over. Is there something wrong with me?

There's nothing wrong with you, but there's something wrong with our consumerist society.

First of all, it's important to realize what secular society calls "the Christmas season" isn't the Christian season of Christmas. That begins on the evening of December 24 and lasts through Epiphany. During Advent, we prepare spiritually for Christmas without any Christmas decorations or songs in our churches. The frenzied buildup to Christmas in the secular world only proves the ancient wisdom of our Christian custom of celebrating feasts after they occur rather than before.

The reason for this pre-Christmas season, of course, is that retailers run at a deficit until the end of the year. They want to maximize their most profitable time as long as they can. So they've created a situation where people shop starting around Halloween. By the time Christmas finally comes around, it lasts one day and many are only too glad to have it finally over.

Too often Christmas becomes an orgy of materialism, with people spending far too much money on things others do not need. There's nothing wrong with Christmas gifts—in fact, they're meant to symbolize God's gift of his Son. But if a loot of gifts becomes what Christmas is all about, and more loot means a better Christmas, then we need to stop and take a look at what this situation is doing to us and what we're teaching our children. With all due respect to retailers and their need to turn a profit, maybe fewer and more personal gifts might help us enjoy Christmas a little more. And who knows, we may even want to stretch it out a bit past December 25, as our ancient Christian liturgical calendar teaches us to do.

in the media

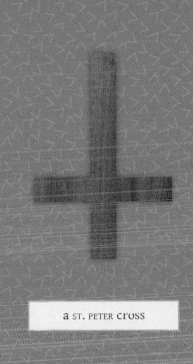

a ST. PETER CrOSS

BERNARDINE
OF
SIENA

THOMAS
AQUINAS

KATHARINE
DREXEL

JOHN
OF
GOD

MAXIMILIAN
KOLBE

BONAVENTURE

PETER
CLAVER

ANDREW

FELICITAS PERPET

Those who trust in the LORD are like Mount Zion,
which cannot be moved, but abides forever.

PSALM 125:1

We Stand on the Shoulders of Those Who Came Before Us

THE SAINTS

Do you have a photo album? Whether it's on your coffee table, iPhone, or hard drive, your photo album probably has images of family, loved ones, and friends, and pictures of important events in the course of your relationships with them. And there's probably a story behind each photo. In the same way, we as the Church maintain memories of and relationships with the faithful Christians who have gone before us, the saints.

You can probably see parts of the Church's photo album in your own parish church. In our rich tradition, this vast, worldwide album is presented in many media: sculpture, icons, paintings, mosaics, stained glass windows, prints, and maybe even in little "holy cards" you received as a child at school or at a loved one's funeral or ordination. Our virtual album extends from humble murals deep in jungle communities to world-renowned Renaissance paintings in the great museums of the world. And behind each picture is a story.

Each image reminds us of a particular family member. We may have never met them in person, but they're our brothers and sisters because our family in faith transcends time and space. You might place an old photograph of your great-grandmother on your mantel to remind yourself of the stories about her, to spark conversation, to compare her features with your own daughter's. So we as the Church keep reminders of those who offer us good example, who teach us, who inspire us, or even make us laugh a little!

There Are Countless Numbers of Saints

These brothers and sisters, the saints,[1] are a living presence to us, the Church. A saint is anyone who's died and experiencing heaven. You probably have saints in your own family. Our connection to them doesn't end at death. We refer to this eternal link as the **communion of saints**; that's what we're talking about when we say this term in the Creed every Sunday. Revelation 7:9–17

Along with all your loved ones who have died and are experiencing heaven, there are also people now with your loved ones who gave witness in an extraordinary way to the Good News. These are the people we generally refer to as "the saints," those you've heard about, like Francis and Clare of Assisi, Stephen the first martyr, Teresa of Ávila, and thousands of others.[2] By a process called

....

1   We know you're itching for another Latin word, so here goes: the word saint comes from the Latin word sanctus, meaning "holy." You might know of churches with names like "Saint Cross," or "Saint Sophia." They're not named for people, but for "Holy Cross" and "Holy Wisdom," an older usage of the word saint.

2   Also included among the saints honored by all the Church are the patriarchs, matriarchs, and prophets of the Hebrew Testament.

canonization, they've been selected from among the millions in heaven because they give us an outstanding example of how to live as Christians. Sirach 6:18–37

Saints Are Chosen at the Grassroots

The saints we honor are chosen by the Christian people. After a person who has made a dramatic impact on their community dies, that community begins to tell stories of how that person enriched the lives of those around him or her. The people of that community will generally begin to honor images of that person—photos, paintings, statues— and to treat with great respect their graves and the personal belongings they left behind. They go to visit places associated with that person. Because the people feel a close bond to that person, they begin to share with him or her their longings, needs, and love—for we know that death does not end our connection to each other.

Once it's become apparent this public devotion to that person isn't just a passing fad, the bishop may petition the pope[3] to recognize that person as an outstanding example of the Christian faith, a saint, to be honored by Christians throughout the world. After a process of investigation, the pope may agree, and that person is canonized, meaning devotion to that person has spread from his or her own local community to the whole world.

The canonized saint is someone who has demonstrated what we call **heroic virtue.** This means he or she lived a life in which at least one special characteristic of the Christian life shone forth in such a way that he or she is a wonderful example for the rest of us. 1 Corinthians 12

Being honored as a saint by the whole Church doesn't mean that person was sinless. All saints were sinners. But they all discerned God's will for their own lives with such fidelity that they were able to be fully alive as themselves. They were able to identify the gifts they were given by God, and to grow those gifts with a single-minded enthusiasm for the benefit of others in such a way that everybody around them stopped and took notice.

Some saints had a gift for learning, and they became great theologians. Some had a gift for social justice, and they became great champions of the outcast. Some had a gift for service to the poor, and they became great in that ministry. Some had a gift for speaking, and they became great preachers. Their gifts varied,[4] but one thing they all had in common was great love. 1 Corinthians 13

A Personal Connection

As you get to know the saints, you'll discover a bond growing between you and them. There are stories about them that'll make you laugh. You'll begin to learn about their personality quirks, what they liked and didn't like, what their failings were. You'll hear people say something like, "Well, there goes another of Paul's run-on sentences," and others will laugh with knowing affection. Or someone might comment, "Hey, you know about Augustine and sex," and people will smile and nod. Don't you talk about your loved ones this way at family gatherings, sharing your intimate knowledge of them with affection?

This personal connection with the saints extends even to conversation between them and us who are still on Earth. They're our mentors. They still can be involved in our lives.

"Therefore, … we are surrounded by so great a cloud of witnesses…" (Hebrews 12:1). From millions who now enjoy eternal happiness, we as a community have selected some to honor in a special way. But we must remember our relationship with them is two-way. We benefit far

---

3 Why involve the pope? Because this process provides an objective review of that person's life that may not be possible in their home community, where only the good things about him or her may be known. We don't want to hold someone up as an example for everybody and later find that something horrible comes to light about him or her!

4 Because each saint is honored for his or her specific gifts, it would be a mistake to assume each is an "expert" in all subjects. For example, if a saint is known especially for serving the poor, that does not necessarily mean his or her views on liturgy have special weight. If a saint was known primarily as a poet, his or her views on moral theology could be a bit off.

more from their example, advice, and intercession[5] than they do from the honor we give them.

....

5 *Just as we may ask our living friends and relatives to pray for us, so we can also ask the same favor of those who have gone before us marked with the sign of faith.*

ELIZABETH ANN SETON

ELIZABETH OF PORTUGAL

ANDRÉ BESSETTE

You are made to be holy

Holiness: yet another example of a perfectly good English word we've corrupted to mean something entirely different from what it should.

Holiness can mean different things to different people. To your parents, it might bring to mind stories of saints who levitated or saw visions. To your friends, it may mean someone who's scrupulous and maybe a little nerdy, someone you can't tell certain jokes—you know, the Ned Flanders type. Maybe to you it's someone who's undergone a somewhat questionable "conversion" that resulted in him becoming unpleasant and demanding to be around: "He turned all holy on me!" Some in the media may use it to mean someone who feels they're better than everybody else. Others may think holiness is a quality that's automatically acquired through ordination, religious profession, or election as pope.

And real holiness is none of these things. Did you notice that in all these examples, holiness is considered something for someone else, but not for you? What's wrong with this picture?

The word *holy* is related to the English word *whole*. Holiness is wholeness. To be holy means to be fully ourselves, the person God has intended from before the beginning of time. Unless we are truly that unique person, we are not whole. As the great spiritual writer Thomas Merton put it, "For me to be a saint means to be myself."

backstory

Now we may look at ourselves with all our imperfections and ask, "*This* is a saint?" The answer is, "Yes," with this important distinction: you are not yet what you are meant to be. When we talk about holiness as being the person you are meant to be, that means the real you, not the one you think you are today. The writer Oscar Wilde pointed out, "Every saint has a past, and every sinner has a future."

Being a saint doesn't mean copying exactly what canonized saints have done. Each of them was different, and being faithful to the person each was is what made them holy. You can't be Teresa of Kolkata. Only Teresa could be Teresa. You can't be Augustine of Hippo. Only Augustine could be Augustine. Get it? Only you can be the saint, the holy person, *you* are meant to be.

Who's this person God wants me to be? The answer's different for each of us, but the common underlying principle is to put all our individual gifts and talents at the service of God and others. We all achieve this ultimate goal to varying degrees at different times. Being holy doesn't mean being perfect. A truly dreadful pairing of words is when people talk about "saints and sinners," as though they were polar opposites. All saints were sinners. They just tried harder than most.

Being holy does mean being authentically integrated. It means tying together your state in life, those talents God has given only to you, your unique personality, your interests, your sexuality, your intellect, your compassion and every other good thing about you into a coherent package that's open to the grace of God and infused with the Gospel.

There's a song only you can sing. Sing it, and you'll be holy. That's what God and a hurting world are waiting for.

ANGELS

When we die, do we become angels?

See what watching too many sentimental movies can do? Either that or we've been scarred for life by Saturday morning cartoons.

Humans don't become angels. Angels are spiritual beings created by God. Like us, they have intellect and individual personalities. Unlike us, they don't have bodies or an inclination to choose evil over good. Having no bodies, they don't procreate or die—or have wings, as they're often depicted in art and popular media. The Christian belief in angels is shared by Jews and Muslims as well.

The word *angel* means "messenger," and that's how we humans have experienced angels, as messengers of God.

Some people say different angels have different roles, and there are hierarchies of angels. All this may be true; we don't know for sure because these distinctions come from legend, not revelation. Some people today claim they've had encounters with angels. This may also be true, but there's no way to say for sure. It could happen.

What we learn from the existence of angels is that God's Creation is so awesome we will never know in our own lives the full extent of his works. Angels are a tantalizing reminder that God is full of surprises, and his works are so wonderful they surpass our pathetic attempts to categorize them.

in the media

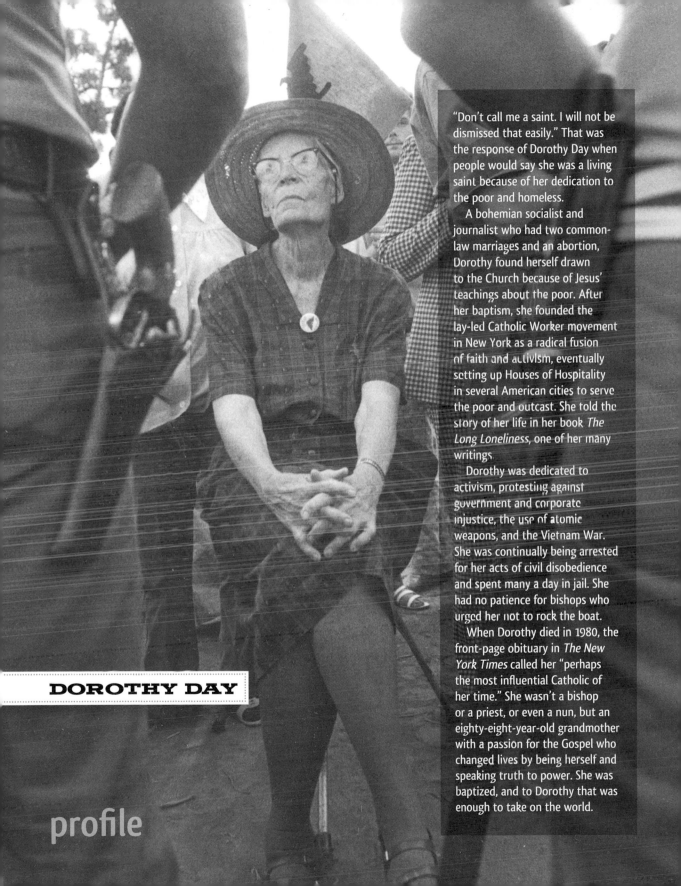

"Don't call me a saint. I will not be dismissed that easily." That was the response of Dorothy Day when people would say she was a living saint because of her dedication to the poor and homeless.

A bohemian socialist and journalist who had two common-law marriages and an abortion, Dorothy found herself drawn to the Church because of Jesus' teachings about the poor. After her baptism, she founded the lay-led Catholic Worker movement in New York as a radical fusion of faith and activism, eventually setting up Houses of Hospitality in several American cities to serve the poor and outcast. She told the story of her life in her book *The Long Loneliness*, one of her many writings.

Dorothy was dedicated to activism, protesting against government and corporate injustice, the use of atomic weapons, and the Vietnam War. She was continually being arrested for her acts of civil disobedience and spent many a day in jail. She had no patience for bishops who urged her not to rock the boat.

When Dorothy died in 1980, the front-page obituary in *The New York Times* called her "perhaps the most influential Catholic of her time." She wasn't a bishop or a priest, or even a nun, but an eighty-eight-year-old grandmother with a passion for the Gospel who changed lives by being herself and speaking truth to power. She was baptized, and to Dorothy that was enough to take on the world.

DOROTHY DAY

profile

For God alone my soul waits in silence;
from him comes my salvation.

PSALM 62:1

She Pondered These Things in Her Heart

MARY

Let it be. With these words a human being gave free consent to the plan of God that his Word should become human too. Pious, cheesy depictions of Mary can obscure the careful consideration this teenage girl gave to God's invitation and the dire consequences she knew could follow her consent. Following Mary's example, we too receive an invitation from God to make Jesus present to the world in ourselves. Mary is the model of Christian discipleship.

While it wasn't actually written with the mother of Jesus in mind, the popular song "Let It Be" by the Beatles evokes the wonder of Mary's assent to bear the Son of God.[1]

These words are especially appropriate because Mary conformed herself to the will of the Father to become pregnant with the Son through the power of the Holy Spirit. Luke 1:26–38 As you already know, the Holy Spirit is the source of Wisdom, and so we also call Mary "Seat of Wisdom," that is, the throne of the Holy Spirit.

Just as each of us has a role to play in God's divine drama, established from before the beginning of time, so Mary also had a role God prepared her for. That's why the angel greets Mary with "Hail, full of grace." From the time of her conception, she had been set apart by God in a special way, through no merit of her own, but by God's free gift. Freed from the heritage of disobedience of our first parents, Mary was inclined by nature to follow the Lord.[2] And yet her free will remained, for God will use no person for his glory unless he first has consent.

Mary's "Yes" Is a Model for All of Us

Mary's consent wasn't given without hesitation. Mary was wise beyond her years. She first questioned the angel and only then agreed. She was right to consider carefully what God was asking of her.

Under the law of the time, she could be subjected to the death penalty for being pregnant

---

1 *We were going to print the refrain for you, but Sony/ATV wanted a large chunk o'change to allow us to quote four lines. So just Google the lyrics and read the refrain, or listen to it on your iPod. You probably know it by heart anyway. Paul McCartney didn't write this song to the mother of Jesus, but rather in honor of his own mother, Mary, who died when he was fourteen. Oh, the things you can learn from Wikipedia! Still it's great as meditation on the Mother of Jesus and the power of her assent.*

2 *Catholics refer to this teaching as the "Immaculate Conception." Mary was conceived without original sin and remained free of sin throughout her life. Note the words of the angel's greeting: not "empty of sin," but "full of grace." This is an important distinction. Mary did not lack something we have; she had something we also have, but more so.*

by someone other than her husband. And Joseph knew the child wasn't his. According to the law she could be stoned to death or "put away" to face a life of shame and discrimination. John 8:1–11 And yet she still submitted herself to God, despite the risk.

This positive response to the call of God, the freely given "Yes" of every faithful person, is the central theme of our Christian community and every Christian as an individual. It's a response we give daily, as we encounter the trials of our own daily lives. When we find ourselves in times of trouble, we follow Mary's example. That's wisdom!

Mary is a teacher of the spiritual life. In Luke's story of the Annunciation and in one other place in the Gospels, Mary is described as one who carefully reflects on the events of her life. Luke 2:41–52 She ponders these things in her heart even as her son grows in wisdom.

Living together for some thirty years, Mary and her son grew in wisdom together. In giving birth to Jesus, loving him, teaching him the Jewish scripture and religion, and sacrificing her own freedom to raise him, Mary is the Mother of God. That's what the ancient Greek word *Theotokos* means. It's our oldest title for Mary. We also are challenged to give birth to God in our own time and place, as members of the Body of Christ baptized to build the Kingdom of God.

Mary Was a Rebel Who Took Risks

Key to the understanding of Mary as a confident and compassionate servant of God is her standing with the outcast. In her hymn of praise, Mary recounts the wonder of God in terms of social justice: casting down the mighty and lifting up the lowly. This was a young girl with a radical, radiating faith, facing the world and its rules head-on. The fact that God chose to become one of us through an impoverished, pregnant, unmarried teenager shouldn't be lost on us, who are so ready to judge others.

God's saving action doesn't take place only in "respectable" settings. In fact, it's often smothered by the smug self-righteousness so prevalent in our communities, where a tame and sanitized form of Christianity is an arm of the Chamber of Commerce, manifested in manicured lawns and social conformity. The prophetic[3] Christian must struggle to be free of this captive Christianity, as Mary willingly stood with God despite the rules of her own society. She continued to defy convention all her life, even standing beside her son as he was executed. John 19:25–30

Mary Is a Sign of Hope for the Unity of All Christians

While Catholics and Orthodox have always treasured the witness of Mary as a faithful disciple, as a loving mother, and as one we can turn to in our distress to offer prayer to the Father for us, some Christians remain wary of honoring Mary.

Anglicans and Protestants have historically been cautious of ascribing too much importance to Mary, largely as a result of excessive devotion to her in the time leading up to the Reformation. But today Anglicans and Catholics have found agreement on virtually every aspect of devotion to Mary, and Protestants have rediscovered her role as a model for the Christian life. Lutherans especially have found new insights in Martin Luther's tender devotion to Mary expressed so often in his writings. Even Evangelical authors are writing books about her as they realize how her example helps us all.

It may be that Mary—once considered a virtually insurmountable obstacle on the path to Christian unity—may now become one of the brightest guiding lights on that very road. For as the angel explained to Mary at the Annunciation, nothing is impossible for God.

---

3 Being a prophet is to stand with God against injustice; to speak truth to power; to align ourselves to the divine pathos, the perfect balance of compassion and justice. This is a dignity we receive at baptism.

JOSEPH

We don't know much about Joseph, the husband of Mary. Scripture tells us he was an honorable man. He struggled with how to deal with Mary's pregnancy; he was engaged to her, but he knew the child wasn't his. Should he lie and say it was, and be less than truthful? Should he say it was not his, and allow Mary to be stoned to death? Joseph faced a moral dilemma that literally involved life and death.

Counseled in his discernment by a messenger of God, Joseph decided to go against everything a man of his time held dear; he decided to help Mary raise a child that wasn't his. Could you do the same if your fiancée told you she was pregnant and the child wasn't yours? In Joseph's macho culture, this was unheard of.

And it wasn't easy for Joseph. Shortly after helping Mary through childbirth in a livestock pen, Joseph had to flee with Mary as refugees into Egypt to save the child's life, leaving everything they owned behind. They hid out until the danger was over, unwelcome immigrants in a strange land where they knew neither the language nor the customs. Probably Joseph earned what he could as a day laborer with work far below his skilled trade as a carpenter.

It's too bad we don't know more about Joseph. But maybe that's for the best, because all around us we can see the face of Joseph, a quiet, gentle, honest, hard-working man who was only trying to care for his wife and son despite great obstacles. Think of Joseph the next time you pass that group of men looking for work in the parking lot at Home Depot.

profile

Our spirits rejoice in God our savior

One of the greatest hymns of our Christian heritage is from the heart of Mary when she greets her cousin Elizabeth.

This ancient song is straight from Mary's Jewish heritage. It echoes the song of Hannah on giving birth to the prophet Samuel. 1 Samuel 2:1–10 Called in our Catholic tradition the *Magnificat*[4] (Latin for the first words: "My soul proclaims"), it's a remarkable summation of God's saving power throughout the Hebrew Testament reaching its summit in the incarnation:

My soul magnifies the Lord,
  and my spirit rejoices in God my savior,
for he has looked with favor on the lowliness of
    his servant.
  Surely, from now on all generations will call me
    blessed;
for the Mighty One has done great things for me,
  and holy is his name.
His mercy is for those who fear him
  from generation to generation.
He has shown strength with his arm;
  he has scattered the proud in the thoughts of
    their hearts.
He has brought down the powerful from their
    thrones,
  and lifted up the lowly;
he has filled the hungry with good things,
  and sent the rich away empty.
He has helped his servant Israel,
  in remembrance of his mercy,
according to the promise he made to our
    ancestors,
  to Abraham and to his descendants forever.
(Luke 1:46–55)

---

4   *You may also hear this referred to as the "Canticle of Mary."*

The central theme of this song of praise is God's concern for the poor and outcast. There's no way around it: Mary is saying God humbles the rich and lifts up the poor. The Magnificat is so revolutionary that at times it's been banned by dictators! There's nothing wrong with May crownings and *mañanitas*—in fact, we absolutely love them! But unless we're putting our focus on the poor and outcast, we're not true followers of Mary, or of Jesus.

This special devotion of Mary to the poor was evident in her words to Juan Diego Cuauhtlatoatzin on the hill of Tepeyac in 1531. According to the story, she asked for a church to be built,

so I may give all my love, compassion, help, and protection to you and to all the people of this land and all the rest who love me, invoke and confide in me. I will listen to their lamentations, and remedy all their miseries, afflictions and sorrows, because I am your merciful mother.

Even today, the poorest of the poor know they can go to the Lady of Guadalupe in the church built at her request in Mexico City. There she will share in their trials and sorrows.

The Mary of the Magnificat stands in dramatic contrast to the image of a wimpy Mary portrayed in some forms of devotional art.

A courageous Jewish teenager who was willing to give up everything, even her life, to do God's will, she reminds us in her canticle of what's important in our Christian life.

Because Mary can reconcile simple wisdom with earth-shaking rebellion, she's truly a star of hope for all Christians.

Θεοτόκος

Mother of God: *Theotokos*

The Greek word *Theotokos* means "God bearer" or "Mother of God." It's a title for Mary that began as a way to counter the erroneous idea that Jesus was only a man.

backstory

APPARITIONS OF MARY

My aunt says Mary appeared to someone as a chunk of chocolate. Is that true?

There have been many people who've claimed to have had apparitions, visions and mystical messages from Mary, Jesus, angels, and various saints. Some of the more unusual instances have been "manifestations" in tortillas, tree bark, cinnamon buns, pasta, and even a grilled cheese sandwich with a supposed image of Mary (if you squinted hard enough) that sold on eBay for $28,000.

It's the job of the bishop to evaluate any such report of a "private revelation" in his own diocese. In researching such events, the bishop takes into account the content of any message supposedly received and the effects of the event. Does the "message" go against any Christian teaching? Does the phenomenon increase the faith of the people, causing deeper participation in prayer and the liturgy? If the message is some whacked-out drivel and people start doing weird things because of it, that would be A Bad Thing. And it's happened—a lot.

In most cases involving grilled cheese sandwiches and such, there's no message and the effect is generally idle curiosity, so you can bet no bishop is going to encourage such things.

On the other hand, there are events that have occurred at places like Lourdes and Tepeyac (Our Lady of Guadalupe) where people have claimed to receive messages that don't contradict Christian teaching, don't claim any new teachings, and where the events have resulted in valuable faith experiences for many people. In these cases, the bishops there have stated we are free to believe in such apparitions if we so desire. Or not. The bishop's role is to ensure that people are not taken in by scams or bowing down to tortillas when they should be building the Kingdom of God.

As Catholics we're not required to believe in any such private revelations. Our Christian tradition makes no judgment on private revelation one way or the other. In many cases, claims of private revelations have produced much good by creating places of pilgrimage where people gather to witness to their faith in a valuable way, producing an effect that goes beyond the initial claims of the seers.

Let your work be manifest to your servants,
and your glorious power to their children.

PSALM 90:16

We Pass on a Gift of Great Price to Our Children

RAISING CHILDREN IN THE FAITH

We all love a child's baptism. Baptism is something we arrange for almost as part of the birth process. After all, our parents did it for us, and we need to have our children become Christians in the same way. Some parents just give in to the pressure of grandparents who may continually ask, "Hey, when are you going to get my grandchild baptized?" Some feel they must baptize their child to save him or her from hell.[1] But if baptism is only something we do because we're supposed to, then what's its real meaning for the Christian family?

There's a question asked of the parents[2] right at the beginning of the baptismal ceremony. The priest or deacon says, "You have asked to have your child baptized. In doing so you are accepting the responsibility of training them in the practice of the faith. It will be your duty to bring them up to keep God's commandments as Christ taught us, by loving God and our neighbor. Do you clearly understand what you are undertaking?" And of course every parent answers, "I do."

1 Or they may think they're avoiding something called "limbo," the idea of a state of "natural happiness" that's not official teaching. But baptism is not just fire insurance. It's not magic. It doesn't give good luck.

2 Let's make it clear when we talk about parents that we mean anyone acting as a parent to a genetic or adoptive child, whether it be husband and wife, a single parent, a guardian, or any other form of modern family. So long as you intend to raise your child as a Christian, you are entitled to have your child baptized in a rite that respects your situation in life.

This promise isn't made to the deacon or priest. This promise is made to God. It's a solemn promise that deserves some serious consideration. Immediately following this question the presider asks the godparents if they're ready to help the parents carry out this promise as well. The godparents also assume a responsibility.

Parents Make Decisions for Children

Parents, in every way, are the primary educators of their children. We make decisions for our children at every stage of their lives. What they wear, where they go to school, whom they associate with, and so many other things are decisions made by parents. Good parents have a sincere desire to ensure that their children become well-adjusted adults, fully educated, capable of making good choices for themselves, and responsible members of society.

In the same way, and through the promise made at baptism, parents must educate and guide their children in the ways of faith. That's how Christian tradition is handed down.[3] If all we desire for our children is that they be healthy and prosperous, we've sold them short. "For what will it profit them if they gain the whole world but forfeit their life?" (Matthew 16:26).

Some individuals may feel it's better to wait for the child to come of age and then make up his or her own mind about God and religion. Even if well intentioned, this idea's short sighted. We guide our children in every other aspect of their lives from the moment of their birth. How can we honestly justify leaving formation of their relationship with God and nourishment of their souls to a time later on when they may investigate on their own? If this approach were valid, why not let them decide when and where to attend school beginning in kindergarten and give them similar discretion in other areas of life? Adults are qualified to choose, not children.

We Pass On Our Most Valuable Possession: Our Faith

Most children entering religious education programs have little or no knowledge of the Faith. Why do so many parents entrust their child's education entirely to the parish—or even ignore it altogether?

First, to be a good educator one must have knowledge of the subject and be committed to teaching. Parents must pay attention to their own formation in the Faith so they have something of substance to pass on to their children. (You're doing the right thing by reading this book!) Second, we live in a culture that in many ways opposes the teachings of Christ. This alone can create a tension between what we profess to believe and how we live.

The biggest challenges facing parents are

- How much do I know about what I profess to believe in?
- What have I done to further my own relationship with God?
- How willing am I to demonstrate to my child that I live my faith through my actions and by faithfully participating in the life of the Church?
- Am I willing to spend time educating my children in what it means to be a baptized member of the Christian community?

As parents we can't avoid the world and its wrong-headed view of reality. This is the world we live in as families. But we can continually challenge what the wounded world offers as false faith, false hope, and false love, seeking instead what brings God and what God brings to our lives.

Our children are the greatest gift God has given us. And the promise we make at their baptism creates a sacred trust among God, the children, and ourselves.

As we respond to our vocation as parents, we must be ready to give everything we have to our children, especially those things that transcend material goods. Matthew 13:44–46 Let's pray that as Christian parents we do understand what we're undertaking and to whom we've made that promise. God will no doubt one day ask us how we think we did!

---

3   The role of the parents in passing on the Faith is so important we call the family the "domestic Church," meaning the family's home itself is like a Church, a small community of faith. The family worships together, learns together, and follows the example of other family members as they grow in relationships with God and one another.

Should you have children?

In any discussion of marriage and family we should understand our Church teaching and whether we should have children.

In 1968, Paul VI wrote an encyclical letter called *Humanae Vitae*. This letter taught that artificial birth control isn't to be used by married couples. Most Catholics are well aware of this teaching. It's equally true that use of birth control by Catholics is widespread despite this teaching.

Cooperating in the creation of human life is one of our most precious gifts. Each human person, different from any other animal, is made in God's image and has an immortal soul that's destined to live throughout eternity, a soul that will find its rest only in the presence of God. So we must first examine and form our own beliefs about this reality, because what we believe here will dictate what we may do elsewhere.

Church teachings challenge us to an ideal. It's true the birth control issue is a hard teaching for many Catholics to follow, but so are many others that perhaps don't get as much press or seem less personal.

The sexual act itself is one of many ways married couples express their love for each other. In this act of extreme intimacy there's the potential to create human life. The attitude of the couple is at the heart of this issue.

Some may use contraception for purely selfish reasons. Financial considerations and the like may not be the issue—rather a married couple could decide that children would stand in the way of career, travel plans, or the ability to live a life of freedom without the responsibility of parenthood. These attitudes need serious consideration, to be sure. Yet if they truly reflect the desire of a couple one may have to wonder if they would make good parents, able to give all a child needs in a lifetime, unless they first grow up themselves.

The decision is always ultimately up to the couple. As with any such decision, making the choice by thoughtfully considering the teaching, discussing the issue with each other and people who have life's wisdom to draw upon, and prayer are all important. Such a process can be more personally affirming than merely doing what feels right in the moment, blindly following rules, avoiding a conversation, or simply not dealing with the issue.

backstory

Of course, we all change over the course of our lives. Something we might think undoable now may seem more doable later. Your beliefs, your attitudes, your priorities today are likely not what they were twenty or even ten years ago.

For us as Christians, we hope the life of discipleship and ongoing conversion will mold us over time. Nobody expects total understanding and 100 percent adherence to every Church teaching—Right. This. Minute. (Well, OK, at least reasonable people don't, and neither does God.) But we're challenged to keep our minds open and to continually evaluate our progress toward becoming who we are meant to be.

ANNULMENTS

Isn't an annulment just an end run around the prohibition of divorce, Catholic style?

Through the vows exchanged during the ceremony, it's clear marriage is for a lifetime, "until death do us part." Yet the divorce rate in our country—even among Christians—is alarmingly high. So is the number of subsequent marriages.

How can a couple enter into a sacramental union, pledging their love to each other forever before God's altar, then later separate, divorce, and remarry? This is a serious question and a cause of anxiety for Christians who find themselves in this state.

An annulment is a formal proceeding that gives a divorced person the freedom to marry again in the Church, should he or she choose to do so. Because it's a legal proceeding, there must be legal reasons for the annulment to be granted. Most of the time, these center around issues present at the time the wedding was celebrated, such as lack of freedom due to family or social pressures, lack of communication, or a misunderstanding of what's involved in a Christian marriage. Example: "Huh? You didn't tell me you never want any children, ever!"

Jesus talks about divorce in Matthew 5:31–32: unless the marriage is "unlawful" it will be for life. Of course one need only obtain an annulment after divorce if one intends to marry again. If one doesn't marry again, there's nothing preventing him or her from being fully involved in the ministries and sacramental life of the Church as a divorced person. If someone said you can't receive communion because you're divorced, that person is wrong!

Of the many questions asked about annulment, one concerns the children of the married couple. What is their status after the annulment? An annulment does not dissolve the civil marriage. In fact the couple must seek and obtain a civil decree of divorce before the Church court will begin consideration of any annulment request.

profile

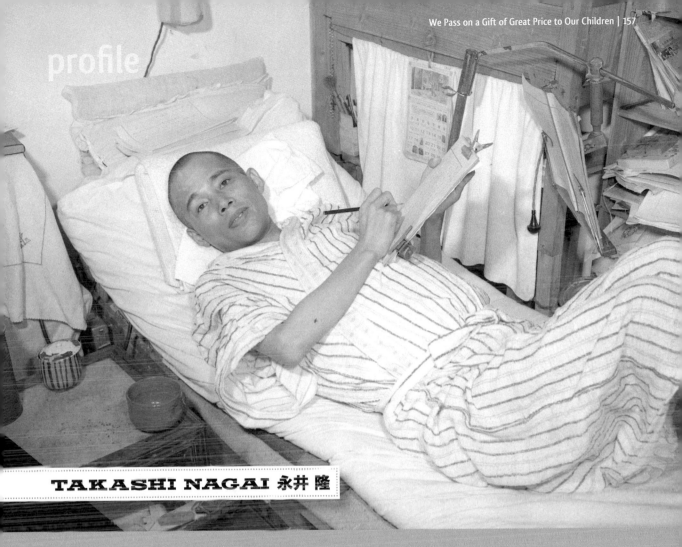

TAKASHI NAGAI 永井隆

Three days after the nuclear devastation of Hiroshima, a Catholic pilot, flying a plane blessed that morning by a Catholic priest, flew over the city of Nagasaki. His sights were set on the Catholic cathedral in Japan's historic center of Christianity. He dropped an atomic bomb over Urakami Cathedral.

Takashi Nagai, a doctor who had decided to share his wife's Catholic faith when they married, was in his office near the cathedral. Amazingly, he lived through the ordeal, even though 75,000 others—including his own wife, Midori—were instantaneously turned to dust. Despite being overcome by the loss of Midori, whose ashes he scooped from the ground into a box, Takashi immediately began to treat survivors. Later he began to lecture, write, and conduct research on radiation poisoning, even as he himself was dying from it.

During these desperate years he lived in a tiny shack amid the ruins of Nagasaki, where he took in many people and cared for them with the help of his son, Makoto, and daughter, Kayano. He called this modest hut *Nyokodo*, "The Love-Your-Neighbor-As-Yourself House" (熊本). He wrote many books during his long, painful illness, including his best-selling personal account of the bomb, *The Bells of Nagasaki.*

Instead of becoming bitter at the hand life had dealt him, Takashi worked tirelessly for harmony and peace in his life and the lives of those around him. He urged forgiveness of those who had destroyed Nagasaki and Hiroshima. When Takashi finally died in 1951 at the age of forty-three, his funeral was held in the ruins of Urakami Cathedral as the bells of churches, Buddhist temples, and Shinto shrines called twenty thousand mourners to honor him.

Takashi's life offers us an example of how to bring up our children to love others as we love ourselves, and even to forgive what may seem unforgivable.

The heavens proclaim his righteousness;
and all the peoples behold his glory.

PSALM 97:6

You Are the Light of the World

CURRENT ISSUES

In the world, yet not of the world. That's how we view ourselves as Christians. Jesus used different metaphors to describe how he sees us: the light of the world, the salt of the earth, a city on a hill. Clearly, he has great things in mind for us. By the royal dignity we received at baptism, we're called to transform our wounded world, which aches for the justice and peace only we can bring. We're in the world not to accept its false wisdom, but to offer it the true Wisdom that comes from God.

The joy and hope, the grief and anxiety
 of all the peoples of this time,
especially those who are poor or in any way
 oppressed,
these are the joy and hope, the grief and anxiety
of all the followers of Christ,
 for nothing genuinely human
 fails to find an echo in our hearts.

These are the opening words of the great Constitution on the Church in the Modern World of the Second Vatican Council (*Gaudium et Spes*). With these words addressed to all the people of the world, the Council described the situation of the Christian in modern society. Though we are witnesses to the trauma the world inflicts upon itself as it stubbornly seeks happiness on its own terms, we can also see the saving grace God offers to heal the wounds of the world. To the world we offer Good News: freedom from slavery, new life, and all that is good, true, and beautiful. Matthew 7:24–29

Reading the Signs of the Times

The world is wounded because it seeks its own wisdom. It seeks to justify violence, revenge, war, torture, injustice, and oppression by appealing to the expedient and the pragmatic. Jesus taught us to evaluate such actions by their fruits. Matthew 7:15–20 And yet we aren't called to judge the individual, but the harmful acts they do to others. Matthew 7:1–5 Still, we can't let injustice pass without action. That's why we're baptized.

Just as the world seeks to justify injustice by appealing to its own wisdom, so some Christians seek to justify injustice by twisting Christian teaching to suit their needs. These are those who begin with a worldly opinion and then look for ways to justify what they already believe

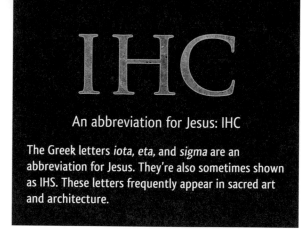

An abbreviation for Jesus: IHC

The Greek letters *iota*, *eta*, and *sigma* are an abbreviation for Jesus. They're also sometimes shown as IHS. These letters frequently appear in sacred art and architecture.

by quoting scripture, appealing to tradition, or selectively citing Church documents.[1]

But the Gospel isn't a fallback position to prove what we already want to believe. We must begin with the Gospel and judge all our beliefs and actions from it. Otherwise we degenerate into an endless spiral of subjective proof-texting that's the stuff of today's shouting-head format of public discourse and bitter bloggers. What we need are not minute declarations of what is right and wrong from Church authorities, but an inner disposition to evaluate what we see in the world by the light of the Gospel. The Holy Spirit is our surest guide.

Church Teaching Develops to Meet New Challenges

While the written form of revelation ends with the last book of the Bible, the understanding of revelation is an ongoing process that will continue until Jesus comes again. Times change, new situations arise. And we the Church continue to discern all God has in mind for us along the way.

Before Christ was taken up into heaven he promised we would not be left alone. He promised the Holy Spirit would be with us as our guide. The Holy Spirit animates the Christian community and guides us in deciding what is right and wrong in our Church and in our world. In fact, this is how our Christian tradition was developed and how we continue to meet the new challenges of every generation.

The pope with the bishops (especially in a council of the Church) are able to teach infallibly—in other words, without error—on matters of faith (what we believe) and morals (what is right and wrong). We, as Catholics, must accept such teachings because Jesus promised that the Spirit would always guide the Church.[2]

Often we encounter teachings in encyclicals[3] from the pope or in pastoral letters from our own bishop. Usually, when such documents come out, they're covered by the mainstream media, and almost always the media don't get it. They either misunderstand the documents or they focus on some random quote or footnote that fits in with what the media thinks the Church is about. So if you hear media reports about some new document from the Vatican or from your own bishop, take what you hear with a gigantic grain of salt. If you want to find out what was said, just look up the document's original text on the Web.

Of course, all teachings must find their roots in revelation. Official teaching isn't based on a whim or the personal belief of any individual. If you don't understand why the Church teaches this or that, seek out the roots of the teaching and see if

1 As an example, a blogger who chides others for not accepting every word that emanates from the Vatican embarked upon an unusual quest. Faced with this passage from the Catechism of the Catholic Church: "Torture, which uses physical or moral violence to extract confessions, punish the guilty, frighten opponents, or satisfy hatred is contrary to respect for the person and for human dignity," the blogger wrote a convoluted argument of some 15,000 words, trying to prove this passage actually permits torture! To say God approves of torture, of course, is blasphemy, no matter how artful your arguments.

2 We call these teachings "magisterial." Magisterium comes from the Latin word magister, or teacher. You might ask about the authority of documents issued by Vatican offices. This is an area of some question. Often such documents are said to be approved by the pope, in which case we can assume they have a lesser weight in magisterial teaching than an encyclical, for example. Note that not all papal teachings are infallible!

3 An encyclical is a letter from the pope, addressed to all the faithful of the Church, to bishops, to a particular nation, or even to the whole world. Generally they have Latin titles and deal with universal concerns, but occasionally they can be very specific, such as the 1937 German-language encyclical Mit Brennender Sorge ("With Burning Anxiety"), written by Pius XI to the German bishops lamenting that country's embrace of Nazism.

that helps you better come to grips with the ideal you are being directed toward.

By virtue of our baptism, we're called to be prophetic witnesses, in every generation, to all Christ taught us by the way we live and love. Together, all believers, who have received the Holy Spirit in the waters of baptism, are guided in the ways of Truth. In fact, together the entire Body of Christ has a supernatural sense of the faith (*sensus fidei* in Latin) that extends from those who hold teaching authority, the bishops, down through all the faithful—yes, even you!

Put more simply, we have a collective sense of the Truth that allows us to remain faithful to God and to God's Church while tradition unfolds over the centuries. For those who think nothing can ever change, think again. Christianity is far from an unchangeable, outmoded set of beliefs, rules, and regulations. Watching the mystery of God unfold in every generation is exciting. We encourage you to be in sync with the communal sense of the faithful as your own understanding of God, faith, and life grows.

As a community, strengthened and sustained by the Spirit, every time we gather to celebrate the mystery of the Eucharist and receive the Body and Blood of Christ we should be nourished and made stronger, and maybe see a little more clearly. God continues to show care and concern for us by enriching us with gifts that draw us closer to him. It's only natural we'd want to know more about the One who loves us so much.

Looking Ahead with Hope

Christianity, especially today, has been the focus of a lot of criticism. Some may be justified, others not. Never let anyone lead you to believe that Christianity isn't relevant to the modern world.

By discerning the signs of the times in light of the Gospel, by paying attention to the *sensus fidei* alive in the Church, and by careful attention to the official teachings of the bishops and the pope, we will always meet the challenges of being "in the world but not of the world." Central to our discernment as Church is the classic Christian maxim, "In essentials, unity, in non-essentials, liberty, in all things, charity."[4]

4 Charity *means "love." So why not just say "love" and be consistent with avoiding words that need explanation? In this case, we just wanted to keep the rhyme!*

Morality is about right and wrong

Probably when they hear the word *morality*, most people equate it with sexual ethics. But sexuality is only a tiny part of what morality deals with.

Morality in our Christian tradition deals with deciding what's right and wrong. In the United States, it's an easy cop-out to debate sexual ethics and call it morality while we oppress people around the world, give ourselves over to greed, and ignore the needs of the poor in our own society. These are gravely immoral acts many Americans overlook as they zealously pursue anyone whose zipper may have gone awry.

One self-professed Christian opined that he would like to see television shows that dealt with "real" Christian issues, like a woman who strove to avoid sex before marriage. That's not the essence of Christianity! It's true we believe people should refrain from sex outside marriage, but this isn't something uniquely Christian—Jews and Muslims also hold this belief. Even atheistic totalitarian states frown upon extramarital sex. So mere sexual abstinence does not set us apart as Christian.

The fact that we hold in common with other people of faith certain aspects of morality shows that part of our Christian moral tradition is rooted in what we call the "natural law." These are the laws of God that any person of good will can discern—the immorality of killing, stealing, lying, adultery, greed, prejudice, slavery, genocide, war, or torture, for example—all those truths enshrined in the Commandments that safeguard justice. By carefully following the path of justice, we can be a moral people along with those who follow other religions.

But we Christians set a higher standard for morality. This higher standard is based on the natural law but is infused with the light of the Gospel. For example, the teachings of Jesus do not just tell us not to kill, but not to even wish misfortune on others. We can't take food from others, but in addition we can't ignore the hungry when we ourselves have food.

In addition to Christian morality that sets a higher standard for the natural law, we also have morality that is based on an even higher law given us by Jesus. As an example, while the

God: *Allah*

The Arabic word *Allah* means "God." It refers to the same God worshipped by Jews and Christians, not a competing deity. In fact, Jews and Christians who speak Arabic use this word just as Muslims do.

natural law may seem to provide for revenge, we are prohibited from seeking revenge. Where the natural law calls for punishment, we are called to extend mercy. Where the natural law provides for self-defense, we are challenged to turn the other cheek.

While Christians may agree that something is immoral, it may be possible to have legitimate disagreement on how to approach that issue in society. As an example, Christian tradition sees abortion as gravely wrong. From our earliest days as Church, we've believed it to be the taking of human life. But while some hold the best remedy is to make it illegal, other Christians are not so sure. They're unconvinced legal prohibition will end abortion and prefer to deal with the root causes that cause people to see abortion as a solution. While agreeing something is wrong, we can legitimately disagree on how to deal with it.

We often hear people complaining about the immorality of our culture. They're right; our culture is immoral. But it's a far cry from the Christian idea of morality to condemn depictions of extramarital sex in a film while ignoring, or even taking pleasure in, the same film's glorification of vengeance.

We see this maladjusted concept of morality, for example, in vehement public complaints about the film *Saving Private Ryan* in which one of the characters says a four-letter word. Proponents of "morality" successfully campaigned to have that word censored, but to leave in the scenes that show people killing each other in gruesome ways. It's like that episode of *The Sopranos* where Tony discovers his "business associate" Vito is gay and must be murdered because Tony claims to be a "strict Catholic."

Now that's messed up.

ISLAM

I was watching Fox News Channel and one of the commentators said Islam is a threat to civilization. Is that true?

Islam is not a threat to civilization. In fact, many aspects of our civilization—such as our number system—come from Islamic culture. It's true there are Islamic fundamentalists who pose a threat, but there are also fundamentalists of Jewish and Christian flavors who also pose a threat to peace.

The Prophet Muhammad was born into a polytheistic culture. He rejected polytheism and taught the Arab people to worship the one God of the Jews and Christians. This one God is referred to by Muslims with the Arabic word *Allah*. It's the same word that Arabic-speaking Jews and Christians use to refer to God. In fact, it's the same God worshipped by Jews and Christians. Every Muslim begins prayer with the opening words of the Qur'an: "In the name of God, the compassionate, the merciful." Muslims believe God is loving and kind.

From the Arabs, Islam spread throughout the world, to the point that today only 15 percent of Muslims are Arabs; most are Asian and African. Of this 15 percent of Muslims, a tiny percentage have embraced fundamentalism. But 95 percent of Muslims are peaceful servants of God, just as only a tiny percentage of Jews and Christians have embraced fundamentalism.

The Second Vatican Council taught that Christians must respect Muslims because they worship the same God; honor the patriarchs, matriarchs, and prophets; and respect the teachings of Jesus, whom they revere as a prophet. They also have a devotion to his mother, Mary. The Council called on Christians to forget the past conflicts between Christians and Muslims and to work together to solve social problems.

It's wrong to accuse all Muslims of being violent, or to suggest they don't worship the same God we do. It's wrong to discriminate against them or to advocate public policy that does. When confronted with social ills, the Christian role is not to seek scapegoats, but rather to humbly reflect upon our own actions that may have contributed to the problem. *Inshallah!*

in the media

THE JESUITS OF THE GUARANÍ

In the sixteenth century, Jesuits came to an area now part of Paraguay, Argentina, and Brazil to bring the Good News to the indigenous peoples. Their approach was unusual. They worked with the Guaraní people to create new forms of community governance deep in the jungles, where they could prosper by their own creativity and skill.

For about 150 years, these "Jesuit Republics" thrived in the jungles. The Jesuits helped the Guaraní build towns, grand churches, schools, prosperous farms, and other forms of industry, such as the manufacture of watches and musical instruments that were highly prized in Europe for their quality. The people enacted their own laws, composed musical masterpieces, provided for the poor, and shared all things in common as they learned from the Gospel. The Guaraní became the first people in history to be entirely literate.

Meanwhile, the Jesuits essentially bribed the Spanish government in the form of taxation to protect the people from the slave trade. At their peak in the eighteenth century, the Jesuit Republics consisted of up to 300,000 native Christians in about thirty missions.

Eventually, the Jesuits could no longer protect the people because the slave trade had grown so profitable. When the area became Portuguese territory through a shameful agreement brokered by the pope, the Jesuits were killed or expelled and the Guaraní were sold into slavery by the Portuguese. The dreams of Christian utopia, the society and structures the people created with the Jesuits were reclaimed by the jungles. You can get some idea of the immorality of the eradication of these South American communities by watching the film *The Mission*.

profile

a METROPOLITAN cross

O sing to the LORD a new song;
sing to the LORD, all the earth.

PSALM 96:1

We Open Ourselves to the Modern World

THE SECOND VATICAN COUNCIL

At least he won't make waves. That's what they thought when John XXIII was elected pope in 1959. An old man at the time, it was thought he'd be a caretaker pope for a few years. But God had other plans. Stunning his fellow bishops, John announced he would assemble a council of all the bishops. The Second Vatican Council (Vatican II; 1962–65), initiated by John under the inspiration of the Holy Spirit and concluded under the ministry of Paul VI, changed the way we as the Church approach and practice our Faith.

At the time the Roman Church still clung to traditions and a philosophy still largely rooted in the Middle Ages. The celebration of the Sunday Liturgy (Mass), the role of laypeople in the Church, and the mission of the Church herself were as dusty as knick-knacks on a shelf, seen but never touched. And the world was racing by this collection of antiques.

A New Approach for a New World

The world was becoming a much smaller place. At the dawn of a new era of communications, people had access to information from the scientific, secular, faith, and social communities in ways never before thought possible. We see the culmination of that today in the Internet and satellite communication. In this new world it would be impossible to believe people would remain isolated and wait for direction from Church leaders. Information challenges people to think, question, and look for answers.

Councils of the Church are rare. Only twenty-one have been called (not counting the very first in

Jerusalem during the time of the Apostles) in the two-thousand-year history of the Church.[1] They were usually convened when some crisis existed about an article of faith. That wasn't the case with Vatican II. John XXIII, aware of how the world was changing—and how the Church had not—called for a breath of fresh air in the Church. He knew that deep down the Gospel speaks to the human heart, but we Christians can sometimes make it difficult for people to hear it when we get caught up in peripheral matters or old habits.

Vatican II affirmed Roman Catholic theology. But it did change the emphasis on how we think, celebrate, and live our faith. The bishops of the Council created sixteen documents, four of them considered major constitutions. (You can search the Internet or pick up a book on the conciliar documents for specific details; see the "Learn More" section of this book).

....

1 *The Catholic Church recognizes twenty-one ecumenical councils (councils of all the bishops). Various Orthodox Churches recognize fewer councils, some only five, some seven.*

Christianity: Not a Spectator Sport

So why is Vatican II considered the most profound event in the modern era of the Roman Catholic Church (and even the single most important even of any religion in the twentieth century)? Listen to these words from the Pastoral Constitution on the Church in the Modern World (*Gaudium et Spes*):

The Church has always had the duty of scrutinizing the signs of the times and of interpreting them in the light of the Gospel. Thus, in language intelligible to each generation, she can respond to the perennial questions which men ask about this present life and the life to come, and about the relationship of the one to the other. We must therefore recognize and understand the world in which we live, its explanations, its longings, and its often dramatic characteristics.

This major document addresses the place and relevance of the Church in the modern world. It calls all those who believe in Christ to be a Church of mission reaching beyond personal levels of comfort and entering into one Body for all humankind. No more private worship, one-on-one salvation. Believe in the mission and message of Jesus Christ and take it into the world where you encounter others to love and live your faith. At the time these ideas were scary and yet exciting; no different today. Luke 5:36–39

Changes in the Way We Live Our Faith

Vatican II reformed the way we celebrate liturgy. We were now free to pray in our own languages and to see more clearly what was happening at the altar rather than having the priest remote and distant from the assembly. People were challenged to be part of the Eucharistic celebration rather than silent spectators. The way we celebrate all the sacraments was changed to conform more to the practices of the early Church rather than the medieval Church.

Laypeople were challenged to live their baptismal call in innovative and inspiring ways. Lay leaders were encouraged to carry on the work of Christ in parishes and in the streets.

Much of the work of carrying out the Council's reforms fell to Paul VI. He was a tireless servant of the people, devoted to working out the details of what the Council ordered in dozens of documents that implemented reforms. We owe a great debt of gratitude to him.

In the aftermath of the Council there's still tension in the Church. Some say the changes called for have been slow in coming if not completely thwarted by those in power. And there are those who want to undo the reforms, to move backward. One of the major criticisms in implementing the conciliar documents is the lack of knowledge or ignorance among Catholics of Christian tradition.

There's a real need for ongoing adult education and evangelization. It's impossible to change from the "old" to the "new" if the faithful (you and I) have no understanding of our journey. In this brief discussion of the Council it's impossible to adequately lay out the work ahead of us. The work of reform launched by the Council is not yet ended; it will take generations until its fruit is fully realized in our lives.

Live the Heritage of the Second Vatican Council

Because it happened in the 1960s, many young Catholics are unaware of the importance of the Second Vatican Council. In one poll that asked young people what Vatican II was, the most common answer was, "The pope's summer home!" Every Catholic must become familiar with the challenges placed before us by Vatican II and we must continue, both together and each in our own way, to move ahead with the work of the Holy Spirit started for us so many years ago by a very wise and beloved pope.

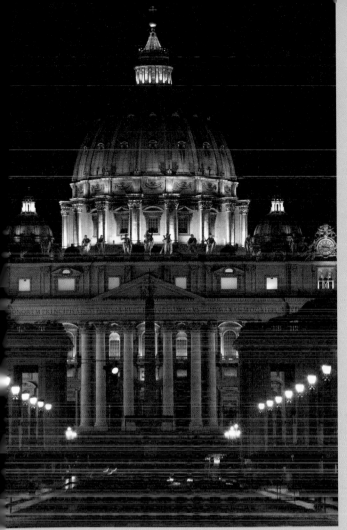

issues of financial abuse and corruption as well. For example, Luther was justly horrified that Julius II was financing the construction of St. Peter's Basilica by the sale of indulgences (a cancellation of "punishment in purgatory," widely misunderstood—without correction by those who wanted to maximize income—as a get-out-of-jail-free card that allowed people to sin).

In the midst of this crisis, the Council of Trent was convened in Italy. Bishops were commissioned to reform the way the Church was structured and administered. Many of these reforms were valuable and necessary.

So the Counter-Reformation was a movement, over hundreds of years, that attempted to defend and repair a Church that had lost her course and was under attack. As you might expect, some things went well, others not so much.

The good: Several popes continued the efforts toward reform begun by the Council of Trent with wonderful results. An increase in learning, new approaches to spirituality, efforts to improve the morality of the clergy, new religious orders, reforms in the education of the clergy, a new way of designing church buildings, liturgical reform, and the creation of a uniform catechism are examples of the issues Church leadership successfully addressed.

The bad: Paul IV was no fan of Protestantism. Two of his efforts to fight it were the Inquisition and prohibiting the faithful from reading books that were thought to be critical of Catholicism (the list of forbidden books called "The Index"). Yes, some people were even burned at the stake for so-called heretical beliefs, which were often nothing more than creative approaches. Emphasis on absolute Church law (canon law) became so severe that personal religious experience in the Faith was in many ways almost destroyed. Controlling the faithful was the issue of the day.

The ugly: The Counter-Reformation would be best characterized as the Church in a defensive mode, sometimes referred to as the "fortress Church." In modern times we've acknowledged that some of the Church's actions resulted in deeper wounds in the unity of the Body of Christ, wounds that exist to this day.

Counter-Reformation: The good, the bad, and the ugly

In the sixteenth century, Church leaders were challenged by the Protestant Reformation. In fact, much of the criticism directed at the institutional Church by the Reformers, history would later show, was valid. Example: Many practices since adopted by the Church were also points made in the 95 Theses by the great theologian and Reformer Martin Luther.

At that time, many bishops had become politicians and wealthy administrators of land rather than shepherds of their flock. Priests were not well educated, nor did they relate to the faithful in meaningful ways. The laity were relegated to an inferior status. There were

backstory

Part of the healing in any such circumstance is the acknowledgment of one's part in these divisive actions as a member of the People of God. The Second Vatican Council brought the five-hundred-year period of the Counter-Reformation to an end. The first steps have been taken in reconciling the Christian world, but we have a long way to go.

οἰκουμένη

Everywhere: *Oikoumene*

The Greek word *oikoumene* means "the whole world." From it we get the word *ecumenism*, which refers to the movement for full, visible unity of all Christians. Ecumenism is different from interfaith activity, which refers to our dialogue and working relationships with non-Christian religions we do not seek unity with.

In contrast to Trent stands the Second Vatican Council. To study the purpose and intention of both Councils presents us with a valuable contrast. On the one hand, there was self-preservation when threatened; on the other hand, a reaching out to all people of good will in an effort to understand and reclaim what Jesus lived and died to establish.

SCHISM

In my neighborhood there's a chapel with a sign saying it's Catholic, but I heard it's not connected to the diocese. How can that be?

Each of the twenty-one councils of the Church was called to deal with particular issues, and after each Council there were always people who disagreed with what that Council decided. These conflicts often resulted in schism (SIZ-um), the breaking away of a group from union with Rome. In almost all cases, such schismatic groups claim to be conservatives who keep the "true faith" against what they perceive as innovations of a council.

The defining characteristic of schism is when a group ordains bishops without consent of the pope and sets up its own organizational structure and parishes that are not in communion with the local bishop.

For example, after the First Vatican Council (1869–70), the bishops' affirmation of papal primacy disappointed some people, who then set up the Old Catholic Church (also called the Union of Utrecht, after the city in Holland where it was established). From this community others sprang; they have names like American Catholic Church, Independent Catholic Church, Liberal Catholic Church, and so on.

The same thing happened after the Second Vatican Council. Some people rejected the Council. The main leader of this faction was a French bishop, Marcel Lefebvre. He and his followers insisted on doing things the old way and refused to accept the teachings and reforms of the Council. Lefebvre ordained his own bishops in defiance of John Paul II, who pleaded with him not to take this radical step. This act resulted in the excommunication of Lefebvre and the four bishops he ordained. This schismatic group is the Society of St. Pius X, also called the "Lefebvrites." They're the largest of dozens of similar groups of estranged people—often calling themselves "Traditional Catholics"—who reject the Second Vatican Council. Some have even elected their own "popes."

Because the defining characteristic of the Catholic Church is unity, schism is a very serious matter for us. It's the job of the pope to do whatever he can to heal schisms. So in the case of the Lefebvrites, Benedict XVI lifted the excommunications of the four bishops in 2009 (Lefebvre himself had already died in 1991) as a gesture of peace, hoping that dialogue and eventual reconciliation would then follow.

For our part, we should avoid attaching ourselves to groups that claim to be Catholic but are not in communion with our local bishop, yet always treat those affiliated with these groups with respect and compassion, hoping and praying for their reconciliation with the Catholic Church.

in the media

Circa 1880

JOHN HENRY NEWMAN

At the age of fifteen John Henry Newman converted to Christianity, becoming a member of the Church of England. As an Anglican priest he was outspoken against the Catholic Church, especially on the issue of papal authority. Once in a letter he described Catholicism as "polytheistic, degrading, and idolatrous."

John Henry became noted for his scholarly writings, sermons, and intellectual influence in religious circles of his day. In the course of his study he slowly reversed his thinking. He took back all the negative comments he had made regarding Roman Catholicism. He urged the Anglican Church to rediscover its Catholic heritage, and his influence through the Oxford Movement is still felt in that tradition. His best-known book, *Apologia pro Vita Sua*, is an account of his decision to become a Roman Catholic.

Having suffered discrimination from Anglicans because of his embrace of Catholicism, John Henry then suffered rejection from Catholic leaders because of his writings on the dignity of the laity. The English Catholic bishops resented his efforts to explain that the Church wasn't just the clergy, that the laity also has a role in how Christian teaching evolves to meet new challenges. He was accused of heresy. After much turmoil, his thoughts were finally accepted, and he was made a cardinal. When John Henry died in 1890, he was buried in the same grave as his best friend. His writings are considered a major influence on the Second Vatican Council, and Catholic centers at many universities are named for him.

John Henry's life is a study in searching with openness for truth even when what you may come to discover is different from what you comfortably know. His approach is expressed in the motto he chose as a cardinal: *Cor ad cor loquitur*, "Heart speaks to heart."

profile

From the rising of the sun to its setting
the name of the LORD is to be praised.

PSALM 113:3

We Look Forward to the End of Time

THE SECOND COMING

When is Jesus coming back? The early followers of Christ expected him to return soon after he ascended to heaven. They were anxious for the Kingdom Jesus so often talked about to arrive in a blaze of glory. Some of Paul's writings warned people not to get too attached to things of this world and prepare for the Second Coming. 1 Corinthians 7:29–31 Then time went by, lots of time. Where was Jesus?

Soon Christians realized that while Jesus promised to return, their conception of how that would happen and God's plan might not be the same. It's another great example of how the mystery of God unfolds for us as we read and study scripture and as we have time, even centuries, to ponder the working and will of God in salvation history.

Looking Back to Look Ahead

In the Synoptic Gospels (Matthew, Mark, and Luke), Jesus talks about the Son of Man coming again in glory into his kingdom. Luke 17:20–37

In the Gospel of John, Jesus again uses the image of the Son of Man when he talks about the last day, John 6:39–54 and the evangelist connects this to the resurrection of the dead. Martha talks about Jesus' second coming as both a resurrection and an ongoing process. John 11:24–27

Study of these passages over time has led some theologians to believe Jesus' prediction of his coming in glory was fulfilled on the cross. Our salvation was assured through an obedient act of love when Christ sacrificed his mortal body for humankind. It's in this way the messianic

prophecy was fulfilled and we were all saved. The visual may not seem all that glorious according to our human ideas, but the achievement on behalf of us all certainly leaves no doubt as to its significance for every human person. Hebrews 12:18–24

Still, others are waiting for Christ to come again, although no one knows just how that will happen. The Nicene Creed tells us, "He shall come again in glory to judge the living and the dead." In the Roman Catholic, Anglican, and some Protestant liturgies we hear the acclamation, "Christ has died, Christ is risen, Christ will come again!" referred to as the "mystery of faith."

Can I Get an ETA on That?

Over the centuries there have been a lot of people who've tried to predict the exact date Jesus will swoop down out of the clouds and fulfill the scriptural passages that they'd obviously misinterpreted. Some have even changed the expected arrival date more than once when the original prediction didn't come true! These predictions are no more than they appear on the surface, an attempt to upstage God who will act at a time and in a manner we obviously can't even comprehend. Matthew 24:3–44

Mainstream Christianity doesn't attempt to predict the date of the Second Coming or even what it will be like. After waiting more than two thousand years, those who believe the Second Coming may be an extraordinary event still recognize that it's not integral to anyone's day-to-day life in faith.

Do We Have a Role?

Let's, for a moment, return to the prayer Jesus taught us. "Our Father who art in heaven, hallowed be thy name. Thy Kingdom come, thy will be done on earth as it is in heaven." Jesus talked a lot about the Kingdom of God. He even asked us to pray that God's Kingdom would come about here on Earth as it exists in the perfection of heaven.

The challenge for all who call themselves Christian isn't to say the words, "I am a follower of Christ," or accept Jesus as your personal savior and then go on with life feeling saved by this acclamation alone. The life of Christ is a life lived for us as the perfect example of what God desires each one of us to be here on Earth.

Look at our world today. It's far from the Kingdom of Heaven. Human pride, selfishness, arrogance, and the like all keep us from living in relationships as Jesus challenges us to do. The Book of Genesis tells us right from the start that God's Creation was perfect and human nature rejected this perfect gift. Perhaps the Second Coming will occur when we as a people accept Christ in a way that allows all humankind to live filled with the love of God and the true Peace of Christ we so casually offer each other every time we celebrate Mass.

Trust God

We love to be in control. Yet two of the most significant events in our lives we have absolutely no control over at all: the moment of our birth and the moment of our death. It's all that in-between stuff we spend a lifetime trying to engineer!

Somewhere along the way we have to learn to trust. It's not uncommon in our journey to be disappointed more than once. That makes our need to control and our ability to trust, really trust, that much more difficult at times.

To trust we have to believe someone has our best interest at heart and will always be there for us, especially when we're at our worst or need to know we're loved without condition.

Can Others Experience a Second Coming through You?

Whatever the case, the Second Coming is not an event to hold our breath and wait for in anxious anticipation. We—you and me—make Christ present every day in this world by what we do and who we are. If we do it well, even though it may not be perfect, we have made Jesus present, and we can celebrate "Emmanuel" in our little victories each day. God with us again and always!

People of faith learn to trust God above all others. Ultimate control rests with the Creator who has concern for all things, who loves the human person beyond any words we can express, and who is the ultimate master of his plan.

At times Jesus encouraged us to be like children as we face life. One aspect of this learning from children is to trust our Father to give us what we need:

Therefore I tell you, do not worry about your life, what you will eat or what you will drink…. Your heavenly Father knows that you need all these things. But strive first for the kingdom of God and his righteousness, and all these things will be given to you as well. (Matthew 6:25, 32–33)

Try as we might, we will never know the future. For the Christian, control of our destiny, even with our free will, must be placed in the hands of God. This trust in Divine Providence is part of our lifelong faith journey. Jesus himself had to develop a relationship with his Father through study and prayer that ultimately gave him the courage to face the cross with the certainty of resurrection.

This is the Christian story, and each day we write another page of our own journey from this world home to our loving Father. Trusting in Divine Providence, we become confident of our destination no matter where we may stop along the way.

backstory

Ἔσχατον

The end: *Eschaton*

Eschaton is a Greek word we use to refer to the end of the world and the Second Coming of Jesus. The study of this subject we refer to as "eschatology," which in a broader sense also includes our individual judgment, the afterlife, and the final resurrection.

THE RAPTURE AND ARMAGEDDON

Will the world end with the "Rapture" and a great war?

Hollywood has produced lots of movies depicting the end of the world. They're both entertaining and scary—and sometimes just kitsch!

Scientists have looked into outer space to track the path of giant asteroids that might collide with Earth and destroy the planet; others are concerned about the effects of global warming. These concerns are different from our Christian concept of the end of the world, although science and theology may converge on some points.

The Book of Revelation, with its awesome imagery, has also been used by some to predict how the world will end. Actually, Revelation was written for a persecuted Church, to people who were oppressed by the Roman government. This book inspired those readers to have faith in Christ, through whom all things will be made new, even in the midst of their oppression.

There's no inside scoop in the Book of Revelation. And it's kind of creepy that some have taken a book of consolation and made it into a book of fear.

Fundamentalists claim the good people will be sucked into heaven as driverless cars career about our cities ("The Rapture"). They say those "left behind" will endure a period called "The Tribulation." They say a literal World War called "Armageddon" will bring about the Second Coming—and some of them are actively trying to spark such a war because they think they have power over when Jesus will come again.

Oh come on now. That's hardly the imagery of the Body of Christ. Don't let anyone scare you into a false faith by persuading you to join the "Christian Club" or else! If it's God who will initiate the end of Earth, the love of the Creator will fill even that event, and true justice will be ever-present for everyone. Divine Providence will be in full swing. To suggest otherwise is to deny the very nature of God. We should not fear the end of the world or try to predict when it will come, but welcome it with joy when it does!

in the media

MYCHAL JUDGE

Mychal Judge had two ambitions growing up: to be a priest and a fireman. Mychal did both by following in the footsteps of Jesus as a follower of Francis, a Franciscan, and as a chaplain for the Fire Department of New York.

Mychal's entire life was characterized by his compassion toward all people. His presence was felt by those suffering from AIDS, and he worked among the homeless and those on the margins of society. It was said he treated all people, without reservation, like family. Because of his personal experience as a gay man and a recovering alcoholic, he brought special empathy to those communities. He traveled to Northern Ireland to work for peace.

To the firefighters of New York he was a brother who went with them on dangerous missions. This ministry eventually led him into action on September 11, 2001, as the Twin Towers were in flames. Mychal lost his life while anointing a dying firefighter and a woman who had fallen on the fireman.

Moved by his life, sacrifices, and death, his fellow firefighters gently carried Mychal's body from the devastation to a local church and placed him in front of the altar. Covering the sheet over his body were his priestly stole and chaplain's badge.

Mychal was always grateful to God for his vocation and constantly acknowledged the presence of God in all things. His life was filled with a joy he shared with all he met. When a day arrived that must have seemed like the end of the world, Mychal continued to do God's work, for he had been working for the Kingdom his entire life.

profile

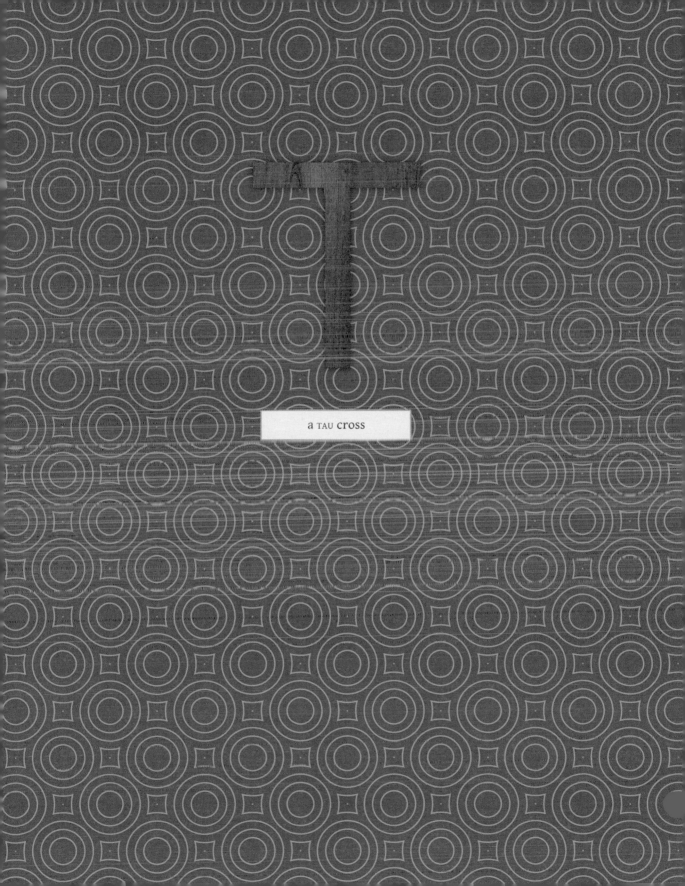

a TAU cross

Choose the Red Pill

THE DISMISSAL

Go in peace! That's the dismissal from the deacon at the end of the Eucharist. And it doesn't mean, "Get out of here so we can clear the parking lot for the next Mass." The deacon's dismissal is a charge to take what you've experienced in the liturgy, to make it a part of your life outside the church building and a part of the lives of all those you meet. To go in peace means the hard part has just begun.

In the pop classic sci-fi film *The Matrix*, a lonely computer programmer named Neo is approached by the shadowy figure Morpheus,[1] who police say is the world's most dangerous criminal. Morpheus tells Neo the world is an illusion, and he gives Neo a choice between two pills: If he takes the blue pill, his life will go on as it always has been. If he chooses the red pill, he'll see reality as it truly is.

Neo takes the red pill and awakes in a pod filled with fluid and with tubes stuck in his body. As he coughs and pulls out the tubes, he sees his pod is one of millions around him, each with a human in it. It turns out what he thought was reality is actually an elaborate computer program, called "the Matrix," that keeps the mass of humanity in a dream state, thinking they're living real lives while they're really just passive energy sources for intelligent machines.

When he chose the red pill, Neo knew he could never go back to his life of comfortable illusion. His choice led to a life of risk, of danger and deprivation, but at least it was real. And that made all the difference.

Living a Countercultural Life

The Gospel of Jesus Christ is the red pill that opens our eyes to the wisdom the blue-pill world thinks is just plain foolish. But as the world seeks to polarize issues into simple black and white options, living a Christian life isn't that simple. We walk in that purple haze, the gray area between the world and the Kingdom of God. But we are children of the Light.

At times, people will hold out to us choices that may seem to be the Gospel but are not. They're seductive proposals because they're cloaked in religious language: "Say your prayers and go to Mass; that's all you need to do." "Christianity is just about believing the right things; that's what God wants of you." "Being a good Christian means voting for this political party." "It's dangerous to think for yourself; just believe everything that comes from Rome." "All these other Christians support war; why do you think you're better than them?" Hmm. Tastes gospely, but something's wrong.

---

1 *The name* Morpheus *comes from a Greek root meaning to "form" or "change." The pagan Greek god Morpheus communicated by dreams.*

In his novel *Les Misérables*, Victor Hugo describes the compassion of a saintly bishop that amazes his people: "As we see, he had a strange and peculiar way of judging things. I suspect he acquired it from the Gospel."

Christians are called to live a radical life that evaluates everything through the lens of the Gospel. The Good News is meant to conform us to Jesus; we're not to conform Jesus to what we already want to believe. It's our Christian *sensus fidei*, sense of the faith, that guides us, not the sense of the world that seeks to justify itself by Googling scripture passages to make a case. We call that "proof-texting." It puts the cart before the horse. For example, if I'm in favor of the death penalty, I start hunting for scripture passages or official documents to support my position. This is the way of spiritual decline. It begins with a worldly position and seeks to clothe it in Christian garments. That's totally messed up.

Seek Understanding

Faith seeks understanding. This is a central concept in the Western Church. While we must balance our rational Western approach with the wisdom of the East, it's still important for all Christians, East and West, to learn more about our faith.

When you stop learning, you die. That's how life works. Don't die to learning before your body gasps its last breath. Your decision to read this book is an important step along the way to lifelong learning. In "Learn More," we provide some book recommendations for you. Choose some that can help you grow in those area of the Faith you are most interested in. That's how your personal gifts will flourish.

You may also want to explore some of the opportunities for learning provided by your parish or diocese, such as the "Theology on Tap" series offered in many dioceses for young adults. Who knew faith and a little microbrew beer could make a revolution! If your diocese offers Theology on Tap, you should definitely check it out. As the Catholic writer Hillaire Belloc points out:

Wherever the Catholic sun does shine
There's laughter and good red wine
At least I've always found it so
Benedicamus Domino! [translation: "Let us praise the Lord!"]

Let the Spirit Work in Your Life

Our Christian tradition—expressed in scripture and our ancient beliefs—is a living thing, not some dusty old rule book. There's no time in history when our Christian story has been completed and set in stone. Our belief, our way of life, is continually evolving under the guidance of the Holy Spirit. Otherwise, why would we even need the Holy Spirit? We could just look up words, and that would be all she wrote.

The source of our faith is not a written text, but the very person of Jesus, who directs us to the Father by the guidance of the Spirit. If we truly believe this, a vast new horizon opens before each of us. We're set free from the old rules and can live lives of total honesty and integrity; the new rules are those things others can discern by observing our lives. As John Henry Newman explained, "The perfect Christian state is that in which our duty and our pleasure are the same, when what is right and true is natural to us, and in which God's service is perfect freedom." Paul famously wrote, "For freedom Christ has set us free. Stand firm, therefore, and do not submit again to a yoke of slavery" (Galatians 5:1).

The freedom of the Christian is not the freedom of American consumerism. It's the freedom of service. In service, you'll discover the real you, the unbound, happy person God has envisioned from before the beginning of time when he called you by name.

The freedom of the Christian is not the freedom of relativism. We have our tradition to guide us; we don't reinvent the wheel of belief to suit ourselves or our times. We're faithful to the teachings we've received from countless Christians before us. We pass them on as members of the Body of Christ, eager to provide the healing only the Gospel can give the world.

Born at a time when the buffalo were still plentiful on the plains, Black Elk was a witness to the battle of Little Bighorn; his cousin Crazy Horse was among the chiefs who defeated the invading army of General Custer.

The plight of the Native Americans—especially Black Elk's own Lakota people—grew increasingly desperate due to their land being taken from them. Black Elk became caught up in the Ghost Dance movement, involving a long and ecstatic dance the Lakota believed would restore their way of life to them—a sort of Native American rave. This messianic movement alarmed the U.S. government, which massacred hundreds of Lakota at Wounded Knee in 1890. Black Elk escaped the carnage.

After learning about Christianity from Jesuit missionaries, Black Elk was baptized and took the name Nicholas. Because of his respected standing in the community as a medicine man, he was made a catechist. For decades he ministered to the Lakota, teaching them the faith using examples from traditional Lakota culture. He was a gifted preacher. He conducted Sunday services in the absence of priests, baptized his people, prayed with the sick and dying, and buried the dead.

Black Elk and his wife, Brings White, lost several children to tuberculosis and other effects of poverty in their South Dakota reservation. Only one daughter, Lucy Looks Twice, survived. Yet he continued to teach, preach, and invite the Lakota to a life of constant prayer. He even traveled to other tribes to teach them the Faith, enduring the ridicule and hatred of white people along the way. He died in 1950.

Having lost their ancient way of life, the Lakota were in dire poverty and were only occasionally visited by priests, Black Elk brought the Good News to his people and sustained the Christian community from births to deaths by his quiet faith and way with words. His example can inspire lay leaders in today's Church as they teach, preach, and guide faith communities to a deeper prayer life.

Wakhan Thánka níci un. May the Great Spirit go with you and guide you.

BLACK ELK (HEȞÁKA SÁPA)

profile

The freedom of the Christian is not the freedom of rugged individualism. It's finding true individuality in community. We Christians are saved in a community, the Church. This complicates matters. It's not just you and Jesus, your MySpace BFF! Being a community means accepting everybody else in the Church, with all their faults and annoying personalities, and even their crazy ideas—some of which you can probably learn from. And it also means they have to accept your faults, your annoying personality, your crazy ideas they can also learn from. See how it works?

Finding a Faith Community

Because you can only be fully Christian in a community, you must find one. You'd think we could just tell you to go to your local Catholic church, but you'd be wrong. McDonald's fries will be the same uptown and downtown, but not so much parishes. You'll probably have to look around a bit, but hey, you're an American. You know how to shop.[2]

You have a right to a parish where you can flourish. What are you looking for? A parish where they understand their role in building the Kingdom of God. Is the celebration of the Eucharist welcoming and enriching? Will they accept you as you are? Are there ministries you can be involved in?

Here's a hint: Call and ask what ministries they have. If you hear a puzzled silence followed by, "Um, well, we have Mass," ask if they have outreach ministries for the homeless, or prisoners, or the sick, or the poor. If they still respond, "Well, we have Mass," look elsewhere. This isn't to judge parishes that offer only liturgy; maybe they just haven't grown enough as a community to provide the environment you need. Who knows? Five years from now, that parish may be alive with the Spirit. If you sense some openness to that possibility there, maybe your gifts can help them get to that point.

Of course you can be involved in other programs to serve people, but it's so much better to worship God with the same people you serve others with. And a life-filled and life-giving parish makes all the difference in your growth as a Christian.

Engagement with the World

At times in this book, you may have noticed many negative examples of how the world views reality that are not how we as Christian view reality. Please don't allow the differences between the world and us as the Church to obscure the Christian virtue of hope, to become cynical when faced with the faults of worldly "wisdom" from our countercultural approach of the Gospel.

In his homily opening the Second Vatican Council, John XXIII offered a wise approach:

As we have learned in the daily course of our apostolic ministry, it often happens that we become aware of rather offensive words of certain people, who, though enkindled by religious zeal, do not weigh matters with a fair evaluation and prudent judgment. For these people are able to see only ruin and calamity in the present condition of human society. They insist that our times, in comparison to past generations, have utterly slid into an inferior state. They conduct themselves as if they have nothing to learn from history, the teacher of life, and as though in the times of past councils, everything concerning Christian doctrine, customs, and the just liberty of the Church had proceeded favorably and properly.

Yet we think it necessary for us to disagree plainly with these prophets of doom, who always predict further deterioration, as though the end of all loomed near.

In the present course of human events in which society appears to be progressing to a new order, there is rather the necessity to acknowledge the hidden plans of Divine Providence, which attain their end through successive generations and the deeds of human beings—often even beyond human expectation—and which in wisdom arrange all things, even unfortunate human disasters, for the good of the Church.

---

2 *Are we telling you to "church shop"? Yes. You may be thinking you must belong to the parish in whose geographical boundaries you reside. That was true in the old days, but no more.*

TRULY I SAY TO YOU · TO THE
THAT YOU DID IT TO ONE
BROTHERS OF MINE, E
LEAST OF THEM · YOU

This is the optimism a Christian must nurture when faced with the wounded world.

Keep Your Eyes on Jesus Christ

We offer you the words of someone much wiser than us, Teresa of Ávila:

Christ has no body now on earth but yours,
no hands but yours, no feet but yours;
yours are the eyes through which Christ's
*   compassion looks out on the world,*
yours are the feet with which He is to go about
*   doing good*
and yours are the hands with which He is to bless
*   us now.*

Peace: It's Portable

At Eucharist each Sunday, your authors, who are deacons, send our communities forth with peace. Because we're deacons, this may be a different book than might be written by a priest, a bishop, or a layperson. And as much as we want to offer you a clear and contemporary explanation of our Christian faith, we know correct belief will not set you free. It will not make you happy. It will not save you. Only the red pill of grace can do that. Its active ingredients are faith, hope, and love—above all, love.

Don't despise the failings of the world. It's true the world is lying by the roadside, bathed in the blood of self-inflicted wounds. But we cannot walk by. We must tend the wounds, self-inflicted as they are, and with compassion seek to heal the world. We are our brother's keeper. Luke 10:29–37

εὐαγγέλιον

Good News: *Euangelion*

The Greek word *euangelion* means "Good News," and this is where our word Gospel comes from. From its Latin form, *evangelium*, we get the word *evangelization*, which means to spread the Good News, and *evangelists*, the authors of the four Gospels.

We hope and pray this book has given you some foundation to claim your Christian identity, to understand the living tradition we share, to reflect on your place in the Church and the world. Recall these words of Jesus: "See, I am sending you like sheep into the midst of wolves; so be wise as serpents and innocent as doves" (Matthew 10:16).

Go in peace.

BE STILL

Let the calm, calm blue waters through
Wash your soul, passing right through you
Like the smallest rose out of the hardest ground
Like a tiny hand reaching up for the sun
Let us pray that our hearts are one
The toughest love is the strongest one
Like a crippled man fights his bitter pain
On two tired legs that hope to walk once again
Stay gold and be still.

As we grow, a river flows
Through our hearts
Finding peace wherever it may go

Let the pure, pure blue waters through
Don't let the wind take 'em away from you
Like the smallest star shines in the darkest night
Like a mother's egg brings in a new life
Stay gold and be still
Pray that we can all stay gold and be still.

— David Hidalgo and Louie Perez, Los Lobos

Learn More

This book is not meant to be comprehensive. No doubt some readers will complain that we did not include this or that point they feel is vital. But we wanted the book to be readable and to offer paths for you to learn more as you have time or interest. So in this section, we provide books we think will help you advance your understanding of and appreciation for your Faith and heritage.

Rather than directing you to dusty old tomes, we've tried to emphasize contemporary books, especially best-sellers, along with a sprinkling of must-read classics from the past. We've also tried to use this section to introduce you to some of the best contemporary spiritual writers.

We know how disappointing it is to order something from Amazon and get a big brick of a book when you were hoping for light reading, or vice versa. So we've categorized them by chapter according to the level of commitment each represents. We hope you will use this section as a guide to personal growth, so you can be an effective proclaimer of the Good News.

If you'd like a single book that will be a great reference for you to look things up, we recommend *The HarperCollins Encyclopedia of Catholicism,* edited by Richard P. McBrien. Of course, the definitive source is *The Catechism of the Catholic Church*, although it is rather complex and difficult to use as a reference book. For new suggestions of ways to learn more about your Faith, be sure to visit our Web site at www.catholicstory.org.

1 Knowledge of God and Revelation
God Speaks to a Longing in the Human Heart

Abraham: A Journey to the Heart of Three Faiths, *by Bruce Feiler. This* New York Times *best-seller is an encounter with Jews, Christians, and Muslims in the Holy Land and how they view their father in faith.*

How to Be a Perfect Stranger: The Essential Religious Etiquette Handbook, *by Stuart M. Matlins and Arthur J. Magida. Learn to pray well together in this handy reference guide for anyone who has family and friends of different religions.*

A History of God: The 4,000-Year Quest of Judaism, Christianity and Islam, *by Karen Armstrong. This* New York Times *best-seller explores the history of Judaism, Christianity, and Islam.*

2 The Hebrew Testament
From Age to Age God Gathers a People to Himself

People of the Covenant: An Invitation to the Old Testament, *by Dianne Bergant, CSA. A helpful overview of the history, books, and people we find in the Hebrew Testament.*

Psalms for All Seasons, *by John F. Craghan. A wonderful way to understand and learn to pray the psalms.*

Walking the Bible: A Journey by Land through the Five Books of Moses, *by Bruce Feiler. This* New York Times *best-seller describing a walking tour of the sites of biblical events was made into a popular PBS series, available on DVD.*

The Prophets, *by Abraham Joshua Heschel. A moving, classic work by the renowned Jewish theologian and civil rights-era activist describes the role of the Hebrew prophets and their relevance to modern life.*

The Collegeville Bible Commentary. *If you want to get serious about reading and understanding scripture, this reference work will guide you.*

3 Scripture and Tradition
Revelation Is Alive and Working in Our Own Lives

By What Authority? A Primer on Scripture, the Magisterium and the Sense of the Faithful, *by Richard R. Gaillardetz. A nontechnical exploration by a noted theologian of how scripture and tradition work in the Church.*

4 Faith
God Believes in Us Before We Believe in Him

My Struggle with Faith, *by Joseph Girzone. The best-selling author of the Joshua series of novels narrates his life journey of seeking a reason to believe.*

The Creed: What Christians Believe and Why It Matters, *by Luke Timothy Johnson. Why an ancient confession of faith still makes sense in the modern world.*

5 God the Father
God Is Love

The Shack, *by William P. Young. A man broken by the death of his daughter discovers the power of relationship through an encounter with the Trinity.*

The Space Trilogy (Out of the Silent Planet, Perelandra, and That Hideous Strength), *by C. S. Lewis. What if God created other intelligent beings elsewhere in the universe who did not need redemption? And what would happen if we sinners were to come into contact with them? Find out in this sci-fi trilogy by the author of* The Chronicles of Narnia.

Altogether Gift: A Trinitarian Spirituality, *by Michael Downey. This book shows how the Trinity is not some obscure doctrine, but a way of approaching many facets of the Christian life.*

6 The Son of God
Jesus Changes the World

The Gospels. *Come on now, how can you learn about Jesus without reading the four Gospels? Get to it!*

Consider Jesus: Waves of Renewal in Christology, *by Elizabeth A. Johnson. A fine introduction to the thoughts behind the study of Jesus as the Son of God.*

Easy   Accessible   Advanced

profile

THOMAS MERTON

Born to artist parents, Thomas Merton spent his childhood in various places around the world. During his college years at Cambridge and Columbia universities, he was a heavy party-er and fathered a child out of marriage. Yet he continually felt a longing for God and had a personality that was curious about everything. As a college professor, he explored various Christian traditions and read a lot about religion. Eventually, he became a Catholic, and discerned a call to ordained ministry as a Trappist monk at Gethsemani Abbey in Kentucky.

Thomas's special gift was writing. His most famous book, *The Seven Storey Mountain*, is an account of his conversion and one of the best-selling books of the twentieth century, having sold more than one million copies in fifteen languages. Thomas went on to write more than sixty books on prayer, spirituality, and social justice. He studied Eastern religions and sought to incorporate some of their approaches into Christian spirituality.

Thomas firmly believed that contemplative prayer was not only for monks. His books outline paths to holiness for people of all states in life. Central to his teaching was that we become holy by becoming our true selves. Holiness is not some exterior thing we chase; it resides deep inside us by the grace of God, and our role is to let it flower. And holiness does not exist in a vacuum; Thomas was one of the most prominent voices against racism and the Vietnam War because he saw the connection across prayer, holiness, and the world.

Thomas had his faults. He frequently argued with his abbot over how to integrate his monastic life with the frequent requests to speak and preach outside the monastery. Yet he continued to try to overcome his faults. He finally was able to live a life of solitude at the abbey as a hermit. Thomas died in 1968 and is considered one of the greatest spiritual writers of modern times.

7 The Holy Spirit
The Breath of God Gives Life

The Seven Gifts of the Holy Spirit, by *Mitch Finley. A practical guide to enriching your life through a better relationship with the Holy Spirit.*

Fire of Love: Encountering the Holy Spirit, by *Donald J. Goergen, OP. A contemporary and readable exploration of the role of the Holy Spirit in our lives.*

8 Teachings and Ministry of Jesus
The Kingdom of God Is Here and Now

A Portrait of Jesus, by *Joseph F. Girzone. You may not really know Jesus until you read this best-selling book.*

Desire of the Everlasting Hills: The World before and after Jesus, by *Thomas Cahill. Part of the best-selling* Hinges of History *series, this book examines the impact of Jesus on history and society.*

9 The Life, Death, and Resurrection of Jesus
God Always Wins

The Gifts of the Jews: How a Tribe of Desert Nomads Changed the Way Everyone Thinks and Feels, by *Thomas Cahill. This* New York Times *best-seller tells the story of how the Jews have changed history and our lives in ways we may not have considered.*

The Bible, the Jews and the Death of Jesus: A Collection of Catholic Documents, by *the Bishops' Committee for Ecumenical and Interreligious Affairs, United States Conference of Catholic Bishops. If you really want to know what Catholics are called to believe about the Jews, this book offers the official statements and guidelines.*

10 Grace, Free Will, and Sin
We Don't Choose God, God Chooses Us

The Return of the Prodigal Son, by *Henri J. M. Nouwen. This spiritual masterpiece, raw in its emotion, explores the roles of the people of this parable in eye-opening reflections.*

11 The Great Commandment and the Ten Commandments 1-3
How We Show Respect to God

Jesus for President: Politics for Ordinary Radicals, by *Shane Claiborne and Chris Haw. A young Evangelical Christian examines patriotism gone awry in the light of Christian tradition.*

Losing Moses on the Freeway: The 10 Commandments in America, by *Chris Hedges. The best-selling war reporter offers personal accounts from his experience that dramatically illustrate how the Ten Commandments offer a better life.*

12 The Great Commandment and the Ten Commandments 4-10
How We Act Justly Toward Others

Lights, Camera, Faith: The Ten Commandments, by *Rose Pacatte, FSP, and Peter Malone, MSC. The authors of the popular three-volume movie lectionary offer an assortment of films that illustrate the premises of the Ten Commandments in a dialogue with pop culture.*

Dead Man Walking, by *Sister Helen Prejean. This* New York Times *best-seller describes a nun's ministry with men on death row and the families of their victims.*

The Life of Thomas More, by *Peter Ackroyd. This definitive biography includes all the most recent scholarship on the chancellor of England who tangled with Henry VIII.*

13 Heaven and Hell
We Are Made for Glory

The Gift of Peace, by *Joseph Cardinal Bernardin. The best-selling book written by the archbishop of Chicago as he was dying.*

The Great Divorce, by *C. S. Lewis. What if there were regular bus service from purgatory to heaven, and you could visit there, choosing to stay or return? This short fable will make you look at life and choices differently!*

14 Prayer
God Invites Us to Conversation

Here and Now: Living in the Spirit, by Henri J. M. Nouwen. A concise but powerful approach to the spiritual life; deeply honest.

Everything Belongs: The Gift of Contemplative Prayer, by Richard Rohr. Learn how to find your real center so that you can pray.

The Life of Saint Teresa of Ávila by Herself. The famous and valuable autobiography that contains great teachings on prayer.

The Way of Perfection, by Teresa of Ávila. One of the classics on the spiritual life.

The Interior Castle, by Teresa of Ávila. Traces the passage of the soul through successive chambers of a mystical castle of spirituality.

Teresa of Ávila: The Progress of a Soul, by Cathleen Medwick. A Jewish woman, a former features editor of Vogue and Vanity Fair, pays loving tribute to the life and impact of Teresa in this comprehensive modern biography.

15 Discipleship
Following in the Footsteps of Jesus

Father Joe: The Man Who Saved My Soul, by Tony Hendra. The New York Times best-seller describes the amazing relationship between a troubled man and the spiritual director he had since childhood.

No Man Is An Island, by Thomas Merton. An astounding work by one of the great spiritual writers of the twentieth century.

The Irresistible Revolution: Living as an Ordinary Radical, by Shane Claiborne. A twenty-something Evangelical describes his journey to discover what it means to be a disciple of Jesus.

The Cost of Discipleship, by Dietrich Bonhoeffer. This modern classic by the martyred Lutheran pastor is a call to forego the "cheap grace" of routine Church life in favor of the "costly grace" of true discipleship. Written from a wartime Lutheran perspective, but applicable to all Christians.

16 The Church
We Are the Body of Christ

Pope John XXIII, by Thomas Cahill. A very readable biography of John, part of the Penguin Lives series.

Women in Church History: 21 Stories for 21 Centuries, by Joanne Turpin. Learn about some of the contributions of great women in the Church.

What Makes Us Catholic: Eight Gifts for Life, by Thomas H. Groome. Attitudes, beliefs, and approaches that characterize the Catholic tradition, written for young adults with questions and those who consider themselves Catholic but no longer practice their faith.

Models of the Church, by Avery Dulles. This modern classic explores different ways of understanding the Church.

John XXIII: Pope of the Century, by Peter Hebblethwaite. The modern papal biographer tells the story of John's life.

Easy   Accessible   Advanced

17 Church Ministries and Roles
We Are Each Called to Serve

Excellent Catholic Parishes, by Paul Wilkes. If you are clergy or a lay parish leader, you must read this book to understand what makes a great parish tick.

In the Name of Jesus: Reflections on Christian Leadership, by Henri J. M. Nouwen. The great spiritual teacher reflects on what it means to be a leader in the Christian community.

Leadership in the Church: How Traditional Roles Can Serve the Christian Community Today, by Walter Cardinal Kasper. The Vatican's head of ecumenism explains the history behind the hierarchy (bishops, priests, and deacons) and how these roles can be adapted in an ecumenical age.

The Reform of the Papacy: The Costly Call to Christian Unity, by John R. Quinn. The learned former archbishop of San Francisco takes up John Paul II's challenge to rethink the role of the papacy in an ecumenical age.

The Praise of Folly, by Desiderius Erasmus. This popular book written in 1511 wryly describes the state of corruption in the Church that prompted the Reformation.

18 Social Justice
The Lord Hears the Cry of the Poor

Strength to Love, by Martin Luther King Jr. The martyred preacher explains the place of love in the struggle for social justice in a book his wife says is the best explanation of his philosophy.

The Devastation of the Indies, by Bartolomé de las Casas. This book written in 1552, one of the world's first best-sellers, describes in excruciating detail the situation of the Indians under Spanish rule, with Bishop las Casas' anguished plea to recognize them as human.

Bartolomé de las Casas: Great Prophet of the Americas, by Paul S. Vickery. This is an authoritative biography of las Casas.

19 The Sacraments of Initiation: Baptism, Confirmation, and Eucharist
We Have Died to Sin and Risen to a New Life

Signatures of Grace: Catholic Writers on the Sacraments, edited by Thomas Grady and Paula Huston. Beautiful reflections by contemporary writers on each of the sacraments.

Sacraments: A NEW Understanding for a NEW Generation, by Ray R. Noll. Learn the meaning, history and future of the seven sacraments. Includes a CD-ROM of supplemental reading.

The Memory Palace of Matteo Ricci, by Jonathan D. Spence. An account of the great Jesuit missionary's life in Italy, India, and China.

20 The Sacraments of Vocation: Marriage and Holy Orders
God Calls Each of Us to Our Own Way of Life

The Inner Voice of Love: A Journey through Anguish to Freedom, by Henri J. M. Nouwen. The great spiritual writer addresses the issue of relationships in a Christian context in a searing personal testimony.

21 The Sacraments of Healing: Reconciliation and Anointing of the Sick
God Heals Us

Turn My Mourning into Dancing: Finding Hope in Hard Times, By Henri J. M. Nouwen. Focuses not on how to survive hard times but how to live fully in the midst of them and beyond.

The Monks of Tibhirine: Faith, Love and Terror in Algeria, by John W. Kiser. A moving and dramatic account of the murder by terrorists of seven Trappist monks who served their Muslim neighbors and the spirit of forgiveness that followed.

Easy   Accessible   Advanced

22 The Liturgy
Our Celebration Knows No End

Celebrating Good Liturgy: A Guide to the Ministries of the Mass, by James Martin, SJ (ed.). A collection of essays that will help all liturgical ministers (lectors, ministers of communion, ushers, altar servers, presiders, deacons, and so on) better understand their roles and perform them more faithfully.

With Burning Hearts: A Meditation on the Eucharistic Life, by Henri J. M. Nouwen. The meaning of the Eucharist for ourselves and our communities, based on the story of Emmaus.

Liturgy for the People of God (three volumes), by Charles E. Miller, CM. The late professor of liturgy at the Los Angeles archdiocesan seminary explains in simple language (1) The Foundations of Vatican II Liturgy, (2) The Celebration of the Eucharist, and (3) Sacraments and Other Matters Liturgical.

From Age to Age: How Christians Have Celebrated the Eucharist, by Edward Foley. A fascinating exploration of the history of liturgy, complete with illustrations.

Christian Prayer. This is the one-volume version of the Liturgy of the Hours for those who want to try it without committing to the four-volume edition.

A Banqueter's Guide to the All-Night Soup Kitchen of the Kingdom of God, by Patrick T. McCormick. An examination of the moral implications of the Eucharist through the metaphors of bread, table, body, and sacrifice.

23 The Saints
We Stand on the Shoulders of Those Who Came Before Us

Becoming Who You Are: Insights on the True Self from Thomas Merton and Other Saints, by James Martin, SJ. To be a saint is to be yourself. Learn why in this book.

My Life with the Saints, by James Martin, SJ. An often humorous, deeply personal account of how this Jesuit priest rediscovered various saints and how they have affected his life. Short chapters on each saint make it easy to pick up this book as you have time.

Life and Holiness, by Thomas Merton. How to be holy in your everyday life.

The Long Loneliness, by Dorothy Day. In her autobiography, this socialist bohemian describes her conversion to Catholicism and her work with the poorest of the poor in New York.

Making Saints: How the Catholic Church Determines Who Becomes a Saint, Who Doesn't, and Why, by Kenneth L. Woodward. If you've ever wondered how the process of canonization works behind the scenes, this detailed book is enlightening.

24 Mary
She Pondered These Things in Her Heart

Mary of Nazareth, Prophet of Peace, by John Dear, SJ. A collection of short meditations on peace as personified by Mary at the Annunciation, the Visitation, and in the Magnificat.

The Road to Guadalupe: A Modern Pilgrimage to the Godess of the Americas, by Eryk Hanut. An American couple enters into the mystery and meaning of Guadalupe in this travel journal.

All Generations Will Call Me Blessed: Mary at the Millennium, by Jim McManus, CSsR. A discussion of the meaning of Mary in the third millennium, written with an ecumenical tone.

25 Raising Children in the Faith
We Pass on a Gift of Great Price to Our Children

The Catholic Home: Celebrations and Traditions for Holidays, Feast Days and Every Day, by Meredith Gould. Despite some minor inaccuracies (the paperback version has some corrections), this is a helpful guide to living your faith at home.

The Bells of Nagasaki, by Takashi Nagai. Dr. Nagai's firsthand account of the atomic bomb's effects on Nagasaki.

26 Current Issues
You Are the Light of the World

Simplicity: The Freedom of Letting Go, by Richard Rohr. *This popular spiritual writer examines our individual role as Christians in today's world.*

Do We Worship the Same God? Comparing the Bible and the Qur'an, by George Dardess. *A deacon of the Diocese of Rochester offers a fascinating look at the similarities and differences between Christianity and Islam on some basic ideas. His other book,* Meeting Islam: A Guide for Christians, *is also excellent.*

Muhammad: A Prophet for Our Time, by Karen Armstrong. *A newer and simpler biography (2006), different from Armstrong's longer and more scholarly 1991* Muhammad: A Biography of the Prophet. *Have we confused you? Ask for the HarperCollins "Eminent Lives" version if you want the shorter book.*

Reading the Muslim Mind, by Hassan Hathout. *An introduction to Islam and explanation of how the Muslim world is different from the West.*

The Catholic Imagination, by Andrew Greeley. *A cultural and sociological exploration of what it means to be Catholic.*

The Battle for God: A History of Fundamentalism, by Karen Armstrong. *Today's greatest writer on the history of religion examines the roots and nature of fundamentalism in this* New York Times *bestseller.*

27 The Second Vatican Council
We Open Ourselves to the Modern World

Vatican II in Plain English *(three volumes):* The Council, The Constitutions, The Decrees and Declarations, by Bill Huebsch. *If you've ever tried to plow through a Vatican document and found your head hurting and your eyelids drooping, you will appreciate these moving, almost poetic paraphrases of the documents of Vatican II, together with a fascinating account of how they came to be.*

Vatican Council II, by Xavier Rhynne. *This writer used a pseudonym to report on the secret behind-the-scenes activities of the Council as they unfolded in a famous* New Yorker *series.*

On Consulting the Faithful in Matters of Doctrine, by John Henry Cardinal Newman. *The historic essay that made people look at the laity in a new way.*

Easy   Accessible   Advanced

Each one of us is called to a special place in the Kingdom. If we find that place we will be happy. If we do not find it, we can never be completely happy. For each one of us, there is only one thing necessary: to fulfill our own destiny, according to God's will, to be what God wants us to be.

—Thomas Merton, *No Man Is an Island*

What Do You Really Think?

DISCUSSION QUESTIONS

If you're reading this book in a book club, an adult education group, or RCIA, we hope these questions will help you to gain more insights into the various chapter topics. Don't try to make everyone answer all of them! That's way too much like homework. Choose the two or three from each chapter you think are most applicable to your group.

If you're reading this book on your own, maybe these questions can help you to reflect on what each chapter means to you in your own life. Some people find the practice of spiritual journaling helpful. Perhaps you might like to write answers to these questions in a notebook or diary.

As any good facilitator will tell you when offering questions for discussion, this is not a test! There are not right or wrong answers. So dig deep into your mind and heart and give yourself ample time to really get in touch with yourself. That will make for a much more interesting discussion or reflection. We hope you will find new insights into yourself and your relationship with God and your neighbors.

Chapter 1: God Speaks to a Longing in the Human Heart

How is your relationship with God different from the relationship ancient peoples had with false gods? How are your expectations of God different?

How does your belief in a revealed religion differ from how you would perceive God if you followed a natural religion?

What does the story of Abraham mean for your life today?

The Israelites often fell back to polytheism. Can you understand why? Do you face some of the same pressures in your own life?

How do you understand the life, death, and resurrection of Jesus as the ultimate form of revelation?

How does the fact that Muslims honor Mary affect your understanding of your own relationship with her?

Fundamentalism is a negative reaction to social change that seeks refuge in an imaginary past time when everything was better and truth was absolute. Have you ever experienced a tendency to fundamentalism in your own life? How did you deal with this impulse?

Chapter 2: From Age to Age God Gathers a People to Himself

God's covenant with the Jewish people has never been revoked. Does this fact cause you any problems with your faith in Christianity? Why or why not?

How do you integrate the fact that Jesus was a faithful Jew into your own relationship with him?

Does the fact that some stories in the Bible are not literally true make you uncomfortable? Why or why not?

How do you try to be prophetic on your own life?

Do you read the Hebrew Testament? What parts speak especially to you? Why?

Does the story of the prophet Hosea help you to understand your relationship with God? How does it make you feel?

Chapter 3: Revelation Is Alive and Working in Our Own Lives

Have you ever had an overwhelming experience of the presence or love of God? Describe it.

How is the way the authors of scripture were inspired differ from experiences of inspiration you may have had in your own life?

Many Christians lived and died before there was a New Testament. How do you imagine you might have lived a Christian life without the New Testament?

Moses led his people out of slavery to the Egyptians, saying, "Let my people go!" Who are "your people"? What slavery would you like to save them from? To whom would you say, "Let my people go"?

Have you read the Book of Revelation? What does it say to you?

Chapter 4: God Believes in Us Before We Believe in Him

Have you ever had a personal experience that vividly demonstrated to you that faith is a gift from God rather than something you achieve on your own? Describe it.

In whom do you have faith in your own life? Why?

How is your faith in science different from your faith in God?

Do you desire proof of the existence of God? Why or why not?

How does your own faith influence how you act in your everyday life? Give two examples.

Have you ever had an experience when your faith caused difficulties in your life? Describe that experience.

Have you ever really thought about what the Creed says as you recited it at Mass? How do you think this might be facilitated in the liturgy?

If you were a Christian whose loved ones had been persecuted by Paul, or perhaps even died

as a result of his efforts, how do you think you would react to suddenly seeing him preaching at Eucharist?

Do you know anyone who is an atheist? How do you react to that person? What does your interaction with him or her tell an atheist about Christians?

Chapter 5: God Is Love

What is your relationship with your own father like? Is it good or bad? Why? How does this affect your relationship with God as Father?

Can you imagine God as Mother? How does this make you feel? Why?

Has any intense experience of love ever caused you to think of God?

Think of your favorite love song. Imagine yourself singing it to God. How does this make you feel?

Have you ever been afraid of God? Do you still feel this way? Why or why not?

Have you ever been angry at God because he did not give you something you asked for in prayer? What was it you asked for? Did anything good come from the situation you found yourself in?

Have you ever had an experience when you actually heard God speak words to you? Describe it. How did you react?

Does your understanding of the Trinity have any influence on how you live your life? Why or why not?

Have you ever experienced God as the one who liberated you from some oppression or difficult time in your life? What was that like?

Have you ever described yourself as "spiritual but not religious"? Do you still feel that way? Why or why not? What are the pros and cons of religion?

Chapter 6: Jesus Changes the World

Why do you think the religious authorities disliked Jesus so much? How do you see this in relation to your own life, when you may have been hesitant to "rock the boat"?

As a Christian, do you see yourself as a revolutionary? Why or why not?

Is there an example in your life when you were faced with a difficult decision and decided to do what Jesus would have done? Describe it.

How have you experienced Jesus as the Truth in your own faith life?

Do you really believe that following Jesus can make you happy in this life, or do you think following him is a difficult way that requires you to give up things you want for the sake of being happy later in heaven? Can you give some examples?

Have you ever had to change some aspect of your life to be a better follower of Jesus? Did you do this hesitantly, happily, or with resentment?

Aside from your family and friends, how do you express and act upon your love for others?

Can you recall a time you realized that Christianity was more than a set of dogma and rules?

Chapter 7: The Breath of God Gives Life

Sit in silence for five minutes and be conscious of your breathing. Can you feel the breath of God within you? How does it make you feel?

Do you sometimes find yourself acting as though the Church needs you or someone else to save it or defend in some way? How do you reconcile this with the fact that the Holy Spirit will guide the Church?

The word *Paraclete* means "by your side." Have you ever had an experience of being aware that the Holy Spirit was by your side? Describe it.

If you have been confirmed, do you feel "set apart" in your own everyday life? Why or why not?

What is the individual path to holiness you feel you are called to? How does this differ from others?

Do you feel wise? Why or why not?

Who is wise among people you know? Why?

Explain the differences among the following: data, information, knowledge, wisdom. How are they different? How are they related?

How do you share or pass on your wisdom?

Chapter 8: The Kingdom of God Is Here and Now

Do you feel you need miracles in order to believe? Why or why not?

Can you give examples in your community of how the Kingdom of God is present in our midst?

Do you feel as though you belong to a religion that is countercultural or part of the status quo? Why?

Do you think Christianity should be countercultural or part of the status quo? Why?

What does your parish do well in regard to building the Kingdom of God? What could it do better?

What do you feel when you read or hear the Beatitudes? Do you feel a connection to them or do they seem distant and unrelated to your life? Why?

Do you feel the Ten Commandments should be posted in courthouses and public places? Are they posted in a central place in your church? Which is the more appropriate place?

What do you think of the depiction of Peter as a man of doubt and fears? How are you like Peter?

Chapter 9: God Always Wins

Imagine that you are having dinner with one of the religious leaders at the time of Jesus, and he was telling you all the sins that Jesus committed. How do you think you might respond? No, really...

Do you think Jesus could have accomplished his mission if he would have just been a little more careful of what the religious leaders thought? Why or why not?

Do you think that Christian religious leaders today sometimes obstruct the will of God? Can you give an example?

Is the death of Jesus beautiful to you? Why or why not?

The Gospels do not tell us how the disciples felt after abandoning Jesus after he was arrested. Take the role of one of the disciples. Discuss how you felt about your desertion and how you came to terms with it.

Consider a situation in history or current events where it seems like evil won out over good. Can you identify anything good that came out of it?

How do you feel about death?

Have you ever witnessed or heard about the death of someone where you could call that death beautiful? Describe it.

Chapter 10: We Don't Choose God; God Chooses Us

Can you give an example of a time when you experienced grace as amazing?

Do you sometimes feel as though you need to work to deserve God's gifts? Why do you think that is?

How does the Christian concept of free will differ from society's idea of freedom?

Do you think of sin mainly as things you do or as things you don't do? Why?

Describe the feeling you have when you go against your conscience. Does such an act ever result in a physical feeling of discomfort for you?

Do you really believe that true love of God and neighbor will help you avoid sin, or do you think you need external rules to keep you in line?

Do you believe that God wants you to be happy on Earth? How does that happiness differ from what the world might present to you as happiness?

Chapter 11: How We Show Respect to God

Consider some of your closest relationships. How are they like your relationship with God? How are they different?

Which of these descriptions of God best fits how you most often think of him: Lover, Friend, Father, Mother, Lawgiver, Judge. Why? Is that how you would like to think of God?

Why does Jesus make the love of God inseparable from love of neighbor?

What in your life competes with God for your attention? Are there times this thing becomes more important to you than God?

Have you ever claimed God's approval of some idea or action you were looking to justify? Was it a good thing or a bad thing?

Have you ever witnessed someone committing blasphemy—using God's name to justify or bless evil? What was that? Have you ever done this yourself?

How do you keep the Sabbath, aside from an hour at Mass?

Are you afraid of God, or in awe of God? What is the difference?

What is awesome about God's work in your own life?

What do you think is the difference between patriotism and nationalism? When does nationalism become especially dangerous? Can you give an example from American history or current events?

Chapter 12: How We Act Justly toward Others

Have you ever used the phrase, "I've got to look out for Number One"? What did you mean by that?

Do you feel your attitude at that time was fair to others?

Have you ever thought of the Ten Commandments being involved with justice before? Why or why not?

The treatment of Commandments 4–10 in this chapter is very brief. Can you think of other offenses against justice for each of these Commandments?

Can you think of an example of a secular law in your state that should be followed because it serves the common good? Are there any moral exceptions to it? Can you think of a law in your state that does not serve the common good and should not be obeyed?

Take a careful look at today's newspaper or a news Web site. How many stories can you find where someone is advocating the killing of others? What excuses do they give as to why they think this is justified? Do you think they're right or wrong?

All of us have stolen at some point by not giving to the poor what is theirs in justice. Can you think of an example of how you did this recently?

Have you ever spread a rumor about someone that was untrue or that you did not know to be true? What do you think would be the proper way to offer restitution to that person's reputation?

Have you ever coveted? Do you think coveting was more harmful to you or the person whose possessions or spouse you coveted? Why?

Look at the Web site of your representative to Congress. Choose the first piece of legislation you see that congressperson sponsored, cosponsored, or voted for. Was it legislation for the common good or to benefit some segment of the population at the expense of others? Was it just? Why or why not?

Do you think Thomas More should have signed the oath if it meant saving his life and providing for his family? What would you do?

Chapter 13: We Are Made for Glory

Do you do the right thing because you are afraid of hell or because it's the right thing to do? Has your approach changed in your life?

Do you think most people go to heaven or to hell? Why?

Can you think of someone you met who was truly totally selfish? Do you envy that person or feel sorry for them? Why?

Do you have an image of heaven? Describe it.

Do you have an image of hell? Describe it.

Do you seek to put the fear of hell in your children or the desire for heaven? Do you think you can do both? Why or why not?

Do you think the fear of hell is a productive way to get people to do the right thing? Why or why not?

What does Christian hope mean to you?

Can you imagine an eternity without space or time?

Why do you think the people of Chicago were so moved by the death of Cardinal Bernardin?

Chapter 14: God Invites Us to Conversation

Have you ever heard God speak to you in words? Describe that experience.

Can you explain how conversation with God is like the life of the Trinity?

Have you ever asked God for something very specific, only to discover later that it was good that God did not give you that? Describe the request and why it was not what you really needed.

Have you ever been angry that God did not grant something specific you asked for in prayer? Are you still angry? Why or why not?

During the Prayer of the Faithful at Mass, when we pray for the needs of the world, do you feel a genuine experience of prayer? Why or why not?

When was the last time you offered spontaneous prayer to God by yourself? What was the situation that caused you to do that?

Do you find the psalms helpful as prayer? Why or why not?

Have you ever experienced the prayer of union with God? What was it like?

Chapter 15: Following in the Footsteps of Jesus

Do you think of yourself primarily as a Catholic or as a disciple of Jesus Christ? Why?

How do you think you have experienced ongoing conversion in your life? Have you noticed this process in others?

Describe in your own words what the Good News is.

Do you think most people today view themselves primarily by their politics—as "conservative" or "liberal"—or by their faith? What about you?

Have you ever had an argument with someone about religion? How did that make you feel afterward? How would you have changed the way you approached that experience?

Do you think that service is a primary part of the Christian faith, or something for others who live different lives than yours?

Choose one issue from the front page of today's newspaper. Allow yourself at least fifteen minutes to daydream and imagine how that problem might be solved according to the principles of Christianity.

Do you think of yourself as a steward of the Church? Why or why not?

Chapter 16: We Are the Body of Christ

Why do you think the Church exists?

Have you ever feared that the Church may cease to exist unless some particular path was taken? How do you square that with your knowledge that we are guided by the Holy Spirit?

How often do you think of your own bishop? What do you think of him? Do you imagine yourself living within a community under his leadership? Why or why not?

Do you see your primary allegiance to your bishop or to the pope? Why?

How do you think the Church can be universal and still accept local customs?

Do you personally pray and work for the unity of all Christians?

Have you personally experienced in any way the pain of divided Christianity in your own life? How?

Do you think the United States is a "Christian nation"? Why or why not?

Chapter 17: We Are Each Called to Serve

Do you sometimes find yourself referring to "the Church" in the third person, as an entity somehow outside or above you? Why do you think that is?

Do you believe you are called to holiness? Why or why not?

What does "full, conscious, and active" participation in the liturgy mean to you?

Did you know that Church law gives you rights?

profile

CATHERINE OF SIENA

Although Catherine became a member of the Dominican third order in Tuscany at the age of eighteen, she always felt a part of the universal Church. She kept up on what was happening throughout the Church and got involved in her own way.

Catherine wrote letters. Hundreds of them. And not just to anyone: to kings and popes, calling them to account. Catherine was especially concerned about the papacy, which had moved from Rome to Avignon in France, where it remained from 1309 to 1377.

The Avignon papacy was notoriously corrupt. Catherine was disgusted with the greedy, hedonistic papal court and felt the Bishop of Rome should be in Rome. She told him so, repeatedly, and complained of the corruption. Eventually she convinced Gregory XI to return to Rome. Then a schism broke out with two (and later, three) rival claimants to Peter's chair. Catherine backed the pope who was validly elected, even as she noted his corruption.

Catherine warned crusaders to treat Muslims with respect: "They are our brothers, redeemed by the blood of Christ, just as we are," she wrote. She admonished the warring kings of Europe, pleading for peace.

People listened to Catherine because she walked the walk. She dedicated her life to serving the sick and poor. Powerful men stopped and listened when this fearless woman wrote to them, for she spoke the truth with passion.

How does the conduct of priests or deacons in your parish match up with the "job descriptions" outlined in this chapter?

Have you ever thought of the pope as a servant before? How does this make you feel to say this?

Why do you think people are afraid of embracing the Gospel? Do you sometimes feel that way?

When you read about people like Teresa of Kolkata, do you feel inspired to do likewise or discouraged that you could not? Why?

Chapter 18: The Lord Hears the Cry of the Poor

Sometimes people deride those interested in social justice issues as "bleeding hearts." What do you think about that?

Do you think it's possible for a parish community to be faithful Christians by participating in liturgy while having no community involvement in social justice? Why or why not?

Why do you think people can spend so much time arguing about who should clean a chalice and no time helping the poor? Do you ever find yourself slipping into this mode?

What examples of social sin can you think of in the United States?

Do you sometimes find yourself thinking of peace merely as the absence of war? How could you take steps to integrate the idea of true peace into your everyday life?

Chapter 19: We Have Died to Sin and Risen to a New Life

Do you think of the world as "sacramental"? Why or why not?

Many Catholics think of baptism only as something that takes away original sin. Do you think that is a complete understanding? What do you think have been the effects of this emphasis?

Which do you think is a stronger symbolism of baptism, immersion or pouring a little water on the head? Why?

Did you know that you were a priest, prophet, and king (or queen)? If not, how do you think knowing this earlier in your life may have made a difference?

What do you think are the pros and cons of restoring the sacrament of confirmation to its ancient sequence, after baptism and before first reception of Eucharist?

When you receive communion, the minister says "The Body of Christ." A deliberate decision was made in the liturgy not to say "This is the Body of Christ." Why do you think that is? Could it also apply to you?

What do you think are some of the dangers of individualism versus a strong sense of community?

Chapter 20: God Calls Each of Us to Our Own Way of Life

Sometimes we hear people say, "Father So-and-So married us." What do you think are the key differences between such a view and a realization that the couple themselves administers the sacrament to each other?

If you are married, do you feel grace at work in your marriage? Why or why not?

People are sometimes confused as to why someone would become a deacon when he cannot preside at Eucharist. What do you think? Do you think deacons are necessary? What do you think a parish without a deacon is missing out on?

Have you ever thought of the priesthood as a sacrament involving relationships? Why do you think that is?

There was once a reality show that followed several young men as they discerned whether or not they were called to become priests. The name of the show was God or the Girl. Do you think this is an apt way to describe such a decision? Do you think those that "chose the girl" were deciding against God?

Chapter 21: God Heals Us

In the 1950s, many Catholics thought one had to go to confession every week before receiving communion. Do you think this was a good or bad thing? Why or why not?

Do you have generally positive or generally negative feelings about the sacrament of reconciliation. Why?

Have you ever witnessed the sacrament of anointing of the sick? If so, how did it impact you? Do you think it would be helpful if more people could witness its celebration?

What would you say to someone who complained that they were anointed but their illness was not cured?

Do you think most members of your family think of anointing of the sick only for the dying? Do you think they would be receptive to celebrating it in a setting other than a deathbed? Why or why not?

How does the story of the Trappists of Tibhirine affect the way you think we should approach terrorism? Do you think the precepts of Christianity should have any voice in this issue?

Chapter 22: Our Celebration Knows No End

Do you think your local parish experiences liturgy as a celebration or as a rote ritual? Why do you think that is?

Why do you think some people are angry that various laypeople exercise ministries during the liturgy? What would you say to them?

Can you restate the four ways in which Jesus Christ becomes present in the Eucharist?

Would you say that the Eucharist is primarily an action or an object? Why?

Do you think of the homily as a part of the liturgy or a "break" in the liturgy? Why? What about announcements? Could you think of a reason why they should be a part of the liturgy?

Some liturgists have said, albeit with an eye to making us think, that the most important part of the liturgy is when we are told to "Go in peace." Why do you think one might say that?

List the advantages of thinking of the Eucharist as a meal in one column and as a sacrifice in another. Do you see any points that are contradictory? How do you think they can be reconciled?

Chapter 23: We Stand on the Shoulders of Those Who Came Before Us

How is our veneration of the saints like a family photo album? How is it different?

Have you ever thought of canonization as a grassroots phenomenon? How does this differ from how it is depicted in the media?

Do you have a relationship with any canonized saints? What is it like? How is it different from a relationship you may still feel with a dead family member? How is it similar?

How would you answer someone who said your "prayers" to saints were inappropriate because we should only pray to God?

Does it make you uncomfortable to think of saints as sinners? Why or why not?

How do you think society makes you feel as though you cannot really be holy?

Do you feel that to be holy you must become someone different than who you are? Why or why not?

Chapter 24: She Pondered These Things in Her Heart

Do you feel you have a relationship with Mary? Why or why not?

What does it mean to you that Mary is a virgin? Does this make you feel as though virgins are better than those who have had sex? Why or why not?

How does the fact that Mary was a Jew make you feel?

Do you picture Mary as someone passive or active?

Why do you think that some dictators have forbidden the public recitation of the Magnificat? Is there anything there that might challenge American society?

Do you crave miracles to "prove" your faith or private revelation to give you "the inside scoop"? Why or why not?

Chapter 25: We Pass on a Gift of Great Price to Our Children

Some people say a child should not be baptized if there are no plans to raise it as a Christian. How do you feel about that?

Why do you think your parents had you baptized?

If you are a parent, how do you fulfill your duty to be the primary educator of your children in the Faith?

What do you think are appropriate ways to allow children to make their own decisions? What are not?

Have you ever read *Humanae Vitae*, or do you base your thoughts on it primarily on media reports of what it says?

Statistically, most young people stop practicing their faith between the ages of thirteen and eighteen and pick it up again between the ages of twenty-five and thirty. The most common reason for the resumption of practice is the birth of a child. Does this fit your own life experience? How would you react to your own child not wanting to go to Mass?

How has the experience of divorce—in your own life or in the lives of loved ones—affected your relationship with God and the Church? Has it become stronger or weaker? Why do you think that is? What can be done about that?

Chapter 26: You Are the Light of the World

Describe the areas in which your views as a Christian differ from the views of society.

Do you consider yourself "conservative" or "liberal"? Do you think your basic categorization of yourself influences your views of Church life in a positive or negative way?

Do you sometimes find yourself accepting society's pragmatic views over the sometimes harder truths of the Gospel? How do you handle that?

Do you believe you have an innate sense of the Christian Faith?

When a document is issued by the pope or the Vatican or your bishop, do you accept the media's interpretation of what it says or do you try to read it for yourself?

Have you ever had difficulties accepting a Church teaching (not what the media said it was, but what you read yourself)? How did you handle that?

Do you think of morality primarily as sexual ethics? What are other areas of life that deal with morality?

Do you feel that those who believe abortion is wrong must all agree on a single way to deal with abortion? Why or why not?

How do you feel about Muslims? Do you think your opinion might change if you personally knew some Muslims well as friends?

Chapter 27: We Open Ourselves to the Modern World

If you're not old enough to know what it was like to be a Catholic before the Second Vatican Council, ask your parents or grandparents. Do they think life was better before or after the Council? Why? What do you think?

Do you believe the Holy Spirit was at work in the Council? Why or why not?

After more than forty years, why do you think some people are still angry and hurt about the reforms of the Council?

How would your life be different if the Council had never taken place?

Some people think the reforms of the Council should be rolled back, and others say there has not been enough time to allow them to flourish. What do you think?

How does the fact that the Protestant Reformers had many valid concerns make you feel? Do you feel as though you need to somehow defend these abuses? Why or why not?

Chapter 28: We Look Forward to the End of Time

Do you fear the Second Coming and the end of the world? Why or why not?

Do you think the Second Coming will be something joyful or something frightening? Why?

Why do you think so many people are obsessed with the End of Time?

If you knew the end of the world was tomorrow, would that change the way you live your life today? Why or why not?

How do you balance trust in God with the fact that you must plan for the future?

A Vocabulary of Faith

GLOSSARY

Our faith is more than rules, definitions and lists. It's about conversion, discipleship, and evangelization. Still, in our culture, some words that originated in the Church are now used for other purposes and their original meaning can become clouded. We do use words as a community of faith, and it's important to have clear meanings when we talk about faith, especially when others may have different understandings of our words. So here we go!

Abba Aramaic: "Father." This title for God given us by Jesus was so intimate that we might better translate it as "Daddy," or even "Da-da." Don't pronounce it like the Swedish disco group; it's pronounced AH-bah.

Abrahamic Refers to the three great monotheistic faiths that call Abraham their father in faith: Judaism, Christianity, and Islam.

adoration See **praise**.

Advent The liturgical season of four Sundays preceding Christmas. This is not the same as the secular "Christmas season." Advent is a time to prepare for the coming of Christ at Christmas, in our hearts and at the Second Coming. It should be devoid of Christmas decorations, songs, and such in our churches and in our homes.

alms Possessions given to the poor or outcast.

altar The table on which the Eucharistic Prayer is offered and from which we receive the Body and Blood of Christ. The altar is reminiscent of the days of the Jewish Temple, when sacrifices were offered on altars. The sacrifice of the new covenant is offered on the Christian altar. For this reason, the altar is also a symbol of Christ. That's why we bow to it when we pass in front of it.

ambo The podium (sometimes called a "pulpit") where the Word of God is proclaimed during the Eucharist. This is the second of two tables used at the Eucharist. The ambo is the table of the Word; the altar is the Table of the Sacrament.

American exceptionalism The idea that citizens of the United States are better, more moral, or of greater worth than other people, or that the United States government is an institution favored by God. Just for the record, it's wrong and is against Christian beliefs!

anawim Hebrew: "outcast."

angel An intelligent being that is entirely spiritual; that is, without a body. Angels are a different order of created beings from humans and are generally depicted as messengers of God. People do not become angels when they die, no matter how many sappy movies may claim this; people become saints.

Anglican Churches that are members of the worldwide Anglican Communion, descended from the Church of England and under the leadership of the Archbishop of Canterbury. Most Anglicans do not consider themselves Protestant, but rather a separate branch of Christianity. In the United States, Anglicans are members of the Episcopal Church.

anoint To set one aside by placing oil on him or her.

anointing of the sick The sacrament whereby an individual who is sick or dying is anointed to bring about healing. Note: Healing does not always mean a physical cure.

apologetics The study and practice of explaining the Christian faith to non-Christians. By extension, it may also mean explaining the Christian faith to nominal Christians or explaining the Catholic faith to non-Catholics. Many people mistakenly equate apologetics with evangelization; apologetics is an intellectual approach while evangelization calls for a conversion of the heart.

Apostle Greek: *apostoloi*, meaning "emissaries," or "those who are sent." One of the twelve principle disciples of Jesus.

Ascension The event when the body of Jesus was taken up from Earth after the resurrection.

asceticism An approach to Christian spirituality characterized by denial of the senses, such as fasting and poverty, to bring spiritual reality into greater focus.

Annunciation The event when God asked Mary to become the mother of Jesus.

apocrypha Ancient Christian writings that did not end up in the New Testament. These writings occasionally resurface in the media as "lost gospels" that supposedly threaten the very foundations of Christianity. They are then promptly overshadowed by the next celebrity wedding.

B

baptism The first of the sacraments, whereby one becomes a member of the Church.

Beatitudes Nine maxims given by Jesus that characterize the Christian life.

Bible A collection of sacred texts of various genres, inspired by God and written at different times for different reasons.

bishop From the Greek *episkopos*, which means "overseer." A successor of the Apostles. The bishop is a sign of unity. His role is to teach and guide the Christian community and to help us along the path toward holiness. The bishop is the highest of the threefold hierarchical clergy: bishop, priest, and deacon. There is no higher dignity than bishop. Archbishops are bishops. The pope is a bishop.

blasphemy To use God's name for evil purposes.

Body of Christ The Church. Also the Eucharistic element under the appearance of bread.

C

canon law The system of law governing Church life. These laws are contained in the Code of

Canon Law. And yes, there is such a thing as a canon lawyer. Often we in the United States are confronted with matters of canon law that we can misunderstand. Our American system of law is based on English Common Law, which legislates the lowest common denominator to which all are held equally. Canon law, however, is based on the principles of Roman law, which legislates the ideal and allows for exceptions. This difference in philosophy of law often makes for tense relations between Americans and the Vatican when rules are introduced; folks in the Vatican are often amused to hear Americans assume they must follow such laws to the letter.

canonization A formal declaration that a particular person is in heaven. The process leading to canonization is an odd mix of science, bureaucracy, scholarly research, lobbying, public relations, prayer, and faith. As a rule, faith wins out. Chalk up another one for the Holy Spirit.

cardinal An advisor to the Bishop of Rome. While cardinals today are usually bishops (often chosen to represent the major cities of the world), priests and even deacons and laypeople have served as cardinals at various times in history. Applications are not accepted!

catechesis The lifelong process of education and spiritual formation of the baptized. No, you do not know everything there is to know when you are confirmed!

catechumen An adult preparing for baptism.

cathedra The bishop's chair.

cathedral The mother church of a diocese. The word comes from the Latin word *cathedra*, which means "chair." So a cathedral is a church with a chair: the chair of the bishop, the sign of the unity of the local Church (diocese). Some people use the word *cathedral* to refer to any large or especially impressive church building. They are mistaken.

catholic Greek: "universal." When used with a small *c*, refers to the Body of Christ throughout the world. Spelled with a capital *C*? See the next entry!

Catholic When used with a capital *C*, refers to those Churches in union with the Bishop of Rome, the pope. While many think this term is synonymous with Roman Catholics, it's a much broader term that includes twenty-three Churches, of which the Roman (also called the Latin Church) is the largest. Each of the Churches in union with

Rome retain its own liturgy, theology, customs, and system of governance. Here is a list of all the Churches in union with Rome:

Western Church (Roman Catholic Church) Includes the following liturgical traditions, or "rites": Latin (most Roman Catholics are of the Latin rite); Mozarbic; Ambrosian; Anglican Use

Eastern Churches of the Alexandrian Tradition:
• Coptic Catholic Church
• Ethiopian Catholic Church

Eastern Churches of the Antiochian Tradition:
• Maronite Church
• Syrian Catholic Church
• Syro-Malankar Catholic Church

Eastern Churches of the Armenian Tradition:
• Armenian Catholic Church

Eastern Churches of the Chaldean Tradition:
• Chaldean Catholic Church
• Syro-Malabar Catholic Church

Eastern Churches of the Byzantine Tradition:
• Albanian Byzantine Catholic Church
• Belarusian Greek Catholic Church
• Bulgarian Greek Catholic Church
• Byzantine Church of the Eparchy of Križevci
• Greek Byzantine Catholic Church
• Hungarian Greek Catholic Church
• Italo-Albanian Catholic Church
• Macedonian Greek Catholic Church
• Melkite Greek Catholic Church
• Romanian Church United with Rome
• Russian Byzantine Catholic Church
• Ruthenian Catholic Church
• Slovak Greek Catholic Church
• Ukranian Greek Catholic Church

celibacy The state of being unmarried. Diocesan clergy (priests and single deacons) make a promise not to get married for the sake of the Kingdom of God; they do not take vows. By taking on the unmarried state, they accept the responsibility of all single people: not to have sex outside marriage. See **religious**.

chastity The virtue of living one's sexuality faithfully within the requirements of his or her state in life. In the context of the consecrated life, *chastity* means vowed abstinence from sexual activity.

clergy Those ordained to service of the community through the sacrament of holy orders: bishops, priests, and deacons.

Chrism Olive oil mixed with perfume used in the sacraments of baptism and confirmation. The Chrism is blessed each year in the cathedral church by the bishop during Holy Week, along with the Oils of Catechumens and the Sick, for use in the parishes of the diocese throughout the year.

chrismation See **confirmation**.

Christ From the Greek word *Christos*, meaning "anointed" or "chosen." It's a title of Jesus, not, as many suppose, his last name!

Christian A person who has been baptized. As an adjective, it refers to those things pertaining to the teachings of Jesus or the religion founded on those teachings.

chosen people The ancient Israelites and their descendants, the Jews.

church With a small *c*, the building in which Christians worship.

Church Latin: *ecclesia*, from the Greek word *ekkalein*, meaning "to call out of." With a large *C*, a community of Christians gathered around a bishop (the local, or particular Church), which in turn is united to other Churches in the larger (universal) Church.

Christmas English: "Christ's Mass." The celebration of the birth of Jesus, the second holiest day after Easter. The liturgical Christmas Season begins at sundown on Christmas Eve. The traditional Twelve Days of Christmas are from Christmas to January 6, the old date of the Feast of the Epiphany (January 6 is the celebration of Christmas for some Eastern Churches). Christians do not celebrate Christmas before December 24, no matter what Banana Republic may say. See **Advent**.

collegiality/college A *college* is a body, specifically in the Church the body of bishops throughout the world. When we say the bishops are acting *collegially*, we mean they are acting collaboratively as a group. By the way, the word *college* is also used to describe the body of cardinals: the College of Cardinals.

communion From the Latin *communio*, meaning "union with." The state of fraternal and Christian unity with others, for example, to be in communion with the Bishop of Rome, or the communion of saints. It also refers to the practice of receiving the Body and Blood of Christ during the Eucharist, because by that act we are in union with Christ and with the People of God, the Body of Christ.

communion of saints The vast group of *all* people who have died—not just canonized saints—who offered witness to the Gospel during their lives on earth and are now experiencing the joy of heaven.

community The essential forum for the practice of Christianity. Christians are saved in community.

confirmation A sacrament that completes baptism by anointing and the invocation of the Holy Spirit. Contrary to what some may think, it is not a "graduation from church" or the end of learning about the Christian life.

conscience The inner voice God has placed in our hearts to guide us in choosing good and avoiding evil.

consecrated life The life of those who have chosen to live in community according to the evangelical counsels of poverty, chastity, and obedience. Also called "religious life."

consensus fidelium The worldwide unity in faith of all the members of the Church.

consumerism The practice of being so involved in obtaining and hoarding possessions that we are not fully attuned to God or neighbor.

conversion A lifelong process of conforming ourselves to the person and teaching of Jesus.

countercultural Against the common assumptions and beliefs of the dominant culture.

Counter-Reformation The period of history in the Roman Church extending from the sixteenth to the twentieth centuries as a response to the Protestant Reformation. The Counter-Reformation was characterized at first as an institutional reform of the Roman Church but later became a spirit of defensiveness and suspicion, a mindset sometimes referred to as "fortress Church." The Counter-Reformation ended with the Second Vatican Council.

covenant A relationship between God and a people. A covenant is more binding than a simple agreement, and for all covenants mentioned in the Hebrew Testament, God gave signs to seal them.

Creation Everything created by God, known or unknown, visible or invisible.

creed A statement of Christian beliefs. The two most common creeds are the Nicene Creed and the Apostle's Creed.

crucifixion The event when Jesus was executed by being nailed to a cross by the Roman government.

D

deacon From the Greek *diakonos*, which means "servant." The deacon is one of the three orders of clergy. The role of the deacon is as a servant of the Word (proclaiming the Gospel, preaching, and teaching), a servant of the altar (carrying out certain duties during the Eucharist), and a servant of love (ministering to the poor and outcast of the community).

devotion A prayer or ritual that is not liturgical.

deuterocanonical Those books accepted as part of the Hebrew Testament by Roman Catholics or Churches of the East but not typically by Protestants. For Roman Catholics they are the Books of Tobit, Judith, Wisdom, Sirach, Baruch, 1 Maccabees, 2 Maccabees, and portions of Esther, Jeremiah, and Daniel. Most Orthodox Churches also include 3 and 4 Maccabees, 1 Esdras, Odes (Prayer of Manasseh), and Psalm 151. Some Orthodox Churches also include 2 Esdras, Jubilees, Enoch, 2 Baruch, and Psalms 152–55.

deification or **divinization** For Eastern Christians, the crowning summit of the life of grace whereby we share to some degree in the nature of God.

devil The fallen angel who can sometimes prompt us to sin. We should remember that the power of the devil is often overstated. Teresa of Ávila said, "I am more afraid of those who fear the devil than I am of the devil himself." Many people have pointed out that the devil's greatest achievements are not so much to do bad things—"The devil made me do it"—but to not do good things. This is why he is sometimes called the spirit of laziness. And a good point is made by those who say that the devil is happiest when people argue about mind-numbingly insignificant churchy things—like

what color of vestments should be worn, or what kinds of songs should be sung, or whether gold or glass is better for chalices—because then they are distracted from the real mission of the Church.

diocese The local Church, comprised of many parishes and guided by a bishop.

discernment The process of opening ourselves to understand God's will for our own life through prayer and reflection.

disciple A follower of Jesus Christ.

discipleship The practice of following Jesus, characterized by conversion, evangelization, and stewardship.

doctor Latin: "teacher."

doxology A proclamation of praise to God, often ending a prayer. The most common doxology is "Glory be to the Father and to the Son and the Holy Spirit, as it was in the beginning is now and ever shall be, world without end. Amen."

dualism An approach that wrongly teaches an essential division of the world into good and evil forces, sometimes even to the point where good and evil are considered equal.

E

Easter The primary celebration of the Christian year, honoring the resurrection of Jesus from the dead.

Eastern Catholic. Any of twenty-two autonomous Churches of various traditions in union with Rome. Each Eastern Catholic Church maintains a theology, spirituality, liturgy, and heritage remarkably similar to an Orthodox counterpart, with the exception of the Maronite Church, for which no Orthodox counterpart exists. See **Catholic.**

Eastern Church or **Churches of the East** Any of the Churches, whether Catholic or Orthodox, that represent ancient traditions of the Near East. See **Catholic** and **Orthodox.**

ecumenical council One of twenty-one international gatherings of bishops that have occurred since the earliest days of the Church to settle matters of teaching or practice.

ecumenism The movement that seeks to end the divisions between Christians by praying and working for the full, visible unity of all Christians in our lifetimes. All Christians are called to work for ecumenism. The full, visible unity of all Christians presupposes that such a convergence of Christian traditions will be characterized by diversity rather than institutional uniformity.

Emmanuel Hebrew: "God with us." A title of Jesus. See Isaiah 7:14.

Epiphany From the Greek word meaning "manifestation." Epiphany is the celebration of the manifestation of Christ to the world, when the Three Magi, representing the Gentiles, came to worship him. In the West, Epiphany was celebrated twelve days after Christmas, on January 6 (hence the Twelve Days of Christmas); it is still celebrated on that day by some Orthodox Churches as Christmas. But the Roman Church has transferred the feast to the Sunday after the first Saturday of January. Confused? It's still a lot easier than calculating the date of Easter!

eternity The state of existence unconstrained by time or space in which God lives.

Eucharist From the Greek *eucharistia*, meaning "thanksgiving." The central act of Christian worship. It is also called by a variety of names according to various traditions: the Mass, Divine Liturgy, *Badarak*, and other terms. Roman Catholic theology holds that Christ is present in the Eucharist in four ways: in the Word of God, in the person of the priest, in the assembly, and under the appearance of bread and wine.

evangelical counsels The practice of living by poverty, chastity, and obedience, usually by vows. See **religious**.

evangelist/evangelization The act of preaching the Good News to the world. Evangelization begins with self-conversion and applying the principles of the Christian life to ourselves. We then offer witness to those around us by our example and acceptance of our neighbors. Finally, we share our faith in word when appropriate. Evangelization is often confused with apologetics and catechesis, although catechesis is a part of our own ongoing evangelization. Evangelization is also different from the Protestant term *evangelism*, which often involves proselytism. Proselytism, the seeking out of people in an effort to convert them by intellectual persuasion, pressure, or force, is not considered a part of true evangelization.

evil The absence of good. Evil has no existence in and of itself; it is a vacuum where good should be.

excommunication To place oneself outside the Church community. The purpose of an excommunication is to strongly encourage a person to think long and hard about what they have done and to seek reconciliation with the Christian community. See **schism**.

faith A free gift of God that enables us to believe and to act on those beliefs.

Faith When used with a capital *F*, it generally means the Christian religion.

faithful That would be you.

fast To abstain from food as a way of reminding ourselves of our total reliance on God.

Father The first person of the Trinity.

fear of the Lord The sense of awe and wonder toward God.

filioque Latin: "and the Son." These words were added to the Nicene Creed in the Roman liturgy around the year 1000, referring to the Holy Spirit proceeding from the Father and the Son. The Eastern Churches resisted adding this phrase to the Creed. This gave people of both East and West a reason to argue about an obscure philosophical point. Today we realize this supposed disagreement was really only two ways of looking at the same thing.

forgiveness The required approach of the Christian to those who harm us.

free will The capacity of human beings to choose to serve God—or not—without compulsion or force on the part of God.

G

God The one Supreme Being who created and sustains all Creation, reveals himself to humanity, has involvement in human history, and who desires a relationship with each human being.

Golden Rule A teaching of Jesus: "Do to others as you would have them do to you."

good The intrinsic characteristic of God and goodness in humans is the state of conforming to God's plan.

Good News The proclamation of Jesus that we can be free from sin, fear, doubt, and death through the establishment of the Kingdom of God. It refers to all the teachings of Jesus, his saving act in the passion, crucifixion, and resurrection as well as his promise to come again.

Gospel Old English word meaning "Good News." Also refers to one of the four central books of the New Testament (Matthew, Mark, Luke, and John) and the reading from one of those books during the Eucharist by the deacon. If no deacon is present, the priest reads the Gospel.

Gospel Book The liturgical book carried in procession by the deacon during the liturgy. It contains the Gospel readings for each Sunday of the year, read by the deacon.

grace A share in the life of God, freely given by God with no merit on our part.

Great Commandment A teaching of Jesus: "You shall love the Lord your God with all your heart and with all your soul, with all your mind and with all your strength. And you shall love your neighbor as yourself" Mark 12:28–34.

H

heaven The state of eternal union with God.

Hebrew Testament The collection of Jewish scripture that is part of the Bible. Also called "Old Testament."

hell The state of eternal separation from God.

heresy Teaching or holding beliefs contrary to the Faith of Christianity. It is an offense against truth, which is from God and is not relative but is determined from the guidance of the Holy Spirit.

heroic virtue The characteristic of the saints. Each saint has led a life that demonstrates at least one particular virtue we are called to imitate.

hierarchy Greek: "holy order." The established structure for the guidance and order of the Church on Earth

holiness The state of being in alignment with God's plan for our individual life and in right relationship with God. The nature of holiness varies with each of us according to our own personality and talents.

holy orders The sacrament by which one is set aside for service to the community as a bishop, priest, or deacon.

Holy Spirit The third person of the Trinity.

Holy Week The week leading up to the celebration of Easter. Holy Week begins with Palm Sunday of the Lord's Passion and includes the Holy Triduum (Holy Thursday, Good Friday, and Holy Saturday).

homily Also called a "sermon," it is that part of the liturgy where a bishop, priest, or deacon expounds on the scripture of the day or the meaning of the day's celebration.

hypocrisy The state of not practicing what you preach. Hypocrisy is a particularly dangerous tendency in religion, a fault for which Jesus had little patience. See **reform**.

I

icon No, not a little symbol on your computer, but an image of Christ, Mary, a saint, or an event in the life of Christ or the saints. Icons are used primarily in the Eastern Churches, but also in the Western Churches. The proper term for the making of icons is to "write an icon," not "paint."

iconoclast This word is often used today in secular society as a compliment, referring to someone who stands for truth and originality when others cling irrationally to the status quo. That's not what it means for Christians. *Iconoclast* comes from a Greek word that means "breaking of images." They were people who—though rightly concerned about idolatry—took axes into churches and destroyed ancient sacred art in wild frenzies. So unless you think it would be a great adventure to rampage through the Met or LACMA or the Art Institute or the De Young smashing masterpieces, iconoclasm is not a good thing.

idol A physical representation of a false god worshipped as one should only worship the One God, or any other thing or person we make more important than or equal to God. See **idolatry**.

idolatry The practice of worshipping false gods. Idolatry is not limited to formal worship of a supposed deity, but also includes making anything equal to or more important than God. A rule of thumb: If it's something you'd rather do than worship God, you may have a problem with idolatry.

Immaculate Conception The event whereby Mary was conceived without the natural tendency toward evil that characterizes other humans.

immersion The ancient practice of submerging a person during the rite of baptism, now restored in all Catholic Churches.

incarnation From a Latin word meaning "into flesh." The incarnation is the Word (Jesus Christ) becoming human and living among us.

individualism An undue emphasis on the individual rather than the community. Individualism, while considered a great virtue by American society, is contrary to the ideals of Christianity, in which we are saved primarily as a community in and through the Church.

infallibility Being without error in belief.

initiation The three sacraments that bring a person into the life of the Church: baptism, confirmation, and Eucharist.

intercessory The form of prayer in which we make requests of God on behalf of others.

interfaith/interreligious The practice of dialogue and mutual cooperation between Christians and members of non-Christian religions. Interfaith relations are different from ecumenism; while ecumenism assumes the eventual convergence of all Christians, interfaith relations do not assume convergence but rather good will and working together to solve the problems facing society.

J

Jesus From the Hebrew: *Yeshua*, meaning "God saves." The Son of God.

Jew A person faithful to the ancient covenant between God and the People of Israel.

just war theory While war is always evil, Christian tradition does allow for exception as to when a nation may engage in war, based on the right to self-defense. The basis for an exemption to the universal Christian law against war may exist if all these conditions are present prior to waging defensive (and only defensive) war:

The damage inflicted by the aggressor on the nation or community of nations must be lasting, grave, and certain;

All other means of putting an end to the injustice must have been shown to be impractical or ineffective, so that war is the last resort;

War may only be waged by a legitimate authority;

There must be serious prospects of success;

The use of arms must not produce evils and disorders graver than the evil to be eliminated; the actions must be proportionate to the original offense.

And these conditions must be met in the actual waging of war:

No military action may be directed at civilians or with the aim of destroying nonmilitary targets, residential areas, civilian infrastructure, and so on.

Military actions must be proportionate; for example, you cannot destroy a city because the enemy destroyed a building.

All of these conditions must be met for a nation to have just cause to wage war, and even then, that does not make the war good; it only makes it an *unavoidable* evil. The use of nuclear weapons is generally considered by its nature to be incompatible with the theory of a just war.

justice Our responsibility to give God and neighbor what is due them.

K

king/queen One of the three baptismal dignities of a Christian (priest, prophet, and king) that requires us to work for a just society. This dignity is conferred at baptism by anointing with the Sacred Chrism, an ancient part of coronation rites.

Kingdom of God or **Reign of God** The saving reality of God's working among us on Earth.

L

laity From the Greek word *laios*, meaning "initiated." Funny, isn't it; in the secular world, *lay* means uninitiated. In the old days it was kind of the same in the Church. The laypeople were those who weren't ordained, so they pretty much counted for nothing. Now, however, there is a new approach that is more faithful to the original meaning of the word. You are initiated. You are a full member. You are the Church. Act like it. Today.

Last Supper The observance of the Jewish feast of Passover (*Pesach*) Jesus celebrated with his disciples the night he was arrested.

Latin rite The liturgical, theological, and canonical tradition of most Roman Catholics.

Law The 613 commands gleaned from the Hebrew Testament and related commentary. Paul said the Christian was free from the rigors of the Law. Jesus said that he came not to abolish but to fulfill the Law and the Prophets.

lay See **laity**.

lectio divina Latin: "divine reading." The practice of entering into union with God through prayerful reading of scripture.

lectionary The book of scriptural readings used in the liturgy. The lectionary specifies the Sunday readings in a three-year cycle with one of the Synoptic Gospels being used primarily for that year: Year A (Matthew), Year B (Mark), and Year C (Luke). Readings from the Gospel of John are sprinkled throughout each year. The Roman Lectionary is used by Roman Catholics; many other Christian traditions use the Common Lectionary, an ecumenical version based on the Roman Lectionary. Some traditions have instituted minor variations in the Common Lectionary. As a general rule, all Christian traditions that use a lectionary will have the same readings every Sunday: Roman

Catholics, Anglicans, Lutherans, Methodists, Presbyterians, and so on.

Lent The penitential season of forty days preceding Easter characterized by giving of alms, fasting, and prayer.

liturgy From the Greek *leitourgia*, meaning "the work of the people." The public worship of the Church, comprised of the celebration of the Eucharist, the sacraments, the Liturgy of the Hours, and the liturgical year.

Liturgy of the Hours The daily prayer of the Church, made up of collections of psalms and readings specified for various times of each day.

Lord A translation of the Hebrew word *Elohim*, used in place of the name of God in scripture and prayer: LORD. When not entirely capitalized, it can refer either to the Father (*Elohim*) or to Jesus as a translation of the Hebrew or Greek honorifics for "teacher" or "master."

love The highest level of experience, forming the essence of God, of which humans can partake.

M

magisterium The teaching authority of the hierarchy. Our own bishop (and the priests and deacons who have a share in his authority), the bishops of a nation gathered together, the bishops of the world teaching in a council, and the Bishop of Rome all are a part of the teaching authority of the Church. The different levels of the magisterium have various levels of authority to state what we should believe. Often these teachings are expressed in official documents. Within official papal documents, there is a ranking of importance: (1) encyclical, (2) apostolic letter, (3) apostolic exhortation, (4) occasional papal addresses, *motu proprio*, and so on. Bishops may also issue pastoral letters, which are the highest form of official teaching for that diocese.

maranatha Greek: "Come, Lord."

marriage/matrimony The sacrament uniting a man and a woman in a lifelong bond for the purpose of sharing love between them and any children they may have.

Mary The mother of Jesus. She was conceived without original sin, conceived Jesus as a virgin, and is referred to as the "Mother of God."

martyr One who dies for his or her faith.

Mass See **Eucharist**.

meditation A form of silent prayer, generally mystical in nature, but sometimes an intellectual exercise.

mercy God's response to those who act wrongly and would otherwise deserve punishment.

Messiah From the Hebrew *Moshiach*, "anointed one." The promised savior, Jesus.

minister/ministry Any person who performs an act of Christian service. Liturgical ministers include lectors, altar servers, extraordinary ministers of Communion, ushers, cantors, musicians, and others. Other forms of ministry may be in the area of social justice, such as ministry to the homeless or other outcasts.

miracle An intervention by God in the regular course of human events.

monotheism The belief in one God.

monsignor From the French *mon seigneur*, meaning "my lord." An honorary title bestowed on some priests for various reasons. Technically, this means they are members of the papal household. In some countries, this is the title for a bishop.

mystagogy That stage in the process of the Rite of Christian Initiation of Adults (RCIA) when neophytes enter more deeply into the mysteries of the Christian Faith.

mystery A revealed truth that invites reflection.

mysticism An intense awareness or experience of the presence and awe of God.

THÉRÈSE OF LISIEUX

We tend to think of saints as those who have accomplished extraordinary things. Things far greater then we would ever be capable of achieving ourselves. People bigger than life itself! But the witness of Thérèse tells a different story.

Thérèse responded to her calling to consecrated life when she was only a teenager. She became a nun in the Carmelite order. Thérèse was really an ordinary young woman. Nothing fancy for Thérèse; she was sincerely devoted to her God by the simple way she lived her life. Thérèse lived every day with complete confidence in God's love for her and all people. She said what matters in life is "not great deeds, but great love." In fact she described her entire life as "a little way of spiritual childhood." Her heaven was really doing good while she was here on Earth in the little things of everyday life, like washing dishes or doing something extra for a sister who did not like her.

Thérèse died of tuberculosis in 1897 at the age of twenty-four. The last year and a half of her life was a time of physical suffering and spiritual trial. She gives us an example of a life of love and acceptance. By her example we are inspired to respond to the love of God, extend that love to all people, and accept the trials of our life. No matter how quiet or simple our life, we can be great in the eyes of God.

profile

natural religion A religion that does not claim revelation, but was developed through human intellect, contemplation, or philosophy.

neophyte A person recently initiated into the Church.

New Testament The Christian scripture, containing the four Gospels, Acts of the Apostles, letters, and the Book of Revelation.

O

Old Testament See **Hebrew Testament.**

oral tradition The practice of telling stories over and over again, from generation to generation, before they were written down.

Ordinary Time The periods of the liturgical year outside the seasons of Advent, Christmas, Lent, and Easter when the weeks are counted in ordinal numbers.

ordination The ceremony whereby holy orders are conferred on bishops, priests, and deacons.

original sin The tendency we inherit from our ancestors to avoid the good and embrace what is evil, derived from a primordial act of disobedience to God.

Orthodox Greek: "correct belief." Any of the Eastern Churches not in communion with Rome. The *Eastern Orthodox Churches* are generally of the Byzantine heritage, are usually of a particular ethnicity or nation (for example, Greek, Russian), and are in communion with the Ecumenical Patriarch of Constantinople. While the somewhat

arbitrary date of 1054 is often given for the split between the Orthodox and the Catholics, it was a gradual process of separation over centuries brought about by differences in culture, language, geography, and politics. The *Oriental Orthodox Churches* are of five separate traditions (sometimes called pre-Chalcedonian) whose autonomy dates from the fifth century: Armenian, Coptic, Ethiopian, Indian (or Malankara), and Syriac (or Syrian). The Assyrian Church is of a separate tradition. Each Orthodox tradition is present in a corresponding Eastern Catholic Church, virtually indistinguishable in theology, liturgy, and customs.

outcast Those who are rejected by "respectable" society and rely on God—and, by extension, the community of faith—to protect them.

P

parable A type of story used by Jesus to communicate the nature of the Kingdom of God. Parables are drawn from nature or human experience with a twist and are often subject to more than one interpretation. Jesus rarely explained his parables, and they are generally not meant to be read as simple allegories, but invite a deeper form of interpretation.

Paraclete Greek: "One who is with you" or "Advocate." The Holy Spirit.

parish The smallest geographical division of a diocese. It is in a parish that most Christians have their experience as Church in community.

Parousia The Second Coming of Jesus at the end of time.

Passover The Jewish feast of *Pesach* celebrating the liberation of the Jews from slavery in Egypt. The Christian Passover is Easter.

patriarch/matriarch Ancient progenitors of the Israelite people.

peace The state of justice, mutual love, and submission to God's will that should characterize us as individuals, communities and nations.

Pentateuch Greek: "five books." The first five books of the Hebrew Testament (also called the *Torah*): Genesis, Exodus, Leviticus, Numbers, and Deuteronomy.

Pentecost Greek: "fifty days." The event where the Holy Spirit came to the first disciples, popularly called the "birthday of the Church."

perjury A lie told while swearing by God.

petitionary See **intercessory.**

pilgrimage A form of prayer that involves a journey to a sacred place.

Pilgrim Church The concept popularized by the Second Vatican Council that describes the Church as a wanderer in every time and place, bringing the Good News to all people and learning from every culture.

polytheism The worship of or belief in more than one god.

pope The Bishop of Rome. As the successor of Saint Peter, the first Bishop of Rome, the pope is the head of the Catholic Church. Most Christians accept or are willing to accept the primacy of the pope in a united Christianity; however, differences in what that primacy means and how it is exercised in everyday life continue to slow the pace of ecumenism. It is important to remember that the pope is a bishop, not a living saint.

praise The form of prayer that honors God because he is God, with simple wonder at his power and loving kindness.

prayer Conversation with God.

priest One of the three levels of clergy. The priest is the bishop's coworker, along with the deacon. The priest has care of souls and leads the Christian community in the celebration of the Eucharist and the sacraments. All those who are baptized are also priests (the priesthood of the baptized rather than the ordained priesthood), in that they are called to pray for the whole world. This is one of the three baptismal dignities of the Christian (priest, prophet, and king).

prophet One who is driven by an intimate union with God to take a stand for justice and compassion, especially for the outcast. One of the three baptismal dignities of the Christian (priest, prophet, and king).

Protestant Any of several Christian traditions that broke with the Roman Church over issues of reform (the Protestant Reformation) in the sixteenth century. See **Reformation.**

purgatory The concept of a brief state preceding heaven characterized by remorse and contrition for having fallen short of God's plan for one's life on Earth.

R

Real Presence The presence of Jesus in the Eucharistic elements, which have the appearance of mere bread and wine but are actually the living, risen Jesus in our midst.

reason Use of the intellect in understanding Christian teachings and applying them to life. Also used to refer to intellect unaided by revelation that can discern the existence of God and some of his attributes.

reconciliation/penance The sacrament whereby one is reconciled to God and the Christian community after admitting failures in living the Christian life and repenting of them.

Redeemer Jesus Christ, who saves us from our sins. The word comes from one who pays a ransom for another.

reform The continuous process of making the Church ever more aligned to the teachings of Jesus. An ancient Latin phrase best sums up this moving target: *ecclesia semper reformanda,* "The Church is always in need of reform."

Reformation When used with a capital R, refers to the sixteenth-century movement for reform of the Western Church that instead resulted in the establishment of various separate Protestant traditions due to a variety of factors not limited to doctrine and practice, but also economic, political, and cultural realities of the time.

religion Latin: *religio*, "bind together." A system of beliefs and practices intended to unite humans with God.

religious Not what you might assume: in the Roman tradition, this word refers to those who live according to the "evangelical counsels": poverty, chastity, and obedience. They are the members of "religious communities": clergy, brothers and sisters who live the "consecrated life" in orders such as the Franciscans, Dominicans, Jesuits, and so on.

restitution The act of "making good" to one whom we have offended in justice: returning stolen goods, paying for damage to property, restoring another's reputation, and so on.

revealed religion A form of religion that is based on God manifesting himself to its followers, especially through inspired scripture.

revelation The act of God making himself known and teaching humans his will.

Rite of Christian Initiation of Adults (RCIA) The process whereby adults interested in the Catholic faith or seeking to complete their initiation join a group of other adults for the purpose of learning, prayer, faith formation, and personal conversion prior to accepting the sacraments of initiation at the Easter Vigil.

Roman Catholic See **Catholic**.

Roman rite The liturgical tradition and practice of the Roman Church. Also called the Latin rite.

Rome The spiritual center of Christianity since the days when Saint Peter was the first bishop of this city. Rome is the primary of the five ancient patriarchates (or Christian centers): Rome, Constantinople, Antioch, Jerusalem, and Alexandria. Each of these ancient patriarchates (with the exception of Jerusalem) contributed its own tradition, theology, and liturgical usage to various Churches existing today in both the Catholic and Orthodox communions.

ruach Hebrew: "breath" or "wind." From this Jewish concept arose the idea of spirit, especially the Holy Spirit, as *ruach Yahweh*, "the breath of God."

resurrection The act of Jesus being raised from the dead, the first to do what we all will one day do.

Sabbath The seventh day of Jewish observance, a day of rest dedicated to God. The Christian Sabbath is Sunday because that is the day of the resurrection; every Sunday is a celebration of the resurrection.

sacrament Sacraments give us a share in the life of God through the use of ordinary material things or people. While we assign special importance to seven rites—baptism, confirmation, Eucharist, reconciliation, marriage, holy orders, and anointing of the sick—as Catholics we see the sacramental presence of God in many other ways, especially in the community we call "the Church."

saint From the Latin word *sanctus* or *sancta*, meaning "holy." Anyone who is in heaven. Christians also have lists of official or "canonized" saints, those people who have gone before us with lives of heroic virtue who are held up to us as examples. See **communion of saints**.

salvation history The progressive story of God's Creation and involvement with humanity, always leading us toward the future and ever-increasing ways of knowing and serving him.

Satan See **devil**.

schism The act of a community that separates itself from the Church. According to Catholic canon law, schism generally results when a group ordains their own priests or bishops without permission. The resulting community is termed "schismatic."

scripture Written revelation.

Second Vatican Council The 21st Ecumenical Council of the Roman Church (1962–65). Considered the single most important religious event of the twentieth century, the Council decreed wide-ranging reforms in Church life while reinterpreting Church teachings for the benefit of the modern world.

sensus fidei The innate sense of each member of the Church that enables him or her to discern proper teaching by the power of the Holy Spirit.

servant The highest role a Christian can aspire to. All Christians are called to be servants, and this is something we must strive to be every day of our lives. Even the pope is called "Servant of the Servants of God."

Shekinah Hebrew: "dwelling." The Israelite concept of the actual presence of God on earth, considered to be separate from God himself. The *Shekinah* was considered to be feminine and in Christianity is associated with the Holy Spirit.

sin An act or failure to act opposed to the plan God has for our individual life. Sin can also be committed by a community: social sin is that state a society or nation finds itself in when its practices, policies, or laws are in opposition to God's will.

social justice Striving to conform society to the principles of God's justice.

social sin See **sin**.

Son The second person of the Trinity.

soul That principle that is spiritual, eternal, and gives life to our bodies.

spirit We have lots of uses for this word: the Holy Spirit, the soul, noncorporeal beings, and an animating force.

spirituality An approach to prayer and living in the presence of God. There are many different schools or forms of spirituality in the Christian tradition.

steward One who administers and cares for the gifts and belongings of his or her Master.

Suffering Servant The description of Jesus as one who willingly undergoes pain and suffering for others.

Sunday The Christian Sabbath, the Day of the Lord. Christians observe the Sabbath on Sunday because that is the day of the resurrection of Jesus. Every Sunday is a celebration of the resurrection.

supersessionism The idea that Judaism has been replaced by Christianity. This concept is rejected by the Catholic Church, as God's covenant with the Jews has never been revoked.

superstition The belief that rituals or verbal formulas can affect our lives by causing God to conform to our human wills. Superstition exists in some forms in Christianity, when people think they can get what they want by using a special prayer or by repetition of certain words or rituals, or giving gold and silver stuff to the Church or making "deals" with God. This is not Christianity; it's magic, and it doesn't work.

synoptic Greek: "viewed together." Refers to the Gospels of Matthew, Mark, and Luke, which are similar in their structure and content.

T

tabernacle Originally the tent that housed the presence of God among the Chosen People in the desert, today it is the box where the Eucharistic Bread, the Body of Christ, is reserved for the sake of the dying, the sick and the homebound that they may share in the community's Eucharistic celebration.

Tanakh The term for the Hebrew Testament, the Jewish scripture (also called the "Old Testament"). It is an acronym of the first letters of three Hebrew words, *Torah*, *Nevi'im*, and *Ketuvim* (the Law, the Prophets, and the Writings).

Ten Commandments Also called the *Decalogue* (Greek: "ten words"), the guide for living given to the people through Moses by God on Mount Sinai. These are the basic precepts for respecting God and neighbor.

thanksgiving The form of prayer in which we express gratitude to God for all he has done for us.

theology The study of God. Theology is broken into subsections, among which are christology (the study of Christ), pneumatology (the study of the Holy Spirit), soteriology (the study of salvation), ecclesiology (the study of the Church), mariology (the study of Mary), eschatology (the study of the last things and the Second Coming), sacramental theology, and moral theology.

Torah See *Pentateuch*.

Tradition With a capital *T*, refers to teachings handed down to us from the earliest Christians that are not recorded in the New Testament. Tradition always safeguards the true meaning of scripture.

Transfiguration The event recorded as occurring on Mount Tabor, when Jesus became radiant with light and was seen conversing with Moses and Elijah.

transubstantiation The act whereby bread and wine become the Body and Blood of Christ, although the appearances of bread and wine remain.

Triduum Latin for "three days," the holiest time of the Christian liturgical year: Holy Thursday, Good Friday, and Holy Saturday (Easter begins on Holy Saturday evening with the celebration of the Easter Vigil).

Trinitarian The state of seeking to imitate the divine life of the Trinity as a community of love, spirituality, or teaching seeking to emulate the Trinity.

Trinity The teaching that God is one being in three "persons," Father, Son, and Holy Spirit.

U

uniate A pejorative term referring to any of the Eastern Catholic Churches.

union One of the forms of prayer.

Vatican II See **Second Vatican Council**.

vestment Clothing worn for liturgical services. Here are some of the basic vestments:

alb: the basic liturgical vestment. A long white garment symbolizing baptism. It is not a clerical vestment, but all the baptized have the right to wear an alb. Any liturgical minister, clergy or lay, may wear an alb. The traditional white christening gown is a baby alb.

cassock: A long, plain black garment worn by bishops, priests, and deacons on rare occasions. The cassock may be different colors for clergy of various ranks.

chasuble: The ample sleeveless garment worn by bishops and priests over the alb during the celebration of the Eucharist.

cope: A long cape worn by bishops, priests, and deacons for certain worship services outside the Eucharist.

dalmatic: Similar to the chasuble, but with wide sleeves, worn by deacons.

miter: A triangular headdress worn by bishops. It is removed and replaced several times during Mass. The basic rule is that bishops remove it when they lead prayer, invite the assembly to prayer, or when the Gospel is proclaimed.

stole: A symbol of ordained ministry. A long strip of cloth worn by bishops and priests around the neck and by deacons on the left shoulder.

surplice: A white garment with sleeves and reaching to about the knees, worn by bishops, priests, and deacons over the cassock.

zuchetto: That vaguely Jewish beanie worn by bishops. They remove it during the Eucharistic Prayer.

vigil Following Jewish custom, the Church begins the celebration of any Sunday or major celebration at sundown of the day preceding the celebration. Thus, each Sunday begins at sundown on Saturday,

Easter begins at sundown on Holy Saturday, Christmas begins at sundown on Christmas Eve...well, you get the picture.

Virgin Birth The teaching that Mary gave birth to Jesus without having sex with a man.

Visitation The event when Mary went to visit her cousin Elizabeth, who was also pregnant.

vow A promise made to God. Religious take vows of poverty, chastity, and obedience. Contrary to popular misconception, diocesan clergy (priests and deacons) do not take vows at ordination. They promise obedience and celibacy, if unmarried, to the bishop.

war The absence of peace.

wisdom The state of conforming one's self to the eternal truth of God and reflecting that truth to others. When capitalized, it refers to the Holy Spirit or a gift of the Holy Spirit.

witness A person who provides a good example or proclaims Christian truth. Note the difference between Christian and secular uses of the word. If I am a witness to Jesus Christ, I am not testifying against him in a court of law.

Word The eternal manifestation of God to Creation, accomplished at various times through scripture and ultimately in the person of Jesus Christ.

world In scriptural usage, the dominant society, its practices and priorities, which are generally in opposition to Christian teaching.

Sources

Chapter 2

Thomas Merton, *A Year with Thomas Merton*, Jonathan Montaldo, ed., HarperCollins, 2004, p. 240.

Chapter 4

The English translation of The Nicene Creed by the International Consultation on English Texts.

Thomas Merton, *New Seeds of Contemplation*, New Directions Publishing, 1972, p. 177.

Chapter 5

Benedict XVI, Homily on the inauguration of his pontificate, April 24, 2005, official English translation from the Vatican Web site, vatican.va.

Ann M. Brown, *St. Bakhita: From African Slave to Servant of the "Good Master,"* New Hope Publications, 2000, pp. 20 and 32.

Chapter 11

Paul VI, *Populorum Progressio*, Encyclical Letter on the Development of Peoples, March 26, 1967, no. 62, official English translation from the Vatican Web site, vatican.va.

Chapter 13

Excerpt from the English translation of *Pastoral Care of the Sick: Rites of Anointing and Viaticum* © 1982, International Committee on English in the Liturgy, Inc. (ICEL). All rights reserved.

Augustine, traditional poetical paraphrase adapted from *The Confessions*.

Chapter 15

Day By Day, from the musical GODSPELL. Music by Stephen Schwartz, lyrics by Richard of Chichester (1197-1253). Copyright © 1971 by Range Road Music, Inc., Bug Music-Quartet Music and New Cadenza Music Corporation. Copyright renewed. Publishing and allied rights for "Day By Day" administered by Range Road Music, Inc., c/o Carlin America, Inc., and Bug Music-Quartet Music, c/o T/Q Music, Inc. International Copyright Secured. All Rights Reserved. Used by Permission.

Bartholomew and John Paul II, *Common Declaration on Environmental Ethics*, June 10, 2002, official English translation from the Web site of the Ecumenical Patriarchate, ec-patr.org.

Chapter 16

Benedict XVI, *Address to the Delegation of the Ecumenical Patriarchate of Constantinople*, June 30, 2005, official English translation from the Vatican Web site, vatican.va.

Bartholomew, *Welcoming Remarks to Rowan Williams, Archbishop of Canterbury*, November 17, 2003, official English translation from the Web site of the Ecumenical Patriarchate, ec-patr.org.

Peter Hebblethwaite, *John XXIII: Pope of the Century*, Continuum International Publishing Group, 2005, p. 131.

Chapter 17

Wilfred Philip Ward, *The Life of John Henry, Cardinal Newman*, Longman, Green and Co., 1912, p. 497.

Benedict XVI, Homily on the inauguration of his pontificate, April 24, 2005, official English translation from the Vatican Web site, vatican.va.

Susan Conroy, *Mother Teresa's Lessons of Love & Secrets of Sanctity*, Our Sunday Visitor Publishing, 2003, p. 113.

Chapter 18

Paul VI, *Message for the Celebration of the Day of Peace*, January 1, 1972, official English translation from the Vatican Web site, vatican.va.

Chapter 19

Dorothy Day, *The Long Loneliness: The Autobiography of Dorothy Day*, HarperCollins, 1981, p. 286.

Chapter 21

Excerpt from the English translation of *Rite of Penance* © 1974, International Committee on English in the Liturgy, Inc. (ICEL). All rights reserved.

Chapter 22

John Paul II, *Mane Nobiscum Domine*, Apostolic Letter for the Year of the Eucharist, October 7, 2004, no. 28, official English translation from the Vatican Web site, vatican.va.

Chapter 23

Thomas Merton, *New Seeds of Contemplation*, New Directions Publishing, 1972, p. 31.

Oscar Wilde, *The Writings of Oscar Wilde*, Keller-Farmer Co., 1907, p. 113.

Robert Ellsberg, ed., *By Little and By Little: The Selected Writings of Dorothy Day*, Knopf, 1983, p. xviii.

Chapter 25

Excerpt from the English translation of *Rite of Baptism for Children* © 1969, International Committee on English in the Liturgy, Inc. (ICEL). All rights reserved.

Chapter 26

Gaudium et Spes, Pastoral Constitution on the Church in the Modern World, no. 1, authors' adaptation of the official English translation from the Vatican Web site, vatican.va.

Chapter 27

Gaudium et Spes, Pastoral Constitution on the Church in the Modern World, no. 4, official English translation from the Vatican Web site, vatican.va.

Choose the Red Pill

Victor Hugo, *Les Misérables*, Charles E. Wilbour, trans., Everyman's Library, 1997, p. 21.

Hillaire Belloc, "The Catholic Sun."

John XXIII, Opening Address to the Second Vatican Council, October 11, 1962. Vatican.va. Translation from the Latin by Michael Boler.

Teresa of Ávila Prayer adapted from the translation in David Foster, Basil Cardinal Hume, and Timothy Radcliffe, *The Downside Prayerbook*, Continuum International Publishing Group, 2005, p. 79.

Be Still, written by Louis Perez and David Hidalgo. © 1990 DAVINCE MUSIC (BMI) and NO K.O. MUSIC (BMI) / administered by BUG MUSIC. All Rights Reserved. Used by Permission.

Learn More

Thomas Merton, *No Man Is an Island*, Harcourt, Brace and Company, 1955, p. 131.

What Do You Really Think?

Duncan MacLaren, "Catherine of Siena," in Gilbert Márkus, ed., *The Radical Tradition: Revolutionary Saints in the Battle for Justice and Human Rights*, Doubleday, 1993, p. 69.

Image Credits

Cover

Looking Upward, © iStockphoto.com/FauxCaster

Frontispiece and Epigraph

Photograph of the Omega Window in the Cathedral of Christ the Light, Oakland, California, © John Blaustein 2008.

Flame in the night, © iStockphoto.com/dtimiraos

Table of Contents

Spiral Staircase, Rome, © iStockphoto.com/cstewart

Red Jug 2, © iStockphoto/Difydave

Crown of Thorns, ©iStockphoto.com/Kiyyah

The Gemmata Paschal Candle. Photo courtesy of Marklin Candle Design. © 2009 M G Marklin, LLC. All Rights Reserved.

Introduction

The Cross Walkers #2, © iStockphoto.com/Sparky2000

Floral background, © iStockphoto.com/awardik

Chapter 1

Buddhist Monks, © iStockphoto.com/Fpless

Photograph of Abraham's Tomb at Machpelah (Haram al-Ibrahimi) in Hebron, Palestinian Territories, by Eric Stoltz.

Space Travelers, © iStockphoto.com/natsmith1

Chapter 2

Jewish Boy Praying in Jerusalem 2, © iStockphoto.com/alvarez

In the Beginning, © iStockphoto.com/Enticnou

Image of the Prophet Hosea by Duccio di Buoninsegna, ca. 1308–1311, tempera on wood, detail of an altarpiece in the Cathedral of Siena. Public domain image courtesy of Wikimedia Commons.

Chapter 3

Golden Gate Bridge, © iStockphoto.com/ChrisMR

Photograph of Ethiopian Orthodox clergy with Gospel book in Addis Ababa, January 20, 2001 © Wolfgang Rattay/Reuters/Corbis. All rights reserved, used with permission.

Image of Moses, detail of a thirteenth-century mural by an unknown artist in the Monastery of St. Catherine, Sinai, Egypt. Public domain image courtesy of Wikimedia Commons.

Chapter 4

Climber, © iStockphoto.com/chphotoworx

St. Paul the Apostle, © 2000 Markell Studios, Inc. Reproductions at www.BridgeBuilding.com.

Blank billboard on cloudy sky, © iStockphoto.com/macroworld

Chapter 5

Photograph of Omega Nebula from the Hubble Space Telescope, NASA, ESA and J. Hester (ASU).

Photograph of Saint Josephine Bakhita, courtesy of the Canossian Daughters of Charity.

Chapter 6

Chakra Fire, © iStockphoto.com/elenaray

Jesus and the Samaritan Woman, ink-on-paper painting by He Qi, Nanjing. © He Qi. All rights reserved. Used by permission.

Feed the World, © iStockphoto.com/jgroup

Chapter 7

Inside Hagia Sophia, © iStockphoto.com/-lvinst-

Hands Holding a Monarch Butterfly, © iStockphoto.com/mikewking

Image of Saint Stephen from *The Demidoff Altarpiece* by Carlo Crivelli (active 1468–1493), tempera on wood, in the collection of the National Gallery, London. Public domain image courtesy of Wikimedia Commons.

Chapter 8

Baptism of the Lord, painting by John Nava, study for a tapestry in the Cathedral of Our Lady of the Angels, Los Angeles. © Archdiocese of Los Angeles and John Nava. All rights reserved, used with permission.

Voodoo, © iStockphoto.com/webking

Image of Saint Peter, fragment of a thirteenth-century fresco by an unknown artist, Vatican Museums, Rome. Public domain image courtesy of Wikimedia Commons.

Chapter 9

Photograph of the Ceremony of the Holy Fire, an Orthodox Christian Easter celebration in the Church of the Holy Sepulchre, Jerusalem, April 24, 2001 by Natalie Behring. © Reuters/Corbis. All rights reserved, used by permission.

Jewish torah scroll in cover, © iStockphoto.com/hsandler

Mary Magdalene by Robert Lentz, OFM, used by permission. Image available at www.trinitystores.com.

Chapter 10

Misty Morn, © iStockphoto.com/Florend

Confrontation, © iStockphoto.com/robynmac

Photograph of Dietrich Bonhoeffer, courtesy of Preußischer Kulturbesitz, Staatsbibliothek, Berlin.

Chapter 11

Drowning in Money, © iStockphoto.com/hidesy

American Angel, © iStockphoto.com/PinkTag

Optimist on the Beach, © iStockphoto.com/The_Flying_Dutchman

Chapter 12

Compass, © iStockphoto.com/JJGutierrez

Portrait of Sir Thomas More by Hans Holbein the Younger, oil on wood, 1527. Public domain image courtesy of Wikimedia Commons.

Photograph of boarded-up Hall of Justice in downtown Los Angeles by Eric Stoltz.

Chapter 13

Stairway to Heaven, © iStockphoto.com/elaine

Photograph of Cardinal Joseph Bernardin by Michael E. Keating, © The Cincinnati Enquirer. All rights reserved, used by permission.

Young Woman Trapped, © iStockphoto.com/ranplett

Chapter 14

Night Scene, © iStockphoto.com/efenzi

Teresa of Ávila by Robert Lentz, OFM, used by permission. Image available at www.trinitystores.com.

Million Dollar City, © iStockphoto.com/JimLarkin

Chapter 15

Crowd Crossing in Hong Kong, © iStockphoto.com/christinegonsalves

Photograph of Archbishop Alexander Brunett washing feet at Holy Thursday liturgy 2006, St. James Cathedral, Seattle, by Mike Penney. © www.photobymike.com. All rights reserved, used by permission.

The Meeting of Francis and Clare by Robert Lentz, OFM, used by permission. Image available at www.trinitystores.com.

Vector Fish, © iStockphoto.com/JJJansey

Chapter 16

Human Pyramid, © iStockphoto.com/Mlenny

Tuscany Doors—Porte della Toscana, © iStockphoto.com/fajean

Acknowledgments

We thank all those who believed in the concept of this book and who worked with us to make it a reality. First we thank our own bishop, Cardinal Roger Mahony, archbishop of Los Angeles, for his support in this effort. We are fortunate to have him as our shepherd and teacher. We thank, as well, Dr. Michael Downey, the Cardinal's theologian, Archdiocese of Los Angeles, for reviewing the text more than once and working closely with us to make this a much better book. His thoughtful and collaborative approach was most encouraging.

We are indebted to Paulist Press for taking a chance on this book. Their commitment to our vision required them to go far beyond business as usual, and their continued dedication required an immense amount of coordination and effort to publish this book. Particularly we would like to thank Father Lawrence Boadt, CSP, Paul McMahon, and our trusted partner and editor, Jim Quigley. Pamela Suwinsky was our dedicated copy editor; Theresa Sparacio and Pamela Stinson-Bell led the book through production.

We are grateful to Cathy Brauer, a parishioner at St. Maximilian Kolbe Church, who helped in proofing, and to Rabbi Haim Dov Beliak, who corrected our Hebrew.

We thank those who formed us to be deacons, for this book is distinctly diaconal; Sister Chris Machado, SSS, Father Frank Ferrante, CMF, and Deacon Cris Vega, who has gone to his eternal reward.

(Deacon Eric here) I'd like to thank all those who have inspired me and those who have encouraged me to write this book. I'm thinking especially of that joyful Christian Archbishop George Niederauer, a shining example of one who teaches with plain language and humor; Bishop Stephen Blaire, who taught me so much in word and example about the role of a bishop; and Bishop Edward Clarke, who introduced me to Takashi Nagai and played a key role in my becoming a deacon. I am grateful to the Jesuits of *America* magazine, who gave me a start by publishing my work in their magazine, despite some risk, especially Father Tom Reese, SJ, and Father Jim Martin, SJ, to whom I owe a special debt for his trust in my abilities and his constant nagging me to write a book.

I thank Monsignor Terry Fleming for asking me to teach the baptismal preparation classes at St. Brendan Church, for that helped me to think some things out, and the parishioners of St. Brendan for their cheerful support.

Most of all, I thank the inmates of the Los Angeles County Men's Central Jail. If not for my experiences with them I may not have even thought of this book.

(Deacon Vince here) I give thanks to our oldest daughter, Maryann, who at a young age taught me the joy and commitment of fatherhood. I thank our youngest daughter Kristina who unknowingly started my journey to the diaconate when she challenged me to teach her confirmation class in 1992. I acknowledge Liz Hise, a wonderfully dedicated director of religious education (DRE), who gently and against my will dragged me through Master Catechist Certification. I give thanks for the people at St. Joseph the Worker Parish in Canoga Park, California, especially Monsignor James Gehl, who was the first to invite me to consider the ministry of deacon. To the community of St. Jude the Apostle in Westlake Village, California, especially Monsignor William Leser, who first recognized in me what I could not see in myself and without hesitation sponsored and supported Susan and me on our way to ordination. For Monsignor Peter A. O'Reilly, who explained what ordination meant and gave me the courage to complete my journey and the friendship, example, and guidance that to this day allows me my small successes. In loving memory of our pastor, Father Patrick O'Dwyer, whom the Lord unexpectedly took home on July 13, 2009. Father Pat gave me space and time to write in the middle of the demands of parish life. To all the parishioners of St. Maximilian Kolbe in Westlake Village, California, whose constant words of encouragement sustain us.

In gratitude to the incarcerated women at California Conservation Camp 13 in the Malibu Hills, who weekly show us that even through the most difficult times of our lives God's Spirit and grace never fail. For Sam, an inmate on California's Death Row, that I have come to know both in person and through our writing. Even from his cell he has given me an appreciation of life that I could not have comprehended elsewhere.

To our adopted son, Blake Gentry Tomkovicz Mahorney, who taught me that we are called to love unconditionally even though it may not be returned to us at the time and in the way we might expect.

Most of all I thank my wife, Susan, whose patient love centers us and remains the glue that holds us together through the messy business of family life!